WILLIAM AT 40

THE MAKING OF A
MODERN MONARCH

Robert Jobson

First published in 2022 by Ad Lib Publishers Ltd
15 Church Road
London SW13 9HE
www.adlibpublishers.com

Text © 2022 Robert Jobson

Hardback ISBN 978-1-913543-08-2
TPB ISBN 978-1-802470-83-3
eBook ISBN 978-1-802470-92-5

A CIP catalogue record for this book is available
from the British Library.

Every reasonable effort has been made to trace copyright-holders of
material reproduced in this book, but if any have been inadvertently
overlooked the publishers would be glad to hear from them.

Printed in the UK
10 9 8 7 6 5 4 3 2

For my mother, Jean.

'My guiding principles in life are to be honest, genuine,
thoughtful and caring'
HRH Prince William, Duke of Cambridge

'I want to say something to the young watching tonight. For too long, we
haven't done enough to protect the planet for your future, the Earthshot is
for you. In the next ten years, we are going to act. We are going to find the
solutions to repair our planet. Please keep learning, keep demanding change
and don't give up hope. We will rise to these challenges.'
HRH Prince William, Duke of Cambridge at the inaugural
Earthshot Prize ceremony, Alexandra Palace, 17 October 2021

CONTENTS

INTRODUCTION AND ACKNOWLEDGEMENTS

As the Bard, William Shakespeare, wrote, 'Some are born great, some achieve greatness, and others have greatness thrust upon them.' In the case of HRH Prince William, Duke of Cambridge, who turns forty on 21 June 2022, it is probably a subtle mixture of all three. As a direct heir to the British throne, he was born to one day lead, as king, the 'great' institution of the British monarchy. Due to a simple twist of fate, being the first-born child of the heir to the throne, William's 'greatness' was undoubtedly thrust upon him. His innate humility would stop him ever claiming to have come close to achieving 'greatness' on merit. He certainly hasn't come anywhere close to the pre-eminence achieved by his grandmother, Queen Elizabeth II. After all, the notable achievements of our oldest ever and longest serving monarch during her long and illustrious reign are too many to list. They include the modernization of the monarchy during her seventy years of leadership, through to the transformation of the Commonwealth, as well as making her succession more equitable. Her service during World War II in which she supported her father, King George VI, during our 'darkest hour' and ground-breaking overseas state visits, such as to Ireland in 2011 and being the first British monarch to address the US Congress, have also set her apart. That said, there is little doubt that when his moment comes, William should have time to make a difference as monarch. Up until now he has made a good fist of it by using his fame and popularity to try to make a real difference in saving our planet. William deserves to be lauded for meeting that critical environmental challenge head on, and he still has time to build on that and perhaps it will be the legacy of his reign.

Instantly recognisable the world over, Prince William is determined to rise to the challenge of serving Crown and country; he is equally set on choosing his own path when that moment for him to reign comes. His public face is that of a loving husband to his beautiful wife, Catherine, and father to his beloved children Prince George, Princess Charlotte and Prince Louis, who are his world. Calm and balanced in public, he is an intensely private man who guards his personal life jealously. As well as being passionate about the environment and sustainability, he has devoted time and energy to saving the endangered species facing extinction on our planet and, indeed, saving the planet itself. His determination to end the despicable illegal ivory trade and his work with the charity Tusk has been commendable. That said, he has made it very clear that he doesn't want to be just a figurehead or a regal voice in the dark demanding action and not following through; he wants to find real solutions to the huge problems facing us and the animals that share our planet. Along with Catherine, William has shown his humanity and compassion; a kind man, his tireless campaigns supporting mental health charities have made great strides in trying to end the stigma surrounding mental illness and depression.

In private, however, William, can be a sensitive and difficult character, with a short fuse and fiery temper that can blow up because of frustration at any time, particularly when it comes to issues regarding his family. He has been known to snap unexpectedly at the press if he feels they are breaching his family's privacy, as he did at a photographer in 2021 when the unfortunate lensman spotted William and the children when they were out on a cycle ride near Sandringham, Norfolk. No photos were taken, but it didn't stop William exploding with rage at the snapper and alerting his police team. Even senior members of his circle will 'check which way the wind is blowing' with William before becoming too self-assured in his presence or raising problematic issues that would be better addressed at another time. Some insiders claim the duke can be an emotional character who is, on occasion, 'difficult to handle'– a description that defies the calm, family-guy public persona he has cultivated. As in any marriage, he and Catherine, whom he married in 2011 but has known since the pair became a couple as undergraduates around 2003, are known to have heated exchanges from time to time. 'He can be a bit of a shouter when he loses it,' one close aide admitted. 'It's fair to say the duke and the duchess give as good as they get if their disagreement results in raised voices, but they know each other so well, it usually blows over quickly and she is, on the whole, a major calming influence on him.'

It is perhaps this chameleon-like characteristic that makes his father, Charles, Prince of Wales sometimes tread carefully when dealing with him. William has been known to insist on deference, too, from those royally ranked below him in the line of succession, but, in truth, when dealing with those above him, he is rarely deferent himself. William, ever since his childhood, has been a pragmatist. He is a doer, and rarely dwells on situations he is not able to change. He is somebody who rises to the challenge. One cannot help but admire his extensive list of accomplishments, such as learning to fly, and the way he has coped and eventually overcome obstacles and emotional traumas in his life. Without doubt he has developed into a focused and accomplished individual, with a broad spectrum of interests and steely determination and confidence that befits his current role and that of monarch which lies ahead of him.

I set out in writing this book to mark the fortieth birthday of the Duke of Cambridge and to try to delve deeper into the complexities of the man behind the public persona: the real character of the man on the cusp of middle age who will one day be our forty-third monarch since his namesake, King William the Conqueror, William, Duke of Normandy, who became King of England in 1066. (Our reigning Queen, Elizabeth II, is the forty-first English monarch since 1066. If Prince Charles outlives Her Majesty, he will become the forty-second. If he does not, William will be the forty-second King of England since William I, rather than the forty-third.) At this transitional time in the history of the modern British monarchy I wanted to explore what makes our future King William V – should he choose that name – tick, what fires him up, and to examine his ambitions, desires and passions in a bid to define him and his core beliefs. Essentially, I wanted to discover what sort of king he will one day become and what path this man will lead our monarchical system along.

William's childhood, with his mother and father's public divorce, and Diana's tragic death when he was so young, undoubtedly shaped him as a person. It could have left him permanently damaged mentally and emotionally, yet we see a boy who refuses to be held back by that inevitable emotional trauma but develops into one who seems determined not to let his problems define him. Instead, he grows into a well-adjusted and level-headed man, anchored by his deep love of his wife and three children. He could so easily have gone the same way as his younger brother Harry, who admits he has turned to therapy to assist his mental health. William somehow developed an inner steel and a focused mind, supported by the level-headed woman he loves, Catherine, to follow his own path. Unlike his brother Harry, he does not wear his heart on his sleeve, quite the reverse. He is a deeply private man, a man who is acutely aware of what is expected of him and the importance of the role he is destined to fulfil.

I have spent more than thirty years chronicling the story of the key characters in the House of Windsor as an author, journalist and broadcaster. I have been fortunate to have met Prince William and many other members of his family, including his wife, Catherine, on countless occasions in my capacity as a royal writer and correspondent. I have travelled across the UK and around the world covering his official overseas engagements, too, sometimes travelling in the same official RAF aircraft, The Voyager. In fact, I was the first person to 'interview' William when I was elected to throw a few cleared questions at him when he was lined up with his brother, Prince Harry, and cousins, Princess Beatrice and Princess Eugenie, on the ski slopes of Klosters, Switzerland, in 1995. In my career chronicling the House of Windsor I have also interviewed members of the royal family, broken many exclusive stories, won awards for my writing as well as penned several acclaimed and bestselling books about William's parents, Prince Charles and Princess Diana, as well as one about the late Prince Philip, Duke of Edinburgh, including Number 1 *New York Times* bestseller *Diana: Closely Guarded Secret*, written with her former Scotland Yard Personal Protection Officer, Inspector Ken Wharfe MVO.

My goal for this book was to explore beyond the sensational headlines which fixate on buzzworthy issues, such as William's recent falling out with his brother, Prince Harry. Whilst significant in my view, such issues should not totally dominate the narrative when assessing William's life so far. Instead, I will draw on my knowledge, memories, and well-placed and well-informed sources, both inside and outside the royal household and past and present, to present a revealing, detailed portrait of the man. To do that I have not only relied upon my extensive knowledge of the House of Windsor but relied on the testimony of many informed sources, including royal aides and palace courtiers past and present. Some I can acknowledge here, others, at their request, must remain anonymous. Among those I would like to thank for helping me with this book and guidance over the years are Inspector Ken Wharfe MVO, Mervyn Wycherley RVM, Colleen Harris MVO DL, the late Mrs Felicity Murdo-Smith CVO, Ailsa Anderson LVO, Dr Ed Perkins MVO, Dickie Arbiter LVO, Patrick Jephson LVO, the late Mr Geoffrey Crawford CVO, Mr Charles Anson CVO, HP. I would also like to acknowledge the hard work of Lily Jobson and Kara Kennedy, whose assistance with research and fact checking was invaluable. I would also like to thank other authors and writers whose work I have read and, in some cases, referred to whilst researching this book. They include Penny Junor, Robert Lacey, Brian Hoey, Andrew Morton, Tom Bower, Christopher Wilson, the late James Whitaker, Christopher Andersen, Colin Butfield and Jonathan Hughes. I would like to thank my good friends and colleagues who have helped me along my royal journey over the years as well as on our travels around the world on royal tours, particularly Richard Kay, Robin Nunn, Arthur Edwards MBE FRPS, Kent Gavin and Ian Walker. Others I'd like to thank include Michael Cole, Camilla Tominey, Katie Nichol, Alan Jones and Charlie Rae. Of course, I would like to thank my publishers John Blake and Jon Rippon and all the first-class editorial and marketing team at Ad Lib for backing this project and making it happen. Finally, I would like to thank my family, too: my son, Charlie; my mother, Jean; and my late father, Vic, whose love, guidance and support have been my guiding light always.

I trust this tome realises what I set out to achieve: to provide both an intimate portrait and a serious study of a man who has come of age as a modern-day crown prince of Britain. For William is not only determined to do his duty and to serve his country with distinction and alacrity, but when his time to reign comes, he will be a king of his epoch, with the leadership qualities that enable him to follow his own path.

Robert Jobson, May 2022

PRINCE FOR OUR PLANET

'The shared goals for our generation are clear. Together, we must protect and restore nature, clean our air, revive our oceans. Build a waste-free world and fix our climate.'

HRH Prince William, Duke of Cambridge

Once we had touched down safely on the runway at Lahore airport, Prince William drew back the cabin divider curtain and walked into the economy section at the back of the Royal Air Force Voyager Airbus 330 jet, where members of the accompanying media and some of the assigned Royal Air Force crew were sitting. It had been an eventful flight, but he was relaxed enough and had a broad smile across his face. 'I was flying,' he joked. At that point most of the press burst out laughing, but our joint relief that the ordeal was over was palpable. Minutes earlier, dramatic lightning flashes could be seen around the right wing through the aircraft windows as giant hailstones, some as big as golf balls, pounded the grey wings of the aircraft carrying the future king, his wife Catherine, his royal household and royal bodyguards, as well as the accompanying press corps.[1]

At one point during the terrifying electric storm the plane had lurched and suddenly dropped more than 120 feet, lifting some members of the fifty or so media party on board and I presume those further forward, too, in the section where the accompanying members of the royal household were sitting, out of their seats as they frantically clung on to heavy equipment such as television cameras, photographic kit and laptops, to stop it smashing and flying around the cabin. One could only imagine what was going through the minds of William and the Duchess of Cambridge, out of sight at the very front of the plane in their private section reserved for the royal family or prime minister. After circling the airport at Pakistan's capital, Islamabad, for just over an hour and after two aborted attempts to land, the experienced RAF pilot decided it would be best to abandon the original plan and return to Lahore.

As a royal correspondent who had been covering the royal family story on overseas tours for more than thirty years and having flown hundreds of thousands of miles all over the world, I regard myself as a relatively relaxed international traveller and flying had never bothered me. But that roller-coaster ride in the turbulent skies over Pakistan on 17 October 2019 was the most nervous I had ever felt as a passenger in a plane. The tour schedule was ripped up and we were all forced to spend a secret, unplanned night in Lahore after the RAF jet had to double back. The British Embassy staff and security teams went into logistical overdrive. William and Catherine were immediately driven away in waiting limousines and checked into a suite at the four-star Pearl Continental Hotel, but not before William had instructed his private secretary, Simon Case, that the accompanying press must be looked after. I was fully expecting to spend the night on the floor of the airport arrivals lounge and had made a mad dash to claim one of the few chairs in the room we were taken to and to find a plug point so I could charge my phone. But soon we were on the move again, being taken by bus to the same hotel as the royals, where Pakistani security forces had formed a cordon around the hotel. The royal security team issued a media blackout on reporting of the royal couple's enforced return to Lahore because of safety concerns. It would remain in place, we were told, until the royal principals had returned to Islamabad.

Prince William's attitude towards the press during that tour was markedly different to that of previous visits. The fact that he was using the RAF Voyager – normally reserved for Her Majesty the Queen, the Prince of Wales, and the current prime minister – seemed to elevate the seriousness of the overseas visit; this was clearly an important high-level diplomatic mission that both the royal family and the Foreign and Commonwealth Office had invested a lot of time and effort in. William's demeanour, too, seemed more statesmanlike. Simon Case, who was soon poached back to run the civil service by Prime Minister Boris Johnson, had been an inspired appointment. A gifted diplomat and public servant, he seemed to know instinctively how to position his new boss to maximise his impact.

On the plane as we flew from RAF Brize Norton to Pakistan, not only did Mr Case fully brief the press on the level of importance being placed on the visit, spelling out the diplomatic and security implications, but he invited the well-schooled, totally prepared William to talk it all through with the media too. It all felt very grown-up for a change. The travelling royals were not kept at arm's length for another series of photo opportunities and smiles (although that was included in the schedule), but were on a mission, and an assignment that the accompanying press, rightly or wrongly, felt they were a part of. After the debacle on the overseas visit by the Duke and Duchess of Sussex to South Africa, where the travelling accredited media felt as though they had been treated like pariahs by Prince Harry and his wife Meghan, William was clearly on a charm offensive. He went on, 'Thanks for coming, you should all take this as a group hug.' It went a long way to restore cordial press/Palace relations that had been at breaking point after the Sussexes' South African trip, helping to smooth the path towards his time as leader of the monarchy.

It was like watching a new Prince and Princess of Wales, in their early days. They had gone to the next level. From the moment William had stepped onto the plane, immaculately attired, he looked like the super-ambassador he has now become. Giving briefings at the front of the plane to reporters, many of whom he was on first-name terms with, and later mingling with ease among the photographers too, he seemed to have a new air of confidence. He was controlled. Gone was the edginess he used to have as he tried to hold back information. He was himself. What followed over the next few days was soft power diplomacy at its slickest.

The electrical storm became a talking point during the rest of the official visit to Pakistan, which had been at the invitation of Prime Minister Imran Khan, a former friend of the duke's late mother, Diana, Princess of Wales. On the third day of their trip, the royal couple travelled by helicopter to the north of the country in the Chitral District of the Khyber-Pakhtunkhwa province to see a melting glacier. That flight, thankfully, was not as dramatic, though the sight of the diminished glacier certainly was. As Catherine remarked: 'Everyone's asking all of us to protect the environment and what comes first is actually just to care about it in the first place. And you're not necessarily going to care about it if you don't know about it. That's why we thought it was so important to come here.'

William, who was being followed by acclaimed documentary filmmaker Nick Kent, was determined to put himself centre-stage in the climate-change debate. The resulting film, *Prince William: A Planet for Us All,* that aired on ITV on 5 October 2020, also underlined where the motivation for his involvement had come from. As a father, William explained, he now sees things differently. 'I feel it is my duty, and our collective responsibility, to leave our planet in a stronger position for our children. My grandfather [the late Prince Philip, Duke of Edinburgh, born 1921, died 2021], my father and I have been in environmental work for many years. My grandfather's well ahead of his time. My father, ahead of his time. And I really want to make sure that, in twenty years, George doesn't turn round and say, "Are you ahead of your time?" Because if he does, we're too late.'

It's no surprise to me that William used television, a platform where his natural warmth comes through, to share his life's mission statement – which is to help save the natural world. It is this road map that drives him. Doing so will help him step from the shadow of his late mother, Diana, Princess of Wales, his environmental champion father, the Prince of Wales, as well as the slightly contrived double-act he shared with his brother, Prince Harry, before he married Catherine.

At forty, William may well be the man who appears to have everything: a devoted and beautiful wife, three healthy children, personal wealth, two amazing homes in London, the vast Apartment 1A Kensington Palace, and a country home, Anmer Hall, in Sandringham, Norfolk, and global respect and growing recognition on the world stage. He accepts he's a lucky man, but we see him at a crossroads, too. He seems a man in a hurry. His earlier television films on mental health have shown part of that progression.

But, in my view, it's his role as a champion of the natural world and his determination to use his fame and influence to be a bridge between the passionate young and sceptical old that appears to drive him and may, in time, define him and his future reign. William has spoken with passion about generational change, particularly apparent in the slight impatience he shows with those who won't commit to action.

'That generational gap has to be bridged, so that the older political leaders understand that the younger generation mean business. They want their futures protected. I owe it to them to help their voices be heard,' he says in Nick Kent's film. It's powerful stuff; a real statement of intent.

When he was growing up, William always loved nature and he went on to read Geography at St Andrew's University, where he met his future wife, Catherine, a fellow undergraduate at the ancient seat of learning in Scotland. His father, Charles, who made his first major speech on the environment in February 1970, always imposed upon him the importance of nature and its fragility. His grandfather, the late Prince Philip, Duke of Edinburgh, was a pioneer, too, who in 1961 had helped form and became the first president of the British National Appeal, the first national organisation in The World Wildlife Fund family.

It is William's love for his own children, and his empathy for the younger generation as a whole, that motivate him to seek change. 'Fatherhood has given me a new sense of purpose,' says William. 'Now I have got George, Charlotte and Louis in my life … your outlook does change,' he said in *Prince William: A Planet for Us All*.

Despite observing some of the damage we've inflicted on the natural world, William remains positive. He has embraced hope as well as a sense of urgency. From inner-city Liverpool to the Scottish coast, it's young people who are leading the way and effecting crucial change. William acknowledges the work of nineteen-year-old Swedish campaigner Greta Thunberg in galvanising the younger generation into action, but he has also been inspired by children making a difference in their own homes.

'I've been very lucky that through the lockdown I've been here, surrounded by wildlife,' he said, while filming on the Queen's Sandringham Estate in Norfolk, where he has a country home, Anmer Hall. He went on: 'And I can't talk about coronavirus without mentioning about how many people sadly lost their lives and how terrible and sad that all is. But I think if there's any ray of light, it's that it allows us to take stock and to refocus our priorities.[2]

'I've been really heartened by what I've been hearing from other people and how they've started to appreciate nature and experience it – and see all the things that they never thought they would.

We've seen organisations mobilising themselves like never before. The research collaboration, the sharing of expertise, money found to support people. If we can provide the same motivation with the environment, we will have truly turned a corner. Investment, green fashion. We need to build back greener. Young people won't stand for saying it's not possible.' He said later, referring to what it's like to live at Anmer Hall, 'It's very special, it's very peaceful. And we feel very, very lucky to be out in the countryside. We've got the sheep in the fields. We've got the pond here with the duck and the geese on. It's a fantastic place to be.'

A huge admirer of Sir David Attenborough, William interviewed him at the World Economic Forum in Davos in 2019. 'The world is facing great problems,' said Sir David, 'and the most aware of that are the young people of today who will inherit this world.' William also appeared in Nick Kent's documentary in Tanzania, where he was filmed being shown an ivory store where 43,000 tusks with a street value of £50 million had been impounded. On his return to London, he invited world leaders to an international conference to combat the illegal wildlife trade. 'If we can't fix that,' said William, 'how can we ever hope to tackle climate change?' It is a powerful point.

William remains an optimist and believes it's possible to give young people hope, and truly believes that things can get fixed. It is that sense of hope, more than anything, that shines through in the man. Just days after the film aired, he launched his most ambitious project to date: the Earthshot Prize, a £50-million drive to repair the planet. Billed as 'the most prestigious global environment prize in history', it aims to find solutions to repair the planet by 2030. His scheme means that five £1m prizes will be awarded each year throughout this decade, aiming to provide at least fifty solutions to some of the world's environmental problems. His mission statement reveals what is at the heart of the man.

'Growing up in my family gives you a certain sense of history,' he said. 'I'm simply the latest in a line that can be traced back generations.' Touching the tree next to him, he went on, 'This oak tree is close to Windsor Castle, which has been home to my family for over 900 years; thirty-nine monarchs have lived here and enjoyed these beautiful surroundings. I've walked here many times myself, and it always amazes me that some of the trees planted here, living organisms, dependent on soil, rain and sunlight, were here as they laid the first stones at Windsor Castle. That makes some of the oaks here almost one thousand years old.

'While these oaks have been growing, around 35 billion people have lived their lives on our planet. That's 35 billion lifetimes worth of hope, love, fear and dreams. In that time, humankind has invented air travel, vaccines and computers. We've explored every part of the globe, sequenced the human genome and even escaped the atmosphere. Our speed of innovation has been incredible. But so too has acceleration of our impact over my grandmother's lifetime, the last ninety years or so. Our impacts accelerated so fast that our climate, oceans, air, nature and all that depends on them are in peril. This oak has stood here for centuries, but never has it faced a decade like this.

'We start this new decade knowing that it is the most consequential period in history. The science is irrefutable. If we do not act in this decade, the damage that we have done will be irreversible. And the effects will be felt, not just by future generations, but by all of us alive today. And what's more, this damage will not be felt equally by everyone. It is the most vulnerable, those with the fewest resources and those who have done the least to cause climate change, who will be impacted the most. These stark facts are terrifying. How can we hope to fix such massive, intractable problems? It may seem overwhelming, but it is possible.

'Humans have an extraordinary capacity to set goals and strive to achieve them. I've long been inspired by President John F. Kennedy's 1961 mission to put a man on the moon within a decade. He named it the moonshot. It seemed crazy. We had just launched the first satellite, putting a man on the moon that quickly seemed impossible. But this simple challenge encompasses so much. He called it a goal to organise and measure the best of our energies and skills in taking that giant leap for mankind. The team behind the moonshot united millions of people around the world, convincing them that this crazy ambition wasn't so crazy after all.'

William stressed that we now need Earthshot, by harnessing that same spirit of human ingenuity and purpose and using it to repair our planet. Together, he said, we must protect and restore nature, clean our air, revive our oceans. His ambition, he added, is to 'build a waste-free world and fix our climate.' He went on to say, 'If we achieve these goals by 2030 our lives won't be worse. We have the power and potential to ensure that they (the Windsor oak trees) and all life on Earth, thrive for another 1,000 years and more, but only if we now unleash the greatest talents of our generation to repair our planet. We have no choice but to succeed.'

Anyone with any reservations about William's sincerity or vision for the future should re-read his inspiring words over and over. They are his roadmap to achieving real change.

CHAPTER ONE

THE LITTLE PRINCE

'I am so thankful I was beside Diana's bedside the whole time because I felt as though I'd shared deeply in the process of birth and as a result was rewarded by seeing a small creature who belonged to us even though he seemed to belong to everyone else as well.'

Prince Charles on the birth of his son, Prince William, in 1982[3]

The Prince of Wales was overjoyed as he emerged from the Lindo Wing of St Mary's Hospital, Paddington, West London shortly after his wife, Princess Diana, had given birth to their healthy, blue-eyed baby son at 9.03 p.m. on 21 June 1982. The prince had been at Diana's side throughout the thirteen hours of labour and was with her when their child came into the world.

'The baby weighed 7 lb, 1.5 oz and he cried lustily,' a Buckingham Palace spokeswoman confirmed. 'The Prince of Wales was present. We have no names which we can announce,' she said. It later emerged that Diana's pregnancy had been induced by the Queen's surgeon gynaecologist, Sir George Pinker KCVO, the internationally recognised obstetrician who had overseen the care of the princess throughout her pregnancy, and that the princess had chosen to have her baby whilst standing.

Moments after the birth of his son, Charles rang the Queen from the hospital, who was said to be 'absolutely delighted' with the news. Queen Elizabeth, the Queen Mother, driving back to her home at Clarence House was said to be 'overjoyed'. Once the monarch had been informed, the news was also flashed to Charles's brother Prince Andrew, then serving as a Royal Navy helicopter pilot in the South Atlantic task force in the Falklands, who became an uncle as well as being bumped down one in the line of succession for the as-yet unnamed

1

infant, who was now second in line to the throne. Then the rest of the royal family were given the wonderful news.

Outside, a large crowd had gathered and shouted, 'We want Charlie!' as they waved their flags. Then Prince Charles emerged, immaculate in a grey suit, accompanied by his Scotland Yard Personal Protection Officer, Superintendent John Maclean. He happily went over to the crowd and one admirer planted a kiss on his cheek. He had a smear of lipstick on his face as he spoke to the media.

'How do you feel, sir?' asked one reporter, thrusting a microphone forward.

'It's a bit difficult to tell at the moment,' Charles replied. Then he added, 'I'm obviously relieved and delighted. It's marvellous. It's rather a grown-up thing I've found. It's rather a shock to my system.'

Asked about the baby, the prince replied, 'He's in marvellous form.'

The media scrum followed and the questions came thick and fast, and became a little stranger. Did he have any hair? 'Yes, fair hair, rather blondish. It'll probably go to something else later,' he replied.

Did he look like Charles or his mother?

'I can't tell yet,' the prince replied. 'I've no idea.'

Then one from left field. Was he the prettiest baby in the world?

'Well, he's not bad,' Charles replied with a smile.

Then a television reporter shoved his way to the front and came up with one of the most impertinent questions of the day: 'They [the crowd] have been singing, "Well done Charlie let's have another one." Is that on the cards?'

A little taken aback, Charles smiled, before adding, 'Have they?! … Bloody hell! Give us a chance … ask my wife. I don't think she'd be too pleased just yet.'

Then he went into the crowd as 'Three Cheers for the Prince of Wales' rang out, before being driven back to the palace.

Charles returned the next day and cheerily faced the battery of photographers, reporters and television journalists again, who were all anxious to glean any snippet of information about the royal birth, but Charles deflected the questions by talking about the dreary, wet weather. 'It's not very nice, is it?' he said. Then he relented and walked over to the press, packed like sardines behind a steel police barrier, in position early to get the all-important picture of the infant.

'Can you tell us how the princess is?' asked one of the television journalists. The prince who was, oddly, carrying some folders and paperwork and accompanied by his Scotland Yard Personal Protection Officer, replied. 'She's very well.'

'And your son?'

'He's in excellent form, too,' said the prince, with the hint of a smile. 'Looking a bit more human this morning.'

Another shouted, 'When do you think your wife will be coming home, sir?'

'I hope as soon as possible,' he replied.

The media and crowd which had gathered outside didn't have much longer to wait. Within a few hours and less than two days after arriving at the hospital, the Prince and Princess of Wales emerged with their baby in Charles's arms. They appeared to be a perfect picture of family happiness.

Despite Diana's smiles, the princess was struggling to cope, both physically and mentally. She could barely put one foot in front of the other and recalled later that she was in agony throughout the photo session and couldn't wait for it to be over. Her stitches were killing her, she recalled later, continuing to say, 'It was such a strain to stand there and smile even just for a few minutes. As soon as the car disappeared around the corner out of sight of the photographers, I burst into tears.'[4]

Within minutes, after posing for pictures with the nursing staff on the steps, they were home at Apartments 8 and 9, Kensington Palace. Diana couldn't wait to lock herself away with her baby and keep him away from prying eyes. This public performance was all new. In the past, royal princes and their parents had been protected from such public intrusion. But this infant was different. Born into the age of modern media with its rolling news coverage, he was the first future British monarch to have been born in hospital and not safely behind the palace iron gates.

The new second in line to the throne, a future king and direct heir to the reigning Queen, was to be named Prince William of Wales, Buckingham Palace announced later. His parents agreed on the name after what was described later as 'a bit of an argument' between them. A compromise was reached: Diana chose William, whilst Charles's first choice, Arthur, went second, followed by Philip in honour of Charles's father, Prince Philip, the Duke of Edinburgh, and Louis after Earl Mountbatten of Burma, his great-uncle who had been assassinated along with three others on 27 August 1979 by Provisional IRA bomb-maker Thomas McMahon off the coast of Mullaghmore, County Sligo, Ireland. McMahon was sentenced to life imprisonment, but was released in 1998 under the terms of the Good Friday Agreement.

From the moment he first set eyes on his son, Charles was besotted. His paternal devotion, for a short period at least, helped heal some of the wounds of his troubled marriage. The arrival of their son meant a great deal to Charles. He was grateful to have been at Diana's bedside throughout, sharing in the birth. Not everyone in the family, however, shared the sentimentality of the new father. He was aware that while William belonged to them, in a sense he belonged to everyone in Britain, too. The Queen, who is well known for her sharp wit, joked when she met her new grandson, 'Thank heavens he hasn't ears like his father.'[5]

The Queen and Prince Philip, both great-great-grandchildren of Queen Victoria and for whom family ancestry and bloodlines mattered, were of course thrilled with the outcome. Royal historians were having a field day too, for Diana's Spencer ancestry meant that she was descended from two of Charles II's illegitimate sons, Henry Fitzroy, 1st Duke of Grafton and Charles Lennox, 1st Duke of Richmond. It meant that the baby boy was destined to become the first blood descendant of the Stuart monarch, who restored the monarchy after Oliver Cromwell's interregnum, to ascend to the throne, three centuries after his death in 1685, from apoplexy, with no legitimate children to inherit the crown.[6]

Despite the public perception of happiness, everything, as Diana would say, was not 'hunky-dory'. Whilst Charles and Diana were both delighted by the arrival of little William, unfortunately the princess began to suffer from postpartum depression. She desperately wanted to be a good mother, but the condition, which left her with a jumble of powerful emotions and raging mood swings, engulfed her and took away the joy of the moment. Still only twenty, a few weeks shy of her twenty-first birthday, Diana would lurch from feelings of happiness to periods of deep, dark fears and profound anxiety. Charles felt powerless as his young, beautiful wife would end up crying herself to sleep. Bemused and concerned, Charles moved quickly and sought professional psychiatric help for his wife. He consulted Dr Alan McGlashan,[7] who was known to Charles's friend and mentor, the philosopher Laurens van der Post, and asked him not only to help his wife Diana but to counsel him too, as he was beginning to struggle to cope with the mental strain of their marriage, caused by incompatibility. The last thing he wanted to do was fail, but it was becoming increasingly apparent to him and to those close to him that something had to change if they were going to last the course.

'In my opinion it was a positive move. It showed that the prince had at least tried very hard to resolve their problems between himself and his wife from the outset and that he was prepared to do anything to give his marriage a chance. He knew his relationship with the princess was in a bad way but he was taking action before it had irretrievably broken down,' said a close friend.[8] He had a point. Sadly, it failed, and Diana retreated more and more into her shell in a state of heightened paranoia.

Her next crisis came when Diana had to brace herself six weeks later for William's christening on 4 August at the palace. Privately, she was furious at the way she had been excluded from the arrangements for the future king. She later claimed[9] that she felt shunned from William's special day. She recalled: 'Nobody asked me when it was suitable for William – 11 a.m. couldn't have been worse. Endless pictures of the Queen, Queen Mother, Charles and William. I was excluded totally that day. Everything was out of control, everything. I wasn't very well, and I just blubbed my eyes out. William started crying too. Well, he just sensed that I wasn't exactly hunky-dory.' At one point, the Queen gestured towards a visibly distressed Diana, appearing to tell her to offer the crying baby her finger to suck. The new mother obliged, and William calmed down immediately. But throughout, he screamed as soon as her finger was removed.

Like his father, Prince Charles, Prince William was christened in the ornate Music Room of Buckingham Palace. The twenty-five-minute-long ceremony took place to coincide with his great-grandmother the Queen Mother's eighty-second birthday. Most of the royal family were there, but Prince Andrew and Princess Margaret were absent, as both were abroad at the time. The service was conducted by the Archbishop of Canterbury, the Most Rev. Robert Runcie and as per tradition, Prince William wore the same gown that his father, grandmother and dozens of other royal babies before him had worn for their christenings: a robe made of Honiton lace, ordered by Queen Victoria in 1841 for the christening of her daughter, Victoria, Princess Royal. The robe has since been retired due to its age and fragility, and a replica has been made by the Queen's dressmaker, Angela Kelly.

The Lily Font, also commissioned for Victoria, the Princess Royal's christening, was used for William's christening too, brought from the Tower of London to the palace especially for the ceremony. Typically, royal babies are christened with water from the River Jordan, where Jesus was baptised, but because the palace's supply of the special water was depleted, they had to use tap water instead. William's godparents, King Constantine II, the former King of Greece and a cousin of Prince Philip, Lord Romsey, grandson of Lord Mountbatten, who was Charles's beloved uncle tragically killed by the IRA, Sir Laurens van der Post, author and a mentor to Prince Charles, Princess Alexandra, the Queen's cousin, Lady Susan Hussey, Lady-in-Waiting to the Queen and the Duchess of Westminster, a close friend of Diana, Princess of Wales, all posed for photographs.

Others on the select list were Diana's family, of course: the Earl and Countess Spencer, her granny, Ruth, Lady Fermoy, her mother, the Hon. Mrs Frances Shand-Kydd, her brother, Viscount Althorp and her sisters Lady Sarah McCorquodale and Lady Jane Fellowes and her husband, Robert. Also included were Diana's gynaecologist George Pinker and his wife, along with Charles's old nanny, Mabel Anderson, and interior designer Dudley Poplak and their close friends, Mr and Mrs Antony Duckworth-Chad. The Queen's Lady-in-Waiting Lady Kathryn Dugdale, Master of the Household, Vice-Admiral Sir Peter Ashmore also made the list. There was even a place for her childbirth guru, Betty Parsons, whose special relaxation methods have been used by more than 20,000 mothers-to-be since the sixties, including the Queen, Diana and Sarah, Duchess of York.

Charles made sure that his personal staff team were there, too, to witness the historic occasion. So along with the elite of society were the Waleses' team of loyal retainers, their nanny, chef, butler, valet and dresser as well as his Scotland Yard police officers. It showed how inclusive the prince was. Also on William's christening list were Diana's dresser, Evelyn Dagley, chef Mervyn Wycherley, senior housemaid Sheila Tilley, Charles's valet, Ken Stronach, as well as their team of

Scotland Yard policemen, Charles's PPO Supt. John MacLean, Chief Inspector Colin Trimming, Sergeant Alan Peters, Sergeant James MacMaster and Diana's PPO Inspector Graham Smith.

Charles was always very loyal to his team and believed, as they served his family with such devotion, that they should be there to witness the historic moment when the future king, baby William, was baptised. Diana, however, not only felt excluded by the arrangements but she couldn't wait for the ordeal to be over: 'I felt desperate, because I had literally just given birth – William was only six weeks old. And it was all decided around me. Hence the ghastly pictures,' she recalled years later, as described in Andrew Morton's book *Diana: Her True Story*. The photographer on the big day was multi-award-winning *Daily Mirror* staff man Kent Gavin, who was highly regarded by Charles and the royal family.[10] He said, 'All I remember on the day was when the shoot was over and I was just about to leave, I realised we hadn't done a very important shot. I thought I had to say something, so I said to the Queen, "There isn't a photograph of the Queen Mother and Prince William on their own together, Ma'am." The Queen made it happen.' It was a historic shot and one of Her Majesty's favourites.

★★★

The original plans for the 1983 royal tour to Australia by the Prince and Princess of Wales had to be postponed due to Diana's pregnancy, but the Queen and Buckingham Palace were keen to capitalise on Diana's popularity and felt she would be a big hit Down Under. They were delighted because the tour had been organised by the pro-monarchist Malcolm Fraser's government before they were defeated by the republican-supporting Australian Labor party Prime Minister Bob Hawke. The Queen believed the Wales's tour would go some way to restoring confidence in the monarchy, which had been seriously damaged by the Gough Whitlam affair in 1975. Her Majesty's appointed representative in Australia, the eighteenth Governor-General of the country, Sir John Kerr, had caused a huge political uproar when he dismissed Gough Whitlam's elected ALP government and replaced it with the opposition party. At the time, most Australians had little idea that the Queen's representative had such power, and the affair prompted questions about the country's political independence from Britain.

Sir John acted after the so-called 'Loans Affair' led Whitlam to mislead parliament. Firstly, Rex Connor, the Minister for Minerals and Energy, resigned from the Whitlam ministry on 14 October, 1975. Connor's resignation was sought by PM Whitlam after revelations in the *Melbourne Herald* newspaper that Connor had continued to seek overseas loans through the Pakistani intermediary Tirath Khemlani. Connor's behaviour constituted misleading parliament. In doing so, Connor had caused Whitlam also to mislead parliament.

What happened next, however, led Australians to question the role of the Queen and her representative, and their system of constitutional monarchy and parliamentary democracy, which mirrored the British system. Whitlam and his government were effectively sacked by the Queen because he had failed to get parliament to approve his government's spending, and then subsequently declined to call a general election. It was revealed in state papers released in 2020 that the Queen had not been informed in advance of the dismissal of Whitlam as prime minister on 11 November. The letters, released after a court battle, show Sir John wrote it was 'better for Her Majesty not to know.' However, it is clear from the papers that he had discussed it with senior figures at Buckingham Palace to ascertain whether he had the constitutional authority to dismiss Whitlam. It seems inconceivable that those senior figures would not have passed on the information to the Queen, even if it was informally.

So, by 6 March 1983, when Charles and Diana arrived in Australia for the start of their six-week tour of Australia and New Zealand, they were joined by nine-month-old William because Diana had refused to leave the infant behind. Upon arrival in Alice Springs, Australia, William, who was affectionately dubbed 'Billy the Kid' by the Australian press, was carried down the steps of the Royal Australia Air Force Boeing 707 by his nanny, Barbara Barnes, who had looked after William since birth. Charles had been instrumental in hiring her because he believed the only way to ensure that his sons grew up with the type of traditional values he cherished was to employ an old-fashioned British nanny. 'There were some experts very certain about how you should bring up children,' he said, 'but then, after twenty years, they said they'd been wrong. Think of all the poor people who followed their suggestions.'

Diana was far more intent on following the teachings of an altogether more modern teacher, in the shape of Dr Benjamin Spock, with whom she claimed a distant blood relationship. Spock was an influential advocate of the new permissive attitude towards childcare, and that was exactly what Diana wanted for her sons. As soon as William was born, Charles wanted to employ his beloved old nanny, Mabel Anderson, as his son's principal carer. She had played such a significant role in his life, he felt she would be perfect for William. Diana forcefully argued that Mabel was both too old and far too traditional for the job she had in mind. 'A mother's arms are so much more comforting than anyone else's,' she told him bluntly.

She did accept that her position as the Princess of Wales meant she would need full-time support if she were to carry out her public duties. Charles soon realised that on this subject, the lady was not for turning. He finally agreed to Diana's choice of Barbara Barnes. As if to draw a line under the past, she was the first royal nanny not to have at least two footmen and two housemaids to help her. 'I'm here to help the princess, not to take over,'[11] Barbara tactfully announced. The daughter of a forestry worker, Barbara had an easy manner to which children responded, and she got on well with Charles.

Others in the party included former palace footman Michael Fawcett, who had been seconded to Charles and would act as butler for the couple, and chef Mervyn Wycherley. The family posed for photographers before Barnes whisked William away to the couple's base at a farm in Woomargama, Albury, where Charles and Diana planned to re-join him the following day.

The couple's press secretary, Vic Chapman, then fifty-one, a six-foot-tall, sharp-witted former press secretary to Canadian Prime Minister Pierre Trudeau and former Canadian Football League player, sensing William was a positive news story, told the press, 'I heard Prince William cry only twice in thirty hours [during the flight].' The decision to bring William represented a marked break with tradition, contrasting with the Queen's visit to Australia in 1954. She would never travel with Charles in case they both were killed in a plane crash, and Charles was not supposed to travel with his new son either. But bringing William was what made the visit a game-changer. There was a huge focus of attention being drawn in the Australian press about Diana being a breath of fresh air and a modern mum.

There was a lot riding on this tour. It was politically sensitive, with a new wave of Republicanism sweeping Australia, championed by its prime minister at the time, Bob Hawke. Before the tour, he had flippantly dismissed the heir to the Australian throne as a 'nice young bloke'. On 6 March 1983, a mere twelve days before Charles and Diana were set to fly to the continent, a television interviewer asked if Charles would make a good King of Australia. 'I don't think we will be talking about kings of Australia forever more,' he replied.[12] Then he said he thought people would eventually vote to have a republic.

If Charles and Diana had really been sent to save the Crown from republicanism in Australia and the monarchy from being dumped, they had probably arrived a little late. It had already been saved, at least for the foreseeable future, by Hawke's election victory; although he was anxious to assert Australia's independence, he didn't believe republicanism was an urgent issue. His priority, as he made clear, was the restoration of the national economy.

Britain's travelling Fleet Street 'Royal Rat Pack' (the name given to reporters and photographers assigned to cover the Windsor story) were always looking for a headline-grabbing angle, and they weren't going to let the truth get in the way of a good story to keep their editors happy and their expenses signed. The British red-top tabloids had already started to paint Diana as erratic. James Whitaker of the *Daily Mirror*, regarded as the doyen of royal reporters, had already run an exclusive about rumours that Diana was suffering from an eating disorder. Under the headline: 'Concern for Di's health', with a strapline, 'Fears over her diet', it may have been exploitative, but Whitaker, not for the first time, had got it spot on.

The press were not the only ones to question Diana's staying power. The Queen and her advisers were worried about how Diana would cope: 'Did she have the stamina?' But Charles said he was confident she would pull it out of the bag. The tour was a gruelling one: a month in Australia and two weeks in New Zealand. The couple were set to cover 30,000 miles and make up to eight appearances in a single day. Charles had been doing work at this pace his whole life, but it proved overwhelming to his twenty-one-year-old wife. 'The Queen was "terribly worried" before the tour because of Diana's youth and apparent shyness,' wrote the Press Association's royal correspondent, Grania Forbes, ahead of the trip, which must have been cleared by a senior adviser. While the international press waited for the couple to land in Alice Springs, Australia, *The Sydney Morning Herald*'s Alison Stuart recalled the reporters gossiping: 'Would she snap, would she cry, would she collapse from the heat?'[13]

In truth, the royal tour got off to a slow start. Crowds who visited royal events in the Northern Territory were smallish, mainly consisting of mums, teachers and children, and a smattering of Union-flag-waving British expatriates. But Diana was an immediate hit with the children and overall received positive press and TV coverage from the Australian media, who were happy to use lots of photos and footage of Charles's beautiful young bride. Diana did indeed show signs of fatigue. She looked uncomfortably sunburnt and her eyes were often downcast. Charles, sensitive to his wife's moods, apologised and said they were both still suffering from jet lag. Three days after they had landed in Australia, an Associated Press reporter ungallantly described Diana as 'red-faced and bare-legged'.[14] Sensitive to such criticisms, Diana told one Australian reporter, 'I can't cope with the heat very well.'

On a visit to Uluru, then known as Ayers Rock, Diana appeared uncertain. She was not nervous, just inappropriately clad in a white dress that immediately blew open, revealing her petticoat and knees. From that moment, Diana battled in vain to keep the dress closed, as the relentless photographers had a field day. She didn't want to climb, not through fear of slipping, but because she knew when she descended it would expose her knees and petticoat to the world's press.

Once over her jet lag, Diana began to shine. Showing her Spencer spirit, she proved she was made of the right stuff. As the royal tour really got into the swing of things Charles and Diana thoroughly charmed the country. They danced at the Sheraton Wentworth Hotel in Sydney, the first time they had ever been filmed dancing together, with Diana donning a spectacular turquoise dress. Charles scored a goal at a polo match in Sydney and the crowd erupted into cheers.

In Perth, they made headlines when Charles tenderly kissed Diana's hand in public. 'Prince plays the gallant at royal party,' read a headline in *The Times* of London, penned by its irrepressible correspondent, Alan Hamilton, whose witty, sometimes irreverent dispatches were a daily pleasure for readers. A pipe-smoking Scot, Hamilton was one of the old school of Fleet Street reporters who needed nothing more than a notebook, a pen and a phone line to file his copy, fuelled by a nip of whisky and a few puffs of his pipe. He refused to be seduced by modern technology, only came to use a mobile telephone late in his professional life and never opened the lid of a laptop. He covered the royals for thirty years, retired in 2008 and died in 2013. He was a good friend and mentor to me.

As they criss-crossed Australia, wowing the crowds, William stayed with his nanny, chef Wycherley, seconded butler Fawcett and his Scotland Yard protection officers at the working sheep ranch, where Ronald Reagan had once stayed. Charles and Diana would visit him as frequently as they could throughout their tour.[15] The travelling staff's improving suntans would elicit comments from the prince. It became a running joke that every time the royals arrived back at the ranch there would be an almighty downpour. Diana just wanted to see her son.

The six-bedroomed homestead was owned by Gordon and Margaret Darling and was set in roughly 2,500 acres. The local New South Wales village was described in the press as a typical Australian country township. The town served as a comfortable hub and safe home base for William, within driving distance of an airport, and roughly in between Sydney and Melbourne. The Darlings were a little surprised but 'absolutely delighted' when the call came asking them if they could host the royal couple and vacate the property.

Members of the New South Wales tactical response group, armed to the teeth, were installed at the gate. The airspace above the property was secured and a helicopter was placed at the ready on the ranch.[16] Chef Wycherley made sure the pantry was fully stocked by making frequent trips to nearby Holbrook, but whenever the royal couple arrived, they tended to ask for simple fare. Diana liked to pick at cold meats.

When Charles and Diana were away from the homestead, Nanny Barnes and William would be driven around the property every day, including near the digs occupied by the jackeroos, men working on a sheep or cattle station to gain experience. He would just sit in his little car seat and smile. Inside the house, the staff would be kept busy chasing after William as he crawled on the carpets.

When Charles and Diana were in town, it was hardly a break from work. They met local children from the town's school and attended a Sunday service in nearby Holbrook at St Paul's Anglican Church, where Charles read a lesson.

Diana's popularity soon started to eclipse that of Charles. 'The Princess of Wales was the woman they'd come to see, and the people of the Riverland weren't disappointed,' said one of her team on the visit. She freely dispensed titbits concerning baby William, about his health and the weather and jokingly inquired of an elderly citizen if she had any whisky in her picnic basket. Diana was mobbed wherever she went. On 15 April, the *Melbourne Herald* published a cartoon with a map of Australia superimposed with a heart. 'Princess Diana,' read a caption, 'a permanent imprint!' Two days later, the *Sydney Morning Herald* echoed the same sentiment: 'Di Thrills the Queen!' said a headline. Charles on the other hand was criticised when some Australians failed to appreciate his Goonish sense of humour. He received scores of letters from disgruntled animal-loving locals after he joked about feeding baby William on 'warm milk and minced kangaroo'.

The *London Evening Standard* reported: 'This tour has set republicanism back ten years.'

Diana had delighted audiences by sharing cheerful tales about their young son. Yes, William did love his stuffed koala. But she was conscious that whilst praising her performance, Charles, who as future king had always been the star of the show, was uncomfortable with all the attention she was getting. In a 1995 interview with the BBC, the princess recalled that the attention she received during the tour's royal walkabouts had upset him. 'We'd be going round Australia, for instance, and all you could hear was, "Oh, she's on the other side." Now, if you're a man – like my husband – a proud man, you mind about that if you hear it every day for four weeks. You feel low about it, instead of feeling happy and sharing it.'

The visit was far from over. They still had a two-week tour of New Zealand to complete. They touched down on 17 April and the following day 35,000 children were there to greet them at a packed Eden Park. Firstly, they had to face a Maori challenge – the first of many on the tour. Facing tattooed and scantily clad warriors, the royal party slowly edged forward as the Maoris stuck their tongues out at them, gesticulated and wielded their weapons. Once Charles had picked up the stick that had been laid down as a challenge to show that they had come in peace, the party could begin. What followed was an exhausting tour, but Diana, now in the swing of it, charmed the huge crowds wherever she went.

The local press praised her style at every turn and were obsessed with her wardrobe of outfits. She wore a dress by David and Elizabeth Emanuel at Parliament House with Prime Minister Robert Muldoon. At a Royal New Zealand Air Force base in Christchurch, she wore a Catherine Walker coat and John Boyd hat; at a visit to Manukau, near Auckland, she wore a Jan Van Velden suit; and she wowed the audience in a Donald Campbell gown at a gala ballet performance in Auckland. As the royal trio journeyed to Masterton, Wainuiomata and Upper Hutt, a demure Diana paraded an array of incredible outfits, the most memorable being a pale blue, sequin-studded evening gown with a diamond tiara for a banquet in the New Zealand parliament. She was a huge hit and, although her husband praised his wife in speeches wherever he went, she sensed he was displeased at being upstaged. There were protests against the monarchy during their trip, and a buttock bared by Te Ringa Mangu Mihaka, but overall, the trip was deemed a success.

Perhaps one of the tour's most endearing moments came when ten-month-old William posed with his parents and played on a Buzzy Bee on the lawns of Government House in Auckland. It was the icing on the cake. Charles and Diana, who was dressed in a somewhat frumpy long, green dress with an exaggerated white collar, happily accommodated the group of jovial photographers' cameras snapping away at what they believed was a happy family.

The royals emerged from the main house for the photoshoot on 23 April on time, with Charles carrying his son. Everyone agreed William had grown a lot in the five weeks since he had last been seen in public when they all arrived in Australia, at Alice Springs. Diana, hedging her bets a little, had told the newsmen she could not guarantee that he would crawl. So, right on cue, he crawled, drawing a laugh from royals and newsmen alike. During the next few minutes William put in an extraordinary virtuoso performance with his proud parents in supporting roles.

The secret of his other family nickname – 'Wills' – was revealed by his parents. The prince and princess knew they were on a roll when William attempted a wave to the photographers, just as they were about to leave. When they were asked by the lensmen for some posed standing shots, they readily complied. The press corps' hunger for pictures had for once been sated. The couple went back to the house and William to his room, his first major public appearance over.

Cracks may not yet have been obvious in Charles and Diana's relationship, but even during this 'happy family' photoshoot a few hairline fractures had emerged. Charles sat cross-legged, away from his wife and child, his arms out of reach for comfort or play, his hands in his lap rather than reaching out to his young family. Diana was clearly deeply engaged with her new baby. Her focus was on William, not on the cameras; and certainly not on her husband.

On 30 April, the New Zealand tour was over and the couple boarded a plane destined for Eleuthera Island in the Bahamas for a holiday in the sunshine. Throughout the tour, Diana's status as a global superstar had become ever more firmly entrenched as she drew massive crowds wherever she went. It was the start of the Diana phenomenon and the birth of the 'People's Princess'. Diana, however, saw it differently. Years later she recalled the tour as 'a test of endurance', as described in Andrew Morton's *Diana: In Her Own Words*. The couple, she said, had been greeted by hysterical crowds in many of the cities they visited and Diana felt, 'jet-lagged, anxious and sick with bulimia'. Perhaps her experiences long after the visit had tainted the memory, for those with the prince and princess on the long trip remembered them as being happy and having, on the whole, enjoyed the trip. 'I really don't remember a row, maybe once, but actually they got on very well and I think they were still in love,' said a close source.[17]

William was a huge hit with the public. Charles and Diana understood the thirst for information and pictures of the prince and arranged several staged photo-calls for the cameras and television. At eighteen months, William toddled out for the ''tographers', as he called them, in the walled garden of Kensington Palace. Six months later, in June, he returned for the sequel, to celebrate his second birthday, performing for the cameras again by kicking a football and blurting out, 'Daddy,' to his father's and the journalists' delight.

William's second birthday was celebrated with a small gathering at Kensington Palace, which included the Queen. Chef Wycherley had prepared a magnificent cake in the shape of a digger – as the little prince would always get terribly excited any time he saw a JCB or big truck – with two candles as the funnel and bright pink wheels, which were edible. Chef Wycherley's fancy cakes became a fixture with the 'Thomas the Tank Engine' cake for William's fourth birthday and a brilliant cake in the shape of a plane, the Queen's Flight jet, for his fifth. Soon, William's world would change forever with the arrival of a new royal baby, his little brother, and he would no longer be the centre of attention.

CHAPTER TWO

SPARE NECESSITY

'My children are the most important things in my life. I love them to death'

HRH Diana, Princess of Wales

The Prince of Wales stayed at his wife's side throughout her nine-hour labour. He handed Diana ice cubes to suck when she was thirsty, he held her hand in support and he encouraged her throughout the exhausting experience, although he later admitted he had dozed off a couple of times. They arrived at the hospital early in the morning and their baby, the couple's second son, was eventually delivered on 15 September 1984 at 4.20 p.m.

It should have been a moment of undiluted joy for the young family. The sad truth, however, was that despite one or two moments of shared intimacy, by the autumn of 1984 the royal marriage, which had promised so much, was already in free fall. Diana, at just twenty-four, felt increasingly abandoned and unwanted by the only lover she had ever known. Charles, now thirty-five, also felt imprisoned in a marriage to a woman wracked by jealousy and mental health issues, with whom he had very little in common. Diana later claimed that their marriage had been in 'total darkness' in between the births of their sons and she had blotted it out because it was 'such pain'. Somehow, she said, 'Harry appeared by a miracle'. (As described in Andrew Morton's book *Diana*, drawing on interviews with Diana in 1991.) Out of nowhere, however, the couple had become 'very, very close to each other' in the six weeks leading up to their second son's birth, Diana later admitted.

Charles had made no secret among the family that he had been hoping for a girl. So, when a second son was born, his first comment was rather thoughtless. 'Oh God, it's a boy,' he said to his wife. Although Charles later dismissed his comment as a joke, Diana, who already knew she was carrying a boy after a scan but had kept it from her husband so as not to spoil their bonding, was cut to the core. Added to that, Charles followed it with an equally barbed second comment: 'And he's even got red hair.'[18] Another 'joke' that tore at Diana's heart. Diana's family tree was full of redheads, so it was insulting on a primal level. With that, 'something inside me closed off … our marriage, the whole thing went down the drain.' Charles was at the very least guilty of gross insensitivity. Diana, after all, had just endured nine hours of natural birth, which had followed a miscarriage before she became pregnant with Harry.

The princess had been mulling over a possible name for weeks and had already made up her mind. Charles's preference was Albert, after his grandfather King George VI, who adopted the name George when king. Eventually, Charles bowed to his wife over the name choice in order to keep the peace. Canadian Vic Chapman, assistant press secretary to the Queen, who handled Charles and Diana's media relations at the time of the birth, made the announcement from the steps of the Lindo Wing. 'OK, the name is Prince Henry … they intend to call him "Prince Harry".'

The press and public gathered outside had to wait until the following day to see the little prince. First, William, wearing red shorts, arrived with his father and protection team, to meet his baby brother. Royal nanny Barbara Barnes was photographed escorting William from the Lindo Wing a short while later. Then PPO Sgt Alan Peters suddenly emerged and dashed down the steps to prepare the car. Moments later, Diana, wearing a scarlet outfit and holding the sleeping baby wrapped in a white shawl, and Charles appeared on the Lindo Wing steps to pose for pictures. This time, apart from a few smiles and waves, the new dad didn't say anything.

They returned to Kensington Palace after posing outside the hospital. To Diana's annoyance, as soon as they returned home, Charles announced he was off to play polo at Windsor, leaving his wife alone with the two children. He didn't think he was doing anything wrong, but Diana again saw it as a sign of his uncaring attitude towards her. She felt abandoned. She went to the kitchen and started picking at the selection of cold meats that chef Mervyn Wycherley had left for her in the fridge. She loved lamb cutlets and would snack on them cold, with caviar. She also enjoyed foie gras. By now, sadly, her bulimia was back, and she had politely asked for a jug of cold custard, too.

Although Charles knew that Diana was deeply sensitive about the topic of Harry's gender, at his second son's christening, he brought it up again. This time he incurred the wrath of Diana's mother, Frances Shand-Kydd. 'We were so disappointed – we thought it would be a girl,'[19] he told her. Frances was furious and bristled at the comment and reported it back to Diana. Harry would have been around the age of seven at the time when Diana was interviewed and said of the young prince: 'Harry was a complete joy and is actually closer to his father than perhaps William at the moment.'[20] Diana didn't stop there. She claimed that Charles took his discontent over not having a girl to her own mother at Harry's christening.

Frances, whose acrimonious divorce from Diana's father Johnny had been finalised in 1969, was not a lady to suffer fools. She made it clear to her son-in-law that she found his attitude disappointing and let him know. 'Mummy snapped his head off, saying: "You should realise how lucky you are to have a child that's normal." Ever since that day the shutters have come down and that's what he does when he gets somebody answering back at him,' Diana recalled. The admonishment irritated him and his relationship with his mother-in-law deteriorated after that.

His lack of compatibility with Diana had been something the prince had agonised over even before their engagement. Prone to procrastination, Charles had been deeply unsure of the then Lady Diana Spencer's suitability as his wife from the beginning. But he felt under pressure, mainly from the Fleet Street press, to wed. There was no doubt a physical attraction and in the early days of their marriage they were tactile and intimate. But Charles soon felt they were totally unsuitable. Many years after Diana's death in 1997 and even after he had married his long-term mistress, Camilla Parker Bowles, his frustration over the matter boiled over into a sense of profound injustice. To this day he is intensely irritated over what he believes are 'lies' that are both deeply malevolent and harmful to his reputation.

Charles has candidly told his close circle of friends, 'I desperately wanted to get out of the wedding in 1981, during the engagement, when I discovered just how awful the prospects were, having had no chance whatsoever to get to know Diana beforehand.'[21] When referring to the 'awful prospects', the prince was speaking of Diana's bulimia and her alarming and irrational mood swings and temper, which he found impossible to deal with.

Charles started dating the beautiful Lady Diana, the third daughter of Earl Spencer, in 1980 at a time when the pressure for him to marry was beginning to gain momentum, but he soon realised just how ill-matched they were. In the middle of one conversation in the weeks leading up to the wedding, Charles spoke to Diana about his day and his work commitments. She stared back at him blankly and seemed incapable of grasping what he was saying. 'She would well up and burst into tears for no apparent reason,' he recalled to friends.[22]

A sympathetic man, Charles was at a total loss about what to do to help his wife. He sought professional help for himself and his bride-to-be. But as the media frenzy reached fever pitch, despite his sense that there was something very wrong, he felt it was impossible for him to back out of the wedding. 'Things were very different in those days,' Charles explained to a friend. 'The power and influence of the media driving matters toward an engagement and wedding were unstoppable.' (This was originally quoted in my book *Charles at Seventy: Thoughts, Hopes and Dreams.*)

Of course, both Charles and Diana, now parents, loved their sons. They knew that the relationship was on a hopeless trajectory and their marriage, that had barely begun, was over. By this time, the autumn of 1984, Diana simply did not trust her husband, and with hindsight, probably with good reason. She was convinced in the months leading up to Harry's birth that Camilla, his former married lover, was back in his life and the two were once again intimate. Despite Charles's reassurances to the contrary, Diana simply did not believe him. She was heartbroken by what she regarded as his overt betrayal.

The fuss around Harry's arrival seemed to upset the rather spoiled toddler, William. Until then, he had been the sole focus of his parents' attention, as well as that of the coterie of staff in the Waleses' household. William, even at a tender age, loved being the star attraction that his status as a future king granted him. Diana noted that William revelled in the attention. He could not even fall over without a member of the Kensington Palace staff rushing over and picking him up and dusting him down.

Harry's birth changed everything. The focus shifted to the rusty-haired baby, at least for a short while. Diana was keen to prevent William's jealousy escalating and did her best to ensure that the two boys bonded. William was taken to the hospital to meet his little brother for the first time, and she organised for him to present the baby with a soft toy. 'William spends the entire time pouring an endless supply of hugs and kisses on Harry, and we are hardly allowed near,' Diana said.[23]

Charles felt his son's resentment over the new baby was only to be expected and urged his wife not to be overly concerned. In truth, the prince was also pleased that his younger son, Harry, was less boisterous than William had been as a baby. Charles noted that Harry was 'extraordinarily good, sleeps marvellously and eats well'. He also said that Harry was 'the one with the gentle nature'.[24]

Four generations of the royal family attended Harry's baptism, and at the photo session that followed there was no mistaking the pride on the Queen Mother's face as the then eighty-five-year-old former Queen Consort took her fourth great-grandchild in her arms, whilst he plucked at the christening robe of Honiton lace that had been used in baptisms since the days of the Queen Empress Victoria. Film footage of the christening and party to follow was shown on Christmas Day in the Queen's broadcast, and William was seen galloping through the corridors of Windsor Castle and chasing round the Archbishop of Canterbury in a game of tag with his cousins, Peter and Zara Phillips. It was later revealed that he used to have a special name for his grandmother. After a fall at Buckingham Palace, the prince cried out for 'Gary, Gary.' When a guest asked who Gary was, the Queen stepped in and explained: 'I'm Gary. He hasn't learned to say Granny yet.'

Conducted by the Archbishop of Canterbury, Dr Robert Runcie, on 21 December in St George's Chapel, within the grounds of Windsor Castle, Harry's baptism broke with royal tradition. Until then, most royal babies – including William – had been baptised in the Music Room at Buckingham Palace. The three-month-old Harry cried for only two or three minutes whilst the archbishop performed the blessing with holy water. 'He was as quiet as a mouse throughout the rest,' said one of the choristers.

Even though the event was a strictly family-only occasion, the Queen agreed that the entire nation could share it, so television pictures were broadcast in her Christmas message a few days later. It went without a hitch, but William stole a large slice of the limelight with his antics and infectious laughter, as Lord Snowdon – Princess Margaret's ex-husband and official photographer on the day – took the official portraits. All eyes were on William as he cheekily twisted and turned in front of the group, causing the Queen and Charles to burst out laughing. William, just two-and-a-half years old, and described by his father as a 'spindly little character with a good sense of humour', loved every minute of it. He was fascinated by a clockwork bird in a cage given to him by Lord Snowdon whilst the pictures were being taken.

William's over-excited behaviour and the happy smiling faces at the christening party delighted millions as they celebrated Christmas at home with their families in front of their television sets, but the public relations masterstroke masked the truth. The on-screen royal smiles belied the painful truth of a 'fairy tale' marriage in free fall and a royal family on the brink of a crisis that would rock a modern monarchy to its foundations. Diana agonised about the best way to raise her sons. She knew they had to be made aware of royal customs that she regarded as stuffy and outmoded, but she wanted them to be free spirits just the same.

Diana spent hours locked in conversations with her older sister, Lady Jane Fellowes, who like her, had married into the royal family system, albeit at a significantly lower level. Jane had wed Sir Robert Fellowes, who rose to become the Queen's most trusted servant, and acted with distinction as her private secretary, one of the most senior positions in the royal household. Diana confided in Jane in the early days and asked for advice on the best way to educate her sons and prepare them for the unique life experiences that lay before them.

Prince Charles felt it was best to follow the traditional royal educational path of employing a governess, preferably one with experience of teaching members of the royal family. He and his mother had benefited from the closeted experience, and he saw no reason why his sons should need anything different. Diana was determined that it was not going to happen. Jane's children – Laura (born in 1980) and Alexander (three years later) – also lived at Kensington Palace, so she and Diana were almost exact maternal contemporaries, and Jane agreed with Diana's thinking about how to raise the children.

Diana believed William and Harry would benefit from mixing with what they termed 'ordinary' children. Of course, these 'ordinary' children would inevitably come from very privileged backgrounds of wealth and social status. Endless rows ensued, during which the princess made it clear to Charles that she didn't want her sons locked in a schoolroom high in the house somewhere, with only a few hand-picked friends as playmates. She wanted them to grow freely and naturally among their peers. In her more vindictive moments, Diana reminded Charles that just because he had been raised badly, it was wrong to inflict the mistakes of his parents on their children. She reminded the prince that his childhood had left him an emotional wreck, withdrawn, socially inept, and unable to cope with personal criticism. How could he argue with her? Eventually, the shutters came down and his wife won the day. After all, how could he bemoan his experiences and then insist his own children should follow the same route?

The princess was keen to send William to Young England kindergarten in Pimlico, central London, an upmarket nursery, where she had worked after leaving finishing school and where the famous back-lit photograph of her was taken on 17 September 1980. When she tried him out, he failed to participate fully with the other children. They all joined in energetically, playing 'Galloping Horses', and Diana was horrified when William appeared to be left out by the rest of the group. Perhaps overreacting, she saw his inability to interact as evidence of the need for decisive action.

Diana cast around for somewhere nearer to send her older son, and eventually picked a small school run by a bishop's daughter, Mrs Jane Mynors, in a tree-lined street a few minutes' walk from Kensington Palace, at Chepstow Villas in Notting Hill. Not for the first time, William blazed a trail for his younger brother; where William went, his younger brother would inevitably follow. The princess prided herself on her abilities as a mother. 'My children are the most important things in my life. I love them to death,' she confided.

In those early days, Diana relied heavily on the judgement of Nanny Barnes and was adamant that her children were not going to have the same kind of upbringing that she had experienced. She told friends that, as the product of a dysfunctional family, she was often left alone in her bed, frightened and confused about what was going on around her. 'A child's stability arises mainly from the affection received from their parents, and there is no substitute for affection,' she would say when describing how she would always make sure that William and Harry came first.

When the boys went away to boarding school, she pined for them, couldn't wait to receive their letters, and wrote to them twice a week. Despite marrying into the royal family, with all its rank and privilege, she was determined that when it came to her own children, she would have her own way. Like many from broken homes, she did her best to give her sons as secure an environment as possible, and fortunately, this was one area in which Prince Charles truly respected her beliefs.

The prince was fairly old school when it came to motherhood and the duties of his wife. Although society's whole attitude had changed towards what women were expected to do, he believed that one of the most important roles any woman could ever perform was to be a mother. 'Nobody should denigrate that role,' he said publicly. Even though Charles respected his wife's role as a mother, the underlying tensions between the couple surfaced almost from the moment William learned to walk.

As their sons grew, they were raised to show, in public at least, the type of good manners that their father expected. When meeting people, they would offer a handshake and always made a point of writing thank-you notes. One of the more charming aspects for visitors to Kensington Palace or Highgrove was when the boys came downstairs in their dressing gowns to say goodnight, although one of the few people not to be immediately bowled over by the young princes was Sir Bob Geldof. He had come to Kensington Palace to discuss African famine with Charles, when William sauntered in. Unsurprisingly, the dapper youngster was taken aback by the Irishman's appearance.

'He's all dirty. He's got scruffy hair and wet shoes,' William remarked.

Never one to suffer fools, Sir Bob retorted, 'Shut up, you horrible little boy. Your hair's scruffy, too.'[25]

'No, it's not. My mother brushed it!' he chipped back.

Sadly, the relationship between Nanny Barnes and her employers began to unravel, mirroring the disintegration of feelings between Diana and her husband. The princess mistakenly began to see her as a rival for her sons' affections, and Charles was disturbed by the publication of pictures taken when Barbara had flown to the West

Indies before Christmas 1986 for the sixtieth birthday party of her former employer, Lord Glenconner, on his private island, Mustique.

She was photographed enjoying herself in the company of such fellow revelers as Princess Margaret, Jerry Hall and Raquel Welch. Charles did not approve, having old-fashioned views about staff knowing their places, and inevitably, on 15 January 1987, it was announced that Barbara Barnes would be leaving. The statement was timed to coincide with William's first day at his new school. 'I thought no one would notice,' Diana later said, 'but I was wrong, wasn't I?' The British press did not miss a trick. Sensing a story, the tabloid editors elevated the news of Barbara's departure to page one, and relegated William's arrival at his new pre-preparatory school to the inside pages. Meanwhile, William was helping to set the stage for Harry to follow in his footsteps two years later. He quickly informed his new classmates, 'My daddy is a real prince.'

Diana was determined that neither of her beloved sons would go to Charles's old school, Gordonstoun. One of her royal relations remarked, 'She's the strong one in the marriage, especially when it comes to the children.' Like many mothers at the time, the princess was adamant that her sons should be dressed in the most up-to-date fashion and was not going to be put off by stuffy royal protocol or so-called tradition. Out went the short trousers and velvet-collared coats of her husband's youth, and in came striped T-shirts by Jean Bourget, and sweatshirts and corduroy trousers from Benetton. She wanted them to be children of their generation, not throwbacks to the fifties.

The princes' parents were becoming ever more estranged over issues such as spending time with the kids. Michael Shea, the Queen's former press secretary, said, 'The only arguments they had were over the children.' It was, of course, untrue. William and Harry reacted to these strains in their own way. William was always described as being 'forceful'; his brother as 'sweet and a little reserved and shy'. At Mrs Mynors's school, Harry had hidden in the playground and refused to join the other children in their games, but as he grew older and his mischievous character came to the fore, it emerged that he was a better rider and more daring skier than his brother. 'Harry's the naughty one, just like me,'[26] his mother said, with a sparkle in her eye. Harry also developed a passion for animals and the countryside, and he started to echo his father's famous belief in talking to plants. 'Harry loves animals and plants,' Charles proudly observed. 'I tell him all about them and say that they have feelings, too, and mustn't be hurt.'[27] By contrast, William became more sensitive, introverted and closer to his mother. 'William is a very self-possessed, intelligent and mature boy and quite shy,' said his maternal uncle, Charles, now the ninth Earl Spencer. 'He is quite formal and stiff.'[28]

From a very early age, Harry understood he was in the shadow of his older brother, aware of the imbalance in the roles they would be destined for as adults in the royal family. Tensions over the drastic differences in their roles blew up during an argument when they were still very young. Ken Wharfe, a long-serving protection officer to the royals, tells the story of Harry's surprising outburst, when he was aged just six: 'Diana would always take the two boys to Highgrove. On one occasion Diana was driving, I was sat in the front, William and Harry in the back, when Harry said, "You'll be King, I won't; so, I can do what I want!" The princess and I just looked at each other, a little shocked by what he said.'

Harry could easily have felt hurt as William was given precedence. It is true that senior members of the family and even some of the staff seemed to show William deference. The Queen Mother used to put a seat next to her and call for William to sit on it, and he also used to go to Clarence House, without Harry, to see her. Harry, however, seemed to revel in the freedom he knew William would never have. He was far more mischievous that his older brother, who would often tell tales on Harry to his nanny or police officer. His nanny Olga Powell felt the best way to deal with his naughtiness was to impose strict rules. Olga took no nonsense from the boys. She would occasionally give them a smack. 'When he was a little older, I remember one of her classic phrases to Harry was "Harry, I love you, but I don't like you," because he was a nuisance. He was vibrant. But she was strong with him, and I think children like that because they know where they stand,' said Inspector Wharfe.

Harry had inherited his mother's wicked sense of mischief, which often irritated his older brother. On one occasion at Mrs Mynors's kindergarten, Harry was frog-marched to the headmistress by the distraught and furious music teacher, Mr Prichard. All through a morning assembly, Harry, who was sitting next to the piano, kept tugging at the teacher's trousers as he was trying to play. Eventually, the teacher had had enough.

'What on earth is it, Harry? Stop pulling my trousers,' he said.

'But Mr Prichard,' Harry piped up, 'I can see your willy.'

Harry's classmates thought it was hilarious. Mr Prichard didn't. He ejected the prince, who was sent straight to the headmistress for a telling off. The head felt that this was the last straw after Harry had been involved in a series of unruly antics which were disrupting the class. Diana was asked to come and see her to address the issue. Ken Wharfe, Diana's personal protection officer at the time, recalled when the headteacher related the incident and her concerns, Diana burst into a fit of giggles.

Inspector Wharfe later recalled, 'By the time I was assigned to head up the protection for William and Harry in 1986, it was already clear that the royal marriage was in serious difficulties. But the role of wife and mother was the one that Diana valued most highly, and she would go to great lengths to protect it.'

Charles, too, loved his sons desperately, but sadly, by this time, he had fallen out of love with his wife. Therefore, Diana focused all her love on her boys. Not everyone saw her as this doting, perfect mother. In truth the boys' care was often left to staff. One of their police officers found Diana difficult to deal with and dismissed her as a mistress of manipulation; some of her security detail found her level of hypocrisy too much to take. One member of the protection team, who had left her service many years earlier, was so frustrated towards the end of his tenure that one morning he discharged all his bullets into a tree in a garden of a landed family where the Waleses were staying. 'That should wake them up,' he said to a shocked colleague. The SO14 colleague with him urged him to reload quickly to avoid a backlash and say nothing about the incident. Before leaving, the same officer, whom I've chosen not to identify, remarked to his replacement, 'Good luck, you're going to need it. If these kids [Princes William and Harry] were brought up on a council estate somewhere in south London they'd have been taken into care by now.'[29] He was deadly serious. Diana let the pair run free and wild as young children.

The prince, perhaps due to work commitments or because he didn't want to upset Diana, was not the most attentive father, but at weekends, he tried to schedule time off. When at home he would often go looking for his sons to check in on them. He seemed to have a sixth sense, always one step ahead of their misdemeanors, whether they had been go-karting around his garden and tearing it up in the process or smashing cricket balls through the ancient glass of his woodshed. On another occasion Harry burrowed himself into a huge haystack and was struggling for breath before eventually being found in some distress just in time by his policeman. On another occasion he caused a major ruckus when he disappeared again on a hot summer's day. He had crawled into one of the prince's giant urns as it was cooler inside and could not hear the increasingly desperate staff and parents calling his name.

There was an understanding between Charles and Diana during this time of mutual estrangement that during the week, the prince rarely went to Kensington Palace and they effectively used Highgrove at weekends on a rota basis, neither being there when the other was. It meant that James Hewitt, Diana's lover by this time, became a frequent visitor to both residences. He would be assigned his own room but would stay the night with Diana, although he took precautions so that his arrivals and departures were not seen by the press.

James would even join in the play fights the protection officers would have with William and Harry around the garden pool at Highgrove. Diana would burst out laughing when she was thrown into the pool fully clothed. Of course, at this time her sons did not know their parents were involved in adulterous relationships, James was just another avuncular chap on the scene.

Unlike the police team – Inspector Ken Wharfe; ex-Royal Marine Commando, Sergeant Reg Spinney; Sergeant Dave Sharpe; and Inspector Trevor Bettles – or cavalry officer James Hewitt, Charles was not a rough-and-tumble-style father. He would leave that side of their childhood to their bodyguards. Wharfe recalled that they would often turn up at his bedroom at Kensington Palace (used by the Scotland Yard officer on duty). As regular as clockwork the princes would knock at the door. 'Ken, do you want to fight?' It was not really a request or even a question: it was a statement of intent. William and Harry would pile in and made a perfect royal tag team. 'One would go for my head and the other attack my more sensitive parts, landing punches towards my groin, which, if they connected, would make me keel over in agony,' he recalled in his best-selling memoir

Diana: Closely Guarded Secret (co-written by the author). Their parents seemed to appreciate that their sons could let off steam in this way. Charles would pop his head around the door and, with a slightly quizzical look on his furrowed face, would ask, 'They're not being too much bother, are they, Ken?'

'No, sir, not at all,' he would gasp as he recovered from another fierce royal punch.

Charles adored his sons, but he rarely actually joined in such horseplay. It was not his style and, often, he was not around or was away on business. One such occasion was when Diana urged her bodyguard to help set up a go-kart race at Highgrove, around Charles's beloved garden without the prince's prior knowledge. Despite their high birth and high-ranking position, William and Harry as boys were at heart just brothers in search of adventure, both thrill-seekers who loved speed.

Wharfe telephoned Martin Howell, boss of Playscape Racing, where Diana herself had become a regular racer at its circuit in Buckmoor Park, Kent, and at another venue in Streatham since the mid-eighties. She was a very keen and competitive racer and had introduced her sons to the junior karting experience at these venues privately on a regular basis. One weekend at Highgrove the boys kept pestering Diana to take them go-karting and so she begged Ken to call Martin and arrange for him to bring down two of the go-karts.

The karts, capable of speeds of up to forty miles an hour, arrived and Wharfe and Howell set up a course around the prince's grounds and within minutes the boys were racing at full tilt, tearing up Charles's beloved garden in the process. Diana, mischievous as ever, cheered on her sons as they skidded through her husband's secret garden, now a chicane as his sons battled for the lead. The prince was of course oblivious to it all. Weeks later, the prince spoke calmly to Wharfe and half-jokingly teased him about whether he fancied becoming 'the next Bernie Ecclestone'.

If anyone overstepped the mark in correcting his sons, Charles, in his idiosyncratic way, would admonish the offender to let him know, albeit gently, who was the boss. On one occasion when it reached Charles's ears that Wharfe had been correcting William's pronunciation, the prince stepped in. As a youngster, William spoke with that slightly clipped upper-class English accent. He persisted in pronouncing 'out' like 'ite' (as in 'kite'), and Wharfe corrected him, but the prince insisted he was right because his father always said it that way.

'Ken, I understand you have been giving William elocution lessons,'[30] he said, his tone just a little critical. Wharfe had clearly overstepped the mark, and in his own gentlemanly way the prince was letting him know. 'When Diana found out about my telling-off, she thought it was hilarious,' Wharfe said, and urged him to retell the story acting out all the voices.

CHAPTER THREE

SOAP OPERA

'What Kind of Dad are You?'

Headline in the tabloid *The Sun* newspaper when Prince Charles went to the
Royal Opera House when William was undergoing major surgery

The sudden departure of Nanny Barnes and Diana's increased workload
as a public figure meant she needed extra help with the boys in the
nursery. She hired another nanny, Ruth Wallace, from her Kensington
Palace neighbours, Prince and Princess Michael of Kent, and Jessie
Webb, who had worked for the interior decorator Nina Campbell for
fifteen years. The whole childcare operation was presided over by the
senior nanny at Kensington Palace, the indomitable Olga Powell, who
had worked her way up from under-nanny.

They were all 'old-fashioned' nannies and subscribed to traditional
parenting and discipline. Both boys were reminded repeatedly to curb
their over-excited behaviour and to show politeness when in public.
William tended to toe the line, but Harry proved a bit too much of
a handful for Jessie Webb. 'She was a good nanny, but more of a fun
person. They used to play Jessie up because she wasn't really their type
and she would come and knock on my door and say, "Ken, can you
have a word with them, they're being very naughty",' said protection
officer Ken Wharfe.

'I would say, "Harry, what's going on, mate?"'

'"I don't like Jessie," he'd say.'

'"Well, you'd better get to like her, OK? I gather you've been rude
to her. What did you say?"'

'"I told her she should lose weight."'

'"Well, that's not very nice, Harry, is it?"'

'He would later apologise to Jessie because he was under strict instructions from Diana to do so,' said Ken.

Harry struggled to focus. His schoolwork was below average and he compensated by being a joker, relying on his boundary-pushing and cheekiness to win favour. Wharfe said: 'He wasn't the brightest academically. But he certainly wasn't stupid. There were too many distractions for him. He was always getting told off. If there was fun to be had, he would do that rather than work. I think he found school a bit of a chore.'

Nanny Webb had her own way of dealing with his bad behaviour. She would frequently sandwich him up against the wall using her frame, saying it was the only way she could catch him and 'gain control'. The boys were a law unto themselves. William and Harry would often roam around Highgrove, like a couple of urchins. They would think nothing of relieving themselves from the top of the giant haystack in the garden when they were so inclined, much to the annoyance of their father, who caught them in the act on occasion, and gave them a dressing down. But he was ignored.

Whilst Diana did not want her sons spoiled in any way, they still ended up showered with gifts. Barry Manilow gave Harry a valuable, five-inch baby-grand piano, and Jaguar presented William with a miniature motor car which he crashed into the garage wall.

The princess smothered her boys with love and was always hugging and kissing them. 'I want to bring them security. I hug my children to death and get into bed with them at night. I always feed them love and affection – it's so important,' she said. This was a difficult time for William and Harry, who were both aware that there was severe tension between their parents. William became concerned that he might be responsible for his mother's unhappiness. When she locked herself in the bathroom to cry uncontrollably, he tried to help by pushing tissues under the bathroom door.[31]

In 1992, King Constantine of Greece gave a 'Cowboys and Indians' party at his home in north London. Diana dressed as a cowgirl, and William and Harry wore cowboy outfits. It was at the height of the speculation about the royal marriage. Charles and Diana presented a united front in the presence of the children, but by now, their problems were too deep-rooted to be dismissed, and Charles was staying away from the family home for days at a time.

Eventually, the couple realised they would have to separate, so the boys were told by their parents. Their Christmas holiday that year came to symbolise the different approaches of Charles and Diana. The princes spent Christmas Day at Sandringham with their father, who had taken on his old nanny, Mabel Anderson – 'It's just like old times,' the Queen is said to have remarked – but when they joined Diana, it was very different. She whisked them off to the Caribbean for sea and sun, quite a contrast to a bleak, flat Norfolk. For Diana, the difference was more than merely symbolic. She was determined that the boys should grow up in an emotionally healthier environment than she had herself.

Many holidays with William and Harry were spent without their father. Security was essential, and the affable Scotland Yard officers accompanied Diana and her sons on most, if not all, of these private holidays. The locations visited were indeed the resorts of the privileged: the island of Nevis, the Bahamas, Necker Island (owned by Sir Richard Branson), but wherever the location, Diana was determined that her sons should have fun, and they did. With a loving, energetic mother, how could they fail to? Irrespective of her royal commitments, William and Harry were Diana's priority, and they knew it.

'With the exception of unavoidable official public duties, I do not recall Diana missing one school run,' Wharfe recalled. 'The opportunity to talk through their school day with Mummy on the short car journey from Kensington Palace to both kindergarten at Jane Mynors's and pre-prep at the Wetherby School, was an invaluable time for the boys, and I felt very privileged to be part of it. Once at school, Diana would take her place in any queue of parents waiting to chat informally with the respective head teachers, something Diana relished. Both William and Harry loved this aspect of their mother's involvement.'

Whatever their personal difficulties, Charles and Diana always put their differences aside when it came to their sons. Happiness and the 'normal' ingredient were always evident, whether it was organising the 'Nevis Toad Derby', a race the boys devised to make money from bets on the island's giant toads, or bombarding the press boats with water balloons for breaking the agreement not to take pictures. This was a fight that the future soldier-princes relished. Diana was always in on their 'Just William' pranks (akin to the exploits described in the popular children's books about an unruly schoolboy), and her authority to proceed was always sought and never denied.[32]

Diana encouraged Harry's mischievous nature. It manifested itself one morning whilst they were on the school run. In the car leaving Kensington Palace to go to Wetherby School were the chauffeur, the police protection officer, the princess and William and Harry. At that time, Diana loved nothing better than telling risqué jokes to her entourage and was apparently unconcerned that her children were all ears.

On this day, the protection officer did his best to dissuade her from telling her latest joke, but in typical fashion she was having none of it. In fact, in true Diana style, the more he tried to stop her, the more determined she was to get the gag in. Unfortunately for Diana, two things were to collide that morning. First, she had an appointment with the headmistress, Frederika Blair-Turner, of whom Diana was terrified, so she was noticeably hyper at the prospect of the meeting, and secondly, also unfortunately for Diana, Harry was listening intently as she told the joke, which he was determined to tell everybody when he arrived at school.

On Diana's arrival at Wetherby School, Miss Blair-Turner was waiting in the hallway, adjacent to the stairwell, and Diana, for reasons known only to herself, decided she would have her meeting there and then. William ran off to his classroom, but by now Harry was all fired up with the new joke he had just learned and began trying to tell it to his headmistress. Diana's face turned lobster red with embarrassment as she realised what he was attempting to do and tried very hard to stop him from telling it. At that point, a sweating princess made a desperate appeal to her protection officer for help, but he declined, much to her chagrin, as she made plain later. Fortunately, with so many interruptions Harry was unable to get the joke out. Afterwards, Diana admitted to her protection officer that she thought she was on the verge of vomiting whilst Harry was holding court.[33]

★★★

Diana and her sons often enjoyed carefree moments along with her bodyguard, who used to join in with the fun. When Diana, accompanied by her PPO Ken, would collect or take him from boarding school or go on a long drive down to Highgrove in her green XJS Jaguar William recalled their carpool karaoke. William said, 'When I was younger, Harry and I, we were at boarding school. And my mother used to play all sorts of songs to kind of while away the anxiety of going back to school. And one of the songs I massively remember and has stuck with me all this time, and I still, to this day, still quite enjoy secretly, is Tina Turner's "The Best", because sitting in the back seat, singing away, it felt like a real family moment. And my mother, she'd be driving along, singing at the top of her voice. And we'd even get the policeman in the car, he'd be occasionally singing along, as well.

'You'd be singing and listening to the music right the way out into the gates of school, when they dropped you off. And that's when reality kind of sunk in that you really were going back to school because before that, you're lost in songs. You'll want to play it again just to keep that family moment going,' he said. 'And when I listen to it now, it takes me back to those car rides and brings back lots of memories of my mother,' he said in December 2021 when he joined forces with Apple in the company's *Time to Walk* broadcast.

Inspector Wharfe recalled, 'They were such happy times. Yes, there was all the issues of the royal marriage, but the prince and princess did their very best at that time to keep their children out of it, so they were largely oblivious and had great fun with their mother. She loved Tina Turner and would put the CD on full blast in the car, sometimes in the green Jaguar XJS she had, or other cars, the CD always came with us. She played "Simply the Best" all the time.

'Before that she used to love playing Cliff Richard, his hit "Some People" was another of her favourites she played over and over,' said Ken, an accomplished singer who still sings bass-baritone in the English Chamber Choir. 'Her love of Tina Turner and "Simply the Best" started when we went to see her in concert in 1990 at Woburn Abbey. I think Elton John and Kate Bush were there too, along with 60,000 fans. We went back to the main house to see Tina afterwards and Diana was thrilled to meet and chat to her. She was given a CD and from that moment it was the anthem for our car journeys, and it would be on full blast when we drove along the M4 to Highgrove. I'm so glad William has such fond memories of our singing in the car,

I do too, they were the best of times. Diana loved music, particularly classical music, a passion we both shared,' Ken said.

On another occasion, the boys visited the Wookey Hole caves in Somerset. Harry was about two years old and was carried around by the adults in the party. He was passed to each in turn, among them the nanny, but to the puzzlement of all present, Harry periodically burst into tears. Each time, the party came to a halt, but the sobbing child was unable to explain what was wrong, so when he stopped crying, the group set off again until the crying began once more.

It wasn't until the fourth outburst that the reason emerged. As Harry was passed from one adult to the next, he was 'bumped up'. The caves have very low ceilings and he kept hitting his head, so Harry ended the day not very happy and with several bumps forming on his head. Fortunately for all concerned, he was not able to tell his mother what had happened.[34]

Harry was about six or seven years old when he showed his willful streak. He was at Highgrove House, being entertained by one of his protection officers, who was giving him driving lessons in his father's Range Rover Discovery. The Scotland Yard officer was in the driving seat, Harry standing in the footwell, having access to the steering wheel, the front edge of the driver's seat and the accelerator. After a while, Harry was informed that it was game over and time to take the car back, but he was having none of it and as one of his protection team observed, he could be like a little Rottweiler when he didn't want to stop doing something.

Despite vigorous protests from the young prince, the protection officer insisted the car had to be taken back to where it had been 'borrowed' from. Harry, still protesting, was now approaching the parking point, which just happened to be face-on to a rather large Cotswold stone wall. As he got closer Harry stamped down hard on the accelerator, pushed his bottom back, and the vehicle smacked into the wall. No damage was ever found on the vehicle!

Another of William and Harry's police protection officers often used the phrase 'I'm going to see a man about a dog' when he wished to go and do something that he didn't want the boys to be privy to, and on one occasion at Highgrove, with both William and Harry present, the officer, having mentioned to both that he would be away for some time, was badgered incessantly by Harry for the real reason he was going to be absent. This badgering was so constant and insistent that even William couldn't stand it anymore – and he wanted to know, too. So, to shut Harry up, William said to him, 'Harry, shut up. He's already told you – he's going dog-watching. Now shut up!'

Along with his propensity for naughtiness, Harry demonstrated that he was a tough little chap from an early age. When he was big enough, he inherited from William a Shetland pony, which was kept at Highgrove. From the moment Harry first rode it, the pony seemed to take on its new owner's personality and started doing exactly as it pleased. It refused to be led or ridden as the mood took it, and it seized every opportunity to bolt off with Harry in the saddle, run for anything from a quarter to half a mile, find the nearest stream and dump Harry in it.

The scene must have looked hilarious to anyone watching, with a groom and protection officer, both on foot, trying to catch up with, let alone catch, the beast. William was also on hand, and they'd find Harry in all sorts of bushes, streams and hedgerows.

Harry's biggest problem was always that he didn't know when to stop. On one particularly long car journey, William and Harry started to be naughty and were really irritating the chauffeur, the nanny and the protection officer. Despite repeated warnings from the nanny, the boys continued to disobey her and it was clear that repercussions were imminent. In fact, it was William, the main offender, who finally got the message, not Harry. Driven to distraction, the protection officer ordered the car to stop. It did, but so suddenly that the back-up car nearly crashed into its rear. The officer dragged Harry out of the car, took him around to the back of the vehicle, and standing in the road, foot on the rear bumper of the royal car, put Harry across his knee, pulled down his trousers and smacked him. Silence ensued for at least half a mile.

In many ways, these two privileged boys lived an idyllic life, shielded from their parents' increasingly dysfunctional marriage, and enjoying luxury holidays with both. Above all, Diana wanted happiness and security for her sons, and she knew that to achieve this the boys needed a stable life that included both their parents. They often travelled to Mallorca as a family, as guests of King Juan Carlos of Spain, and, on a few occasions, Diana relented after William and Harry begged her to accompany King Juan Carlos and Queen Sofia on their yacht *Fortuna* in search of private beaches on which to spend their afternoons.

Charles and Diana were civil to each other in front of their sons, who were revelling in the sunshine, and to be fair, spending quality time with the father they adored, but who was so often taken from them due to his busy schedule. William went on to attend Wetherby School, also in West London. His first official public engagement took place at the age of eight when he accompanied his parents on a visit to Wales on 1 March, St David's Day, 1991.

William's education was continued at Ludgrove School, in Berkshire. Charles felt it was right that William should go to boarding school at the age of eight, which left Diana in tears as she had been reluctant to send him away. William thrived in his new school. He excelled at sport and represented Ludgrove at football, basketball and swimming, also becoming captain of the school rugby team. He was a natural performer on stage, too, and took part in several school plays. It was while he was a pupil there that he was involved in a serious incident, that exposed the void that existed between his parents.

Their differences came to a head in public when William was rushed to hospital in 1991, after being accidentally struck on the head by another boy's golf club at school. The school tried to keep the matter internal, and if it had not been for the quick thinking of William's personal protection officer, Sergeant Reg Spinney, the situation could have been much worse. Whilst the joint headmasters of the Wokingham prep school, Gerald Barber and Nichol Marston, were debating the incident and not really seeing the seriousness, telling William's policeman he could be dealt with by the matron, no-nonsense former commando Sergeant Spinney took charge. Not waiting for an ambulance, he drove straight to the Royal Berkshire Hospital nine miles away in Craven Road, Reading, at high speed. He also contacted his police headquarters and told them to alert the accident and emergency department that the second-in-line to the throne and future king was on his way to them after suffering a serious head injury.

Sergeant Spinney had also bleeped Diana's personal protection officer, Inspector Ken Wharfe, who quietly alerted the princess, who was enjoying a lunch with friends at her favourite restaurant, San Lorenzo in Beauchamp Place. After William was first taken to the

Royal Berkshire Hospital, in Reading, Prince Charles was alerted and drove to the hospital in his Aston Martin. William was transferred to Great Ormond Street Hospital in London, with Diana travelling with him in the ambulance. Once at the specialist children's hospital, William was given a general anaesthetic and operated on for a depressed fracture of the skull.

A Palace statement was released in which a Buckingham Palace spokesman said William had spent a comfortable night at London's Great Ormond Street Hospital following Monday's seventy-minute operation. A fraught Diana had held her son's hand as he was wheeled into the operating theatre. She waited anxiously in a room nearby until Professor Richard Hayward, the consultant paediatric neurosurgeon at the hospital, entered to tell her William was fine. It was, she would admit, one of the longest hours of her life.

When the consultant had earlier said that there was no need for both parents to stay the night as this was a routine operation and there was negligible risk, Charles elected to attend a long-standing appointment instead. He went to see a performance of Puccini's *Tosca* at the Royal Opera House in Covent Garden, where he hosted a dozen European Union officials, including the Environmental Commissioner. Afterwards, he was informed that the operation had been a complete success, so as Diana sat with William in his private room, Charles went ahead and boarded the Royal Train for an overnight journey to Yorkshire where he was due to attend an environmental event. Diana watched as nurses checked William every twenty minutes. She was told he would be fine, but also warned that any drop in blood pressure could still prove fatal. She never forgave her husband for what she saw as his gross insensitivity that night.

Diana worried about William for months, especially after reading newspaper reports saying he could suffer from epilepsy because of the head wound. She was not the only one appalled that Charles had not stayed at her side. His decision to put duty first shocked the public. Diana, however, expected it. *The Sun* newspaper headline the next day screamed, 'What kind of dad are you?' Privately, she was delighted and believed the tabloids had got it right.

Harry was William's first visitor at the hospital and spent fifteen minutes with his brother before going to school. William was 'chatting away', said the Buckingham Palace spokesman. The operation resulted in William having a scar on his forehead much like that of everyone's favourite fictional wizard, Harry Potter. Years later, in 2009, William said, 'I call it [my Harry Potter scar] because it glows sometimes and some people notice it – other times they don't notice it at all. I got hit by a golf club when I was playing golf with a friend of mine. We were on a putting green and the next thing you know there was a 7 iron, and it came out of nowhere and it hit me in the head.'[35] The boy who swung the golf club was never identified.

CHAPTER FOUR

PARADISE FOUND

'I can still picture Diana laughing with William and Harry on the beach
when they were kids. She saw our little piece of paradise as an escape from the
relentless press attention she received and was in her element playing with
her children like any other mum.'

Sir Richard Branson, English business magnate and founder of the Virgin Group

It was for a Diana a little piece of paradise where she could escape
from her troubled life. A private, seventy-four-acre haven in the
British Virgin Islands where she could bond with her boys. During
the school breaks, they often spent the holiday with Diana, without
their father. She would explain that Papa was working, and they simply
accepted it. On the first of her two trips to Necker in January 1989
she was joined by the Honourable Frances Shand-Kydd, her sisters,
Lady Sarah McCorquodale and Lady Jane Fellowes, their children and
her own two sons. It provided her with a perfect excuse for the trip
by saying that she wanted to spend some time with her mother and
sisters, but in fact she was desperate to escape.

Having spent another miserable Christmas at the Queen's
Sandringham Estate, where, she complained, she felt 'totally blanked'
by the royal family, Diana told her PPO that she had decided to take
up business tycoon Sir Richard Branson's offer for her and her boys
to see in the New Year of 1989 on his private island. The princess
made it clear the invitation didn't extend to Charles, who told his
sons that he had to stay at Sandringham. They were heading for
paradise where well-heeled guests go to to 'rejuvenate mind, body
and spirit', according to the marketing brochure. Sir Richard had
bought the island for $306,000 in the eighties and transformed it

from a mosquito-infested atoll to a place where the great and the good could go on holiday in private.

As the boat bringing the royal party from nearby Tortola approached Necker and the island's beautiful white beaches came into view, everyone on board seemed to breathe a simultaneous sigh of relief. William and Harry, alive with anticipation, could not wait to explore. Sir Richard was waiting to greet Diana. The Great House, the main accommodation, looked like a cross between the lobby of a luxury hotel and a Surrey barn conversion. Inside, a snooker table had pride of place beneath a Balinese-style beamed ceiling. For guests for whom being on a private island just isn't private enough, there were separate cottages built in south-east Asian pagoda style, each one equipped with a meditation room. There was also a gym and a swimming pool, as well as four exclusive beaches, with a speedboat and several jet-skis at the guests' disposal. Sir Richard, who covered the cost of the holiday, had instructed his staff to spare nothing to make Diana's stay perfect. On the first evening Sir Richard held a magnificent lobster barbecue and Caribbean music played while they all watched the sun setting.

While Diana sunbathed on the beach, William, Harry and their five cousins romped about in the pool or begged to be taken to the beach to swim in the sea, watched over by the Scotland Yard team. As the princess and the royal party wallowed under heavenly blue skies, the rest of the world was kept firmly away. There were no inhabitants on the island and access was mainly by boat, from Virgin Gorda. Most of the staff came ashore every morning by boat and left each evening after dinner. Inspector Graham Smith had accompanied Diana on the first trip, but by April 1990, when she returned with the boys, he had been struck down with the throat cancer that would eventually kill him and, although in remission, he was no longer fit for protection officer duties. Diana was desperately worried; she had somehow convinced herself that the stress of guarding her had led to Graham's illness. She hoped the holiday would at least help to revive his spirits and insisted that he came as her guest.

Diana had not foreseen that her decision to take a pre-Easter break on the island without her husband would send Fleet Street into a frenzy. Charles was blamed, even though it was Diana who had arranged the solo holiday. Instead, he spent time in the Scottish Highlands, thereby accidentally emphasising the gulf between the couple. Soon the peace was broken when scores of press photographers arrived at the airport on Tortola, desperate for pictures of Diana in a bikini. The local police acted swiftly and simply confiscated several cameras from the paparazzi. They also organised for flights over Necker to be banned and stopped boats within a seven-mile radius of the island. They were taking no chances.

Within days, however, Fleet Street's finest, led by the royal reporting teams of the British tabloid press were back in a flotilla of little boats. James Whitaker, who died in 2012, and Kent Gavin of the *Daily Mirror* and Arthur Edwards and Harry Arnold, who died in 2014, of *The Sun*, were determined to get their pictures. Her haven had been breached, besieged by little boats bobbing around on the sea, filled with photographers, their cameras with long lenses trained on the beach. Although some long-lens shots were taken during the Prince's first trips, they were of poor quality as the security measures had limited the intrusion, much to the relief of the royal party and their protection officers alike. The following year, 1990, Fleet Street retuned. This time they knew what they were up against, and were much better equipped. Their individual editors had made it clear that failure was not an option. Diana was by now the only story that mattered. She sold papers, and pictures of her in a bikini sold even more.

A small armada appeared on the horizon, with more than sixty journalists and photographers packed into chartered boats of all shapes and sizes, cameras primed and at the ready. Diana was furious. 'How did they know we were here?' she demanded, before adding bitterly, 'Someone must have told them.'[36]

Diana became obsessed with the problem and insisted that the media were frightening her sons. It was left to Diana's policeman, Inspector Wharfe, to deal with it. He didn't feel the media presented a major breach of security, and so thought the best course of action was to meet some of the senior Fleet Street journalists to see if a deal could be brokered, in a bid not only to restrain the more intrusive hacks, but also to clip the wings of the rogue element among the foreign paparazzi.

He arranged to meet them at Biras Creek, on Virgin Gorda, about fifteen minutes away by motorboat. Once there, Wharfe made it clear to the press that Diana and her boys were on a private holiday, and under no obligation to give a photo opportunity just because the media happened to be intruding on her privacy, but he agreed to take their case for a photo call to Diana if they would agree that it would be a one-off. Diana trusted her bodyguard and went along with the plan.

The next day, the princess and her family appeared on the beach. Surrounded by her sons and their five cousins, she proceeded to let them bury her in the sand, laughing all the while. Then, having extricated herself, she threw off her sundress, revealing her bikini underneath, and raced William and Harry, then aged eight and five, down to the sea to rinse off the sand. Her body gleamed with water in the hot sun, and the camera shutters clicked in frenzy. It was, as ever, a masterly display by the consummate public-relations professional.

To a man, the Fleet Street press and paparazzi all stopped their intrusive activities immediately. Back in Britain, the newspaper editors were delighted. Diana's image was splashed across the front pages of most newspapers. She had sent her message back to her husband, who she suspected was with his married lover, Camilla Parker Bowles, whilst she holidayed as a family.

'There was no daily plan of activities,' said Ken Wharfe, 'but William and Harry looked to the men in the party to organise their day, so while the princess and the rest of the women lounged around the pool, watched over by Dave Sharp, I was tasked with keeping her two extremely active sons occupied. It was not an onerous task, not least because Branson's island had everything in place to make this their adventure holiday of a lifetime.'

The privacy deal meant William and Harry could enjoy themselves. One of William's favourite games involved the children unleashing billiard balls across the snooker table at high speed in a bid to smash their opponents' fingers – the only rule being that the contestants had to leave their hands resting on the table's cushions until the ball was unleashed. It was not all fun and games. On one occasion even Diana's patience was tested by Harry's unruliness. She was furious when he smashed William with a snooker cue during a fight. 'You had to keep an eye on him,' said Wharfe. 'There was an infinity pool on Necker and the water dribbled over the edge. Harry, inevitably, went and stood on the edge. He was always pushing the boundaries. That was never the case with William, he'd never have done that. He'd say to his mother, "Oh, Harry's done such-and-such again".'

As a diversion, both boys, accompanied by their PPO, went snorkelling with Diana's brother, Charles Spencer, but this was not enough to beguile the inquisitive William. He wanted to explore, so the prince and the detective hatched a plan to recce the island. One morning, the pair set off armed with knives and carrying only bottled water, fruit and some sandwiches to sustain them, they ventured deep into the island's interior for a three-hour mission that involved hacking through the thick undergrowth, climbing rocks and crossing streams.

Sir Richard's manager on the island, Dan Reid, had returned from one of his business and supply trips to Tortola armed with three giant hand-held catapults and hundreds of balloons, which he gave to the children. The catapults were huge. To fire the balloons, which for maximum effect were filled with water to the size of cricket balls, the catapults had to be tied to posts or held by two people whilst a third loaded, aimed and fired the missile. Initially, they caused much hilarity as the children and the protection officers fought pitched mini-battles against each other.

William had a brainwave, to use the catapults to attack the invading press when they returned. Crucially, these newsmen were not abiding by the earlier agreement, that of leaving them alone in return for the generous photo opportunity they had been given. There was a perfect vantage point, on rocks about eighty feet above the shoreline, so William, Harry and their cousins set about constructing two sites in readiness for the return of the press boats. As boats carrying the hardcore paparazzi approached, the boys unleashed their stack of coloured water bombs. The unfortunate photographers did not know what had hit them, and after twenty minutes and several direct hits they retired hurt and did not return. For William, protecting his mother was a matter of personal pride, and he rushed back to tell her of his victory, very much a hero in her eyes. The boys would cherish these memories of laughter and fun with Diana, for the years that were to follow would be testing for them.

In 1992, for their last family holiday with both their mother and father, they boarded the floating paradise, the *Alexander*, loaned to the royals by billionaire John Latsis. When the huge yacht was anchored, both showed their fearlessness; first, Harry leapt more than thirty feet from the stern of the yacht into the sea below, making a huge splash as he entered the water and then, laughing as he surfaced, he dared his older brother to join him. William, who was never one to shirk a challenge, especially from Harry, followed. They were soon joined by bodyguard, Inspector Wharfe, who hit the water with an almighty splash, after being ordered in by Superindent Colin Trimming. As ever, the two princes pounced on him in a play fight, and Diana thought it was hilarious.

No matter how hard Charles and Diana tried to put a brave face on their failing relationship in public, in private they both knew their marriage was over. They were aware that they had both been indulging in extra-marital affairs, Charles with the married Camilla Parker Bowles, and Diana with several suitors, but most notably with the dashing cavalry officer, James Hewitt. Those close to the family knew it was only a matter of time before the marriage would implode; what they did not know was how it would end.

Before the separation was announced publicly Diana drove to see William at Ludgrove School. She told him that although she and his father would always respect each other, they could no longer live under the same roof together. She stressed that she and his papa loved him and Harry. But William was not one to be fobbed off. He wanted answers to his questions – answers she could not give him.

She later recalled that he had asked, 'What was that the reason why your marriage had broken up?'[37]

Diana told him there were 'three of us in this marriage', and the pressure of the media was another factor, so the two together were very difficult. It was a phrase she would, of course, use in the infamous *Panorama* interview with Martin Bashir a few years later. William was always a deep thinker and the princess said it took a couple of hours before she knew his reaction. When his parents' separation was announced in the House of Commons by the Prime Minister, John Major, in December 1992, he was prepared. Unlike his younger brother, William, who always seemed more mature, acted as Diana's emotional crutch throughout her tormented marriage. Diana saw William as her champion, and he had a natural knack of supporting her when she needed it most. He assumed the role of supportive son and had reached that rewarding age when the child becomes a companion and a friend to his parent, able to appreciate, at least in part, a parent's troubles. Whenever Diana felt uncertain, William was there. He once told her he wanted to be a policeman so that he could protect her.[38] When the divorce was finalised and it emerged that the princess would be stripped of her royal title, it was William who threw his arms around her and exclaimed, 'Don't worry, Mummy. I'll give it back to you one day, when I'm king.'[39]

Sometimes, even Diana admitted she went too far and burdened William with problems and paranoia that he should never have been asked to shoulder at such a young age. Royal Navy Commander Patrick Jephson, Diana's private secretary and former equerry to Charles, later revealed that Diana told him that she was afraid that William, like her, was too sensitive for the part he must play in the royal family. He agreed, hoping that the princess would stop passing on her troubles to a mere boy who she had taken to calling 'the man in my life'. It didn't work, Diana continued to load his young mind with her adult troubles, regardless.

CHAPTER FIVE

FLOREAT ETONA

'It's the weird thing Eton does – you're at a school next to lords and earls and, in my case, Prince William, so you end up being used to dealing with those sorts of people'

Oscar-winning actor and Old Etonian contemporary of Prince William,

Eddie Redmayne OBE

He may have been a future king, but from the moment he arrived at Eton College, in the shadow of Windsor Castle, his peers referred to him simply as 'Wales'. In fact, the only pointer that he was special was in 'Fixtures' – a school calendar and list of all the boys in school. The 300-page green booklet informs pupils who all the boys are. If you were a lord, you'd have a 'Mister' before your name. The princes were HRH. 'It was funny though because no one gave a s★★★,' said one of his fellow contemporaries. Founded in 1440, Eton College is seen as the most prestigious school in the world, which counts prime ministers, kings and Hollywood stars amongst its alumni. With sixteen-hour days and reading lists that would make most adults hang their heads in shame, it is no surprise that Eton has so many success stories.

Clearly nervous, Prince William, then thirteen, tried his best not to show it, smiling broadly in all the photographs. He posed alongside his estranged parents, his grinning brother and new housemaster, Dr Andrew Gailey, who headed up Manor House and had taught in the history department since 1981. Charles and Diana had put on a good show of a united front when William enrolled at Eton in September 1995, making him the first senior member of the royal family to attend the elite school with annual fees of over £48,500 per year. His parents watched as he signed the school register with his left hand. Diana was leaning over his shoulder to point out where to make his mark, while his father stood, arms behind his back, smiling. He was assigned to Manor House, whose alumni include the first Duke of Wellington, victor of the Battle of Waterloo. The revered soldier and former prime minister famously said Waterloo had been won on the playing fields of Eton, meaning that Britain's military success was based on the values taught in its public schools.

The prince said his goodbyes to his parents in private and then went to his study-bedroom to unpack, along with the other fifty boys in his house. He then changed into his school uniform – the traditional black morning coat, black waistcoat, starched collar and black pin-striped trousers and later marched out in front of photographers, flashing them a winning smile. He was determined to blend in and make new friends quickly. He didn't want a repeat of that feeling of loneliness that he had experienced when he first went to his prep school, Ludgrove, where he had experienced being a boarder for the first time. After all, becoming more independent from your family, whether you are royal or not, is a huge step. At the beginning his insecurities were bubbling over, and there were even a few tears, but he soon discovered he wasn't the only one experiencing that sense of emptiness. After his initial unhappy prep-school experience, he had eventually grown accustomed to being away from home. He was determined at Eton to hit the ground running and liked the fact that his fellow Oppidans (see below) treated him simply as one of their own, unfazed by his status as a future king. [As the school had grown, more students had been allowed to attend provided that they paid their own fees and lived in boarding-houses outside the college's original buildings, but within the town of Eton. These students became known as Oppidans, from the Latin word *oppidum*, meaning 'town'.]

Although he missed his family, William wrote regularly to his mother, and he loved receiving her warm and loving replies. She missed him dreadfully and took to phoning him, too, sometimes crying hysterically down the line. At first, he found this difficult, but as it increased, he stepped in and asked his mother not to criticise or say things about his father to him. He loved her, of course he did, but he felt she was being unfair to his father, and it made him feel uncomfortable. He didn't want to have to take sides. As his mother's emotions lurched out of control, the teenager found it difficult to cope with his mother's considerable emotional burden, which was hardly surprising for one so young. On a visit to the Royal Shakespeare Theatre in Stratford-upon-Avon with his father, Bel Mooney and her daughter Kitty Dimbleby, among others, William was at a pre-performance dinner with his father. Charles began to chat about his love of the Goons, the comedy group featuring comic geniuses Peter Sellers, Spike Milligan and Harry Secombe. Suddenly, Bel burst into a chorus of 'The Ying Tong Song'. When Kitty turned to William and pointed out how embarrassing parents could be, William's response was very telling, 'Papa doesn't embarrass me, Mama does.'[40]

Eton became a sanctuary for William as the so-called 'War of the Waleses' was fought bitterly, largely through leaks to the tabloid press. He found it all excruciating, particularly when he spotted fellow pupils reading papers with photos of his parents' faces plastered across them. He turned increasingly to Alexandra 'Tiggy' Legge-Bourke, his father's personal assistant, who had been appointed by Charles as a companion to his sons after the formal separation. During term-time breaks with their father and in the school holidays, Tiggy helped entertain them. She was like a big sister and accompanied them on the ski slopes in the swish Swiss resort of Klosters, or on yachts during summer cruises with their father. Tiggy, as was intended, quickly formed a close and affectionate relationship with the boys; she was fun, and the boys liked her. Her presence in their lives, however, infuriated Diana, who was prone to jealousy anyway. Tiggy noted: 'I give the princes what they need – fresh air, a rifle and a horse.'

Sadly, the innocent Tiggy soon found herself cruelly dragged into the mud-slinging of the royal marriage crisis. It got very ugly with the arrival of mendacious BBC reporter Martin Bashir, who had his own agenda after being introduced to the princess by her brother, Earl Spencer, in September 1995, two months before the infamous *Panorama* interview in which she famously claimed, 'there were three of us in this marriage'. At their meeting, Bashir produced an extraordinary dossier of smears about the Prince of Wales and other royals, calculated to feed Diana's paranoia. They included the astonishing, false claim that Charles was 'in love' with Tiggy and that the two were planning a holiday together. As absurd as this sounded, Diana believed it. Indeed, Diana became so obsessed with the idea that Miss Legge-Bourke was pregnant by Charles – and had lost the baby – that she confronted her about it at a Christmas party for palace staff on 14 December 1995 at the Lanesborough Hotel in London. Tiggy was left utterly shocked and embarrassed. She even threatened legal action and Sir Robert (now Lord) Fellowes, the Queen's private secretary and Diana's brother-in-law, launched an internal inquiry, which showed Diana's claims were groundless. Tiggy later married former Coldstream Guards officer Charles Pettifer, in October 1999. Significantly, in 2021, Tiggy, now Mrs Pettifer, was offered 'significant' damages by the BBC for distressing and groundless smears spread by Martin Bashir.

William showed his sensitivity when, aged fourteen, he asked his parents not to attend Eton's Fourth of June celebrations, as he felt the circus their presence would entail, with all the accompanying press and security, would spoil parents' day for his fellow pupils. Instead, he asked Tiggy to attend, which upset Diana and surprised Charles.

During William's time at school, Prince Charles's media team struck a deal with the press through the Press Complaints Commission to leave William largely alone in return for limited access at press and photo calls. It meant William could relax knowing there wasn't a camera around every corner. Although some paparazzi breached this agreement and sold photos to foreign magazines, in the main, it worked. William was accomplished academically and excelled on the playing fields of Eton. He captained his house football team and took up water polo, too. Having proven to be the fastest junior swimmer at Eton in ten years, William also captained the swimming team, holding the title of Joint Keeper of Swimming. His duties included team selection, greeting visiting teams, keeping records, training new boys, and recommending swimmers for their colours. William was also appointed secretary of the renowned Agricultural Club, and received Eton's Sword of Honour, the school's highest award for a first-year army cadet.

During his time there, the palace arranged for William to be photographed inside his private room, as well as in communal areas which he shared with fellow students. His room had light-green walls and a large, white desk, on which stood William's computer, below a pinboard displaying various notes and letters regarding his studies. Beside the window was a small table with a TV and a telephone.

William also had blue-and-white geometric print curtains at the windows. The kitchen featured wooden floors, yellow-and-white walls and white cupboards.

Of course, the proximity of Windsor, the Queen's weekend home, meant William could frequently visit his grandmother there. She was extremely fond and supportive of her grandson and always on hand to help prepare him for his future role. He began visiting the Queen every Sunday from 1995, after he had started at Eton College, although he was very secretive when asked where he was going. He wouldn't even say he was going to the castle. Those relaxed chats were a chance for her to mentor him, as her grandfather, George V, had done for her. They certainly helped him to embrace his destiny.

★★★

William and Harry were fast asleep and oblivious to the first reports which came through that something was wrong. At around 1 a.m., Prince Charles was woken and told by telephone that there had been a crash in the Alma tunnel in Paris. Dodi, he was informed, was dead. His ex-wife was injured. The prince woke the Queen. Then moments later came the call with the terrible news that Diana was dead. The poor man, racked with a combination of guilt and grief, broke down and openly wept. He went to see the Queen who wisely advised against waking his sons. She counselled that it was best to let them sleep, knowing that sleep was something that would not come easily over the following days, weeks and months. Charles paced the corridors as the boys slept. He dreaded the prospect of telling his sons such devastating news and went for a lonely walk. Diana had spoken to her sons just hours before the tragedy. William and Harry had been roaming the Queen's Balmoral estate at the time when the call came from Paris. 'Harry and I were running around, playing with our cousins (Peter and Zara) and having a very good time,' William recalled twenty years later. This is why they kept the phone call brief – something they deeply regret to this day.[41]

When Charles returned at around 7 a.m., William, often an early riser, was already awake. Charles, his eyes swollen and red from tears, walked into William's room, hugged his son and broke the awful news.

The two embraced each other. It was the worst moment of William's life, but he immediately thought of his younger brother, who was still asleep in the bedroom next door. The task of telling Harry was one that Charles and William decided to undertake together. They tried to explain that Diana had been injured and that the medical team had sadly failed to revive her. Now, all three embracing each other, they cried and the sounds of their raw pain could be heard around the old house. Their lives would never be the same again.

The Queen felt her grandsons needed to be protected from the outside world, which meant a great deal to them. She was criticised for keeping them hidden but both boys were grateful for her decision. Speaking in 2017, William said, 'At the time, my grandmother wanted to protect her two grandsons, and my father as well.' He was thankful he was given 'the privacy to mourn – to collect our thoughts'. In GQ magazine, twenty years later, William said he locked his grief inside. 'I am in a better place about it than I have been for a long time, where I can talk about her more openly, talk about her more honestly, and I can remember her better, and publicly talk about her better,' he said. 'It has taken me almost twenty years to get to that stage. I still find it difficult now, because at the time it was so raw. And it is not like most people's grief, because everyone else knows about it, everyone knows the story, everyone knows her.'

William, who had lost so much, showed, in the depths of his grief, a strength of character and dignity that was regal. Charles too, showed warmth and strength that many of his critics believed him incapable of. Diana's brother, Earl Spencer, was certainly not a fan of his ex-brother-in-law. At Diana's funeral in Westminster Abbey, he delivered a eulogy to his sister riddled with both covert and blatant criticisms of the royal family. He insisted that the boys would continue to be influenced by his sister Diana's 'blood family' and seemed to imply that it was her kin who stood the best chance of offering them a rounded upbringing, saving them from the grim clutches of an unadulterated and traditionally royal background.

The words irked and hurt Charles, maybe in part because they struck a chord. Had a traditional royal upbringing been such a success for him? Diana's visits to homeless centres, theme parks and fast-food restaurants seemed gimmicky and had made him cringe in the past. But Charles could see that her devotion and unconventional methods had paid off. William and Harry were well-rounded little chaps with a fresh and confident outlook – despite the turbulence of their parents' love lives and divorce.

William felt that he had let his mother down when he was younger. In a documentary, *Diana, Our Mother: Her Life and Legacy*, speaking on behalf on his younger brother too, he said, 'We feel we at least owe her twenty years on to stand up for her name and remind everybody of the character and person that she was. Do our duties as sons in protecting her.' He went on about his sadness that Diana will never know his children. 'I would like to have had her advice,' he said. 'I would love her to have met Catherine and to have seen the children grow up. It makes me sad that she won't, that they will never know her.'

Charles stepped up, too. He recognised that his sons needed time to be boys, and that he needed to be more of a dad to them. He cancelled all his immediate engagements. Diana's past accusations of his being an absent father echoed in his mind. If he had been a poor husband then, now that she was gone, he was not going to fail her again as guardian to the sons they both cherished. Charles threw himself into the role of devoted single dad. He took Harry with him on an official royal tour to South Africa, listened more to their views and began, tentatively, to embrace modern life. One minute he was posing with the Spice Girls, the next he was embracing children with AIDS. Out of adversity, Charles triumphed – and so did his sons.

There was no great ambition behind the trip. It was another family skiing holiday – some much-needed time for the princes, William and Harry, to spend with their father, just seven months after the appalling loss of their mother. Before the three princes retreated to Whistler and the mountains of British Columbia to enjoy four days on the slopes, a stint of royal walkabouts had been pencilled in for the entourage on arrival in Canada.

Nobody, neither Prince Charles's closest advisers nor the following rat pack of royal journalists – including me – knew quite what the public would make of the beleaguered trio. Charles still had to contend with a great deal of blame and resentment from those among the public who ludicrously viewed him as somehow culpable for Princess Diana's death.

Meanwhile, the very mention of his grieving sons prompted outpourings of public sympathy and heavy doses of galling grief-by-proxy. William and Harry had been largely spared public scrutiny in the months since their mother's death. Nobody could forget their composure on the day of her funeral at Westminster Abbey on 6 September 1997, and during the very public mourning that had preceded it when they had walked among weeping strangers and viewed the flowers and cards laid at the gates and along the paths and roads outside her west London home of Kensington Palace. William had conducted himself resolutely in the face of almost incalculable adversity. He was much taller and seemingly much more mature than Harry, who, not yet thirteen, had appeared heartbreakingly young and vulnerable. It was easy to overlook the fact that William, too, was a boy who had lost his mother. Now, three months short of his sixteenth birthday, he was still camera-shy, by turns sullen, quick to blush and possessed of all the awkward self-awareness of teenage years.

When they touched down at Vancouver Airport, on 24 March 1998, the royal party did so with a great deal of apprehension and few expectations. This was, to all intents and purposes, a family holiday with a few public engagements thrown in – a sop for the devoted royalists and a scrap for the fascinated press. But within minutes of their arrival in the city on the country's west coast something remarkable happened – something that would mark the trip out as a watershed for the teenage Prince William. From the instant he stepped out onto Canadian soil, a new phenomenon was born: 'Wills Mania'.

Crowds of frantic teenage girls, hundreds of whom had waited for hours to see their hero, went wild as they finally caught sight of him. They jostled against police barricades and wept, screamed and waved banners offering to prove to Wills in a variety of forthright fashions just how devoted to the young royal they really were. It was an astonishing spectacle. It would have fazed the most seasoned public figure. This was the sort of adoring hysteria associated with the Beatles in their heyday, when frenzied female fans screamed themselves into fainting fits and had to be pulled unconscious from the crowds.

This was unlike anything William had ever experienced before. There were about thirty of us in the press contingent that had travelled to Canada – photographers, reporters and television crews. If truth be told, 'Wills Mania' caught us all on the hop, but it was a dream story. For the reporters covering the visit, the copy just flowed. It was spontaneously upbeat and everyone, with the exception of William, seemed to get carried along with the surge of enthusiasm.

At first, William did his best to hide his discomfort at the adulation. He hated it. As he arrived at what was supposed to be a private visit to the Pacific Space Centre, row upon row of screaming girls – about five thousand of them – were there to greet him. He was horrified at the heaving mass of adoration.

'Look at him! I've got posters of him all over my wall,' said one.

'They should declare it a national holiday, William Day,' screamed another.[42]

He didn't know which way to look. Eyes downcast, his bashful smile redolent of his late mother, William did his best and showed great resolve, rising to the occasion and spending ten minutes shaking hands with and accepting gifts from well-wishers. On occasion he looked close to tears and could not wait to escape.

Once inside he just flipped. With only his father and the royal entourage in earshot, he refused to go on. Charles was the only one who could talk him round, coaxing the teen back from the brink. While his newly installed PR man Mark Bolland hovered haplessly nearby, Charles's heart-to-heart with William worked. Later, it fell to the PR man to try to negotiate a truce of sorts with the overheated press, but there was little he could do to cool the ardour of a nation's teenage girls. The royal family, the press was told, wanted our coverage to be 'calmer, cooler'.

Back in Britain, the unfortunate Mr Bolland found unlikely allies in the form of various doom-mongering commentators reporting from the comfort of their desks thousands of miles away. The puffed-up self-appointed guardians of the young princes' welfare tried to quell the frenzy. Chief among the commentators was *Daily Express* columnist Mary Kenny, who argued that the boys were being exposed far too soon after their mother's death. She wrote, 'Diana was adored all over the world. And this is a halo effect that William and Harry will carry everywhere: that they were Diana's sons. But would Diana, if she were alive today, want her elder son to start carrying out royal duties at such a tender age?'

The clear implication was that she would not. The finger of blame pointed at Charles, not for the first time, and at his officials for exploiting Diana's sons. As would often happen in the years following Diana's death, Charles's critics would conveniently overlook the fact that he loved his sons unconditionally and would do anything to protect them. But it was a challenging situation. How could the princes visit a country of which, as a realm and part of the Commonwealth, William would one day be king and yet still hide away from an adoring public? Moreover, how could they even begin to control, never mind quash, such a spontaneous outpouring of affection for William? The genie was out of the bottle and not even an accomplished media fixer like Mr Bolland could put it back and seal up the stopper. Besides, the emergence of William as the new royal star was not without its benefits for the royal family.

The natural performer in William emerged. When the three princes were presented with bright-red 'Roots' branded caps – worn by the country's Winter Olympics team – William showed his youthful credentials and a grasp of the real world that his father never possessed. The caps are worn back to front, but Charles inevitably put his on the wrong way round before William, laughingly, corrected him – upstaging his father in the process. They all then headed for the slopes of Whistler for a welcome four-day skiing holiday together as guests of the late Canadian billionaire Galen Weston, a polo friend of Charles's, and Weston's wife, Hilary, who was then Ontario's lieutenant-governor. They stayed in a chalet owned by friends of the Westons. It had been a close call, but William, Prince of Cool, was a media triumph and his father, for one, breathed a huge sigh of relief.

Given William's uniquely close bond with his mother, those close to her were astonished at how rapidly he appeared to cope with his grief. But then William had shown his strength before, back when his mother needed him and used him as an emotional crutch. Now, he showed that same generosity of spirit as he recognised that Harry and his father needed him. Harry was more of a worry. The gregarious, impish little boy all but disappeared; he retreated into himself, as he had done in the wake of his parents' divorce. William gradually re-emerged. The tears still flowed in private moments, but Diana was never coming back, and life had to carry on.

The fact that the media could not do the same upset him. Every time there was another instalment in the Diana saga and another front page of their mother was published, the seething grief with which they were learning to live surged forward with renewed intensity. They grew protective of their surviving parent and were genuinely hurt by what they saw as unfair criticism of him. A year after Diana's death, they decided to do something about it. They issued a touching personal statement calling for an end to the public mourning and what had been called the 'Diana industry' – the commercial exploitation of the Princess of Wales. William was angered by what he saw as calculated profiteering on his mother's name, such as her own Memorial Fund using her signature on margarine tubs.

William decided to speak out. After liaising with his younger brother, the two princes issued a statement in which they insisted Diana would want people to now move on. 'She would have known that constant reminders of her death can create nothing but pain to those she left behind,' they said. They were distressed by the continual references to their mother's death and the endless speculation and conspiracy theories this generated, many of which emanated from Mohamed Al-Fayed. There was a tart response from Al-Fayed's spokesman, saying he could not rest until he knew the full truth about how his son had died.

William returned to Eton on the day they issued the statement. It was also his brother's first day at Eton. Sadly, they would have to live with the conspiracy theories for at least another decade. Still, William continued to flourish at Eton. His housemaster Dr Andrew Gailey, a respected constitutional historian and music lover from Northern Ireland, took the prince under his wing educationally and emotionally and exerted an important and positive influence as William sought to rebuild his life.

For his seventeenth birthday, William was given a VW Golf by Charles, and soon afterwards passed his driving test at the first attempt. Charles was keen for his son to use a four-wheeled vehicle and hoped it would quell his passion for motorbikes. William's passion for motorcycles, and the anonymity it gave him, frightened the life out of people at Buckingham Palace and almost certainly the Queen too. He went on to get his motorbike licence at the age of nineteen, and later owned a range of motorbikes including a 1199cc Ducati.

William had been driving on the private roads of the royal estates from the age of thirteen, but had received just twenty hours of tuition from Police Sergeant Chris Gilbert, an expert in anti-hijack and counter-surveillance techniques, before passing his test in a silver Ford Focus on loan to the Royal Estate. The prince was praised by his instructor for his 'natural flair for driving' and said he would continue lessons to make him more confident at night and motorway driving. Just twenty-four hours after a photocall in which he displayed his driving skills, William leapt from a borrowed Ford Focus car and punched the air in delight on hearing he had passed, according to a watching lorry driver. The unnamed driver realised what he had seen when he watched the L-plates being removed from the car and new green ones used by recently qualified drivers being put in their place. He said: 'I knew then he had passed his test. It was fantastic to witness the moment.'

Perhaps as an escape from his private emotional turmoil, William had thrown himself into his academic work after his mother's death, more so than he had ever done before. 'My boy has got a good brain,'[43] Diana would often say, before adding with her customary giggle, 'considering how hopeless both his parents were.' For some reason he felt he had let her down; there was a sense of emptiness, a void he wanted to fill. Like any son, he just wanted to make her proud of him and his achievements.

He not only wanted to make his late mother proud, but also wanted to prove to himself and the wider world that everything had not been gifted to him. He was, after all, a capable, intelligent and determined student. Close to the first anniversary of his mother's death, the palace announced that William, who had gained three GCSE passes the previous year, had received a further nine GCSEs with top A* and A grades in English, history and languages, and Bs for other subjects including maths and science. He had done Diana, and perhaps more importantly himself, proud. He returned for his final year at Eton on 8 September to take geography, English and history of art at A level.

He was also elected by his peers to be part of a prestigious group of prefects known as The Eton Society, or Pop. They were selected to exercise school discipline and seen as the elite of the elite. His duties included ensuring that younger boys attended a daily chapel service, and serving as an usher at school plays. He was also able to fine pupils for breaking the school rules. The uniform of an Eton Popper was stylish: a black tailcoat with braid piping; spongebag trousers in a houndstooth check; and a starched wing collar with a white bow-tie. It was topped off with highly polished black lace-up winkle-pickers, plus a gardenia or a rose in the buttonhole. While the rest of the schoolboys had been shoehorned into black waistcoats, the Poppers were allowed to wear any waistcoat they pleased. They ranged from waistcoats of green leather to ones spangled with Pearly King buttons, and even a hideous, electric-pink fur number. William, when he was a Popper, tended towards the staid, his most daring outfit was a patriotic Union Jack.

Eddie Redmayne, the multi-award-winning actor who was honoured with an Academy Award for Best Actor in 2015 for his portrayal of physicist and motor neurone disease sufferer Professor Stephen Hawking in *The Theory of Everything*, moved in the same circles as William. There is even a photograph of them together, taken in 2000, showing them in Pop waistcoats. The two were also on the same rugby team at school. Recalling those days recently, Eddie, who went to Eton at thirteen from Colet Court, St Paul's, in west London, said, 'I always felt slightly sorry for him because everyone wanted to tackle the future king of England. He took all the hits.' He went on to add, 'I'm pretty sure Will was more intimidating than I was. I don't think I intimidated anyone in my life. I haven't seen him since school, but he was a lovely man.'

William wanted to show he could get into a good university on merit, not because of who he was. He did well and left school after attaining three A levels: a grade A in geography, another A in history of art and a C in biology. Overall, he was pleased, and so was his father, who had achieved five O levels and two A levels: a grade B in history and a C in French. Charles had subsequently been awarded a 2:2 degree in history from Cambridge University. Charles said, 'I know how hard William worked to achieve these excellent results and I am very proud that he has done so well.' He also let slip that his son wished to attend a Scottish university.

William was 5,000 miles away in the subtropical jungles of Belize when he heard the news of his grades via email. It meant that he had what he needed to go up to read history of art at St Andrew's University in Scotland. In Belize, his travelling companion for part of the ten-week trip was Mark Dyer, a former aide to the Prince of Wales, who had become William's close friend. Dyer, then thirty-four, was also a former captain in the Welsh Guards, and had helped William to plan his year away.

But first, like many teenagers on the cusp of adulthood and readying themselves for life as full-time undergraduates at university, William decided he wanted to take a gap year. He was no longer a self-effacing schoolboy, but he did not simply toe the line either. He was not afraid to buck a few trends and made it clear to his father he would be taking a gap.[44] One former courtier said, 'God help anyone who tried to tell William what to do. He would listen, but he would never be pushed around by the system or anyone who thought they were high up in it.' Never was that more evident than when the issue was raised of where William would continue his education once his schooldays had ended.

Dressed in jeans and a casual fawn crew-neck jumper, he held a press conference outside the Orchard Tea Room in Highgrove and said he would soon join a Raleigh International expedition to Chile, where he would work on community and environmental projects. He said he would also travel to some of the most remote parts of Patagonia and would head to St Andrew's the following year to study for a degree in the history of art.

'Basically, I wanted to do something constructive,' he said, after raising about £5,500 ($8,800) to pay for his trip to Chile by organising a sponsored water-polo match. The money, he said, would also pay for a disadvantaged youngster from Newcastle to share the experience and go on the expedition. Asked if his father had contributed, William, said, 'A bit,' before Charles, standing next to him, drew laughter from the reporters when he said, 'I'm always bloody chipping in.'

In October, November and December, William was photographed in a variety of staged PR opportunities. He was shown sharing a joke with ten-year-old Marcela Hernandez-Rios, whilst helping to teach English in the village of Tortel, in southern Chile, about 950 miles south of Santiago, between the mouth of the Baker River and a small embayment of the Baker Channel. Like everyone else, William arrived at the expedition with a sense of excitement and trepidation, not knowing quite what to expect and what the group of people he was with would be like. But within a short period of time, he just relaxed into the whole Raleigh expedition way of life which helped him develop his confidence. His expedition leaders were thrilled by him.

Marie Wright, the twenty-nine-year-old project manager for Raleigh in Tortel, said, 'He's worked hard. He's laid-back. He's struck a good balance between working hard, having a good time and getting on with everyone. Taking on the team-spirit ethic. He has earned their respect. He's popular on his own merit. He gets on with the work, he's very humble and laid-back and likes to be normal, and there's no reference to his background.' Another said, 'He is very effective as a leader, which is quite evident in the way he manages the group, when he gets the opportunity.'

He agreed to be interviewed about his experience in situ, in an old nursery which was his accommodation for part of the trip, by the Press Association team, who also took photos to be distributed to publications. 'This is luxury,' he said, only half joking, 'Most of the time they didn't have a roof over their heads but were in tents or sleeping under the stars.' He opened up about himself, too. 'You can't have any secrets on Raleigh,' he reflected. 'I found it very difficult to start with because I am a very private person, and I still am a private person, but I love to deal with it more.' Sleeping on a cold and cramped floor, stranded on a remote, rain-lashed beach, and living off rations, doesn't sound like much fun, but he enjoyed the experience and being tested. 'Here you are actually making a difference to other people's lives. The living conditions here aren't exactly what I'm used to, but they are definitely better than I've had in the past six weeks.'[45]

His first brush with adversity during his expedition came when his group was stranded on a beach, while kayaking during a freak five-day storm. 'The wind whipped up into a storm,' he said. 'The tents were flapping around so violently that we thought they were going to blow away. Everything was soaked through. It was quite demoralising.'[46]

William also helped locals build wooden walkways to link their homes and an extension to the fire station. The high points included kayaking in ocean fjords and tracking rare huemul deer in the Tamango National Reserve. Chilean Patagonia, he said, was 'an amazing place'. He was a hit with the locals, too, salsa dancing with them, and enjoyed being treated as an equal by the other volunteers. He also taught English to local schoolchildren. He ran into difficulties explaining the letter 'W' in his name. Standing before a class of ten- and eleven-year-olds, he wrote his name on a board and then had to draw an animal starting with the same letter. Struggling to think of one, he referred to the childhood nickname his mother and father had given him as a baby all those years ago in Australia. 'My name is William. I am a wombat.'[47] Despite his good intentions as a teacher, he was at a loss as to how to draw a wombat.

CHAPTER SIX

SALAD DAYS

'We obviously met at university, at St Andrew's we were friends for over a year first and it just sort of blossomed from then on'

William, on meeting his future wife, Catherine, at university

William wanted to slip quietly into life as an undergraduate, so some concessions were inevitably made due to his status as a future king. He arrived a week late, for a start, having decided to skip freshers' week. 'It had the potential for media frenzy,' William explained, 'and that's not fair on the other students. Plus, I thought I would probably end up in a gutter completely wrecked, and the people I met that week wouldn't end up being my friends anyway. It also meant having another week's holiday.'[48] It was a well-rehearsed script, upbeat and positive. He had chosen to read history of art, geography and anthropology in the first year, but he knew the system gave him flexibility to change, so he could major in history of art.

It had long been assumed that William would follow his father and go up to Trinity College, Cambridge, to further his education. The prince, however, was given much more freedom than his father to choose his own path. He had known for some time that he didn't want to follow the Oxbridge route that had been mapped out for him, and felt that the ancient Scottish seat of learning, St Andrew's, was better suited to him. St Andrew's is highly regarded and counts Alex Salmond, former first minister of Scotland, among its notable alumni, along with Benjamin Franklin, who had received an honorary degree from the university in 1759.

William took the time to explain his choice in an interview published the day before he matriculated. He had, he said, decided against studying at the University of Edinburgh because the city was too big and busy. He also feared he would be swamped by paparazzi. He maintained, 'I do love Scotland. There is plenty of space. I love the hills and the mountains, and I thought St Andrew's had a real community feel to it. I've never lived near the sea, so it will be very different. I just hope I can meet people I get on with. I don't care about their background.'[49] The egalitarian-minded royal was sincere enough even though he had in fact chosen a university with the highest percentage of privately educated undergraduates in the country.

Dressed in jeans, trainers and a pastel sweater, the standard uniform for the modern student, nineteen-year-old William looked a little shaken by the size of the welcoming committee on the morning of 24 September 2001 that had pitched up to mark the occasion. Around 3,000 onlookers lined the streets of the small east-coast town of St Andrew's, a place that revolves around a 'town and gown' divide in much the same way that Durham, Oxford and Cambridge do. The focus fell on the dark-green Vauxhall Omega, driven by Prince Charles, as it attempted to negotiate the narrow cobbled entrance to St Salvator's College. A sharp wind blew across The Royal & Ancient Golf Club as the Prince of Wales nosed his car in under the gothic clock tower. A group of curious students had gathered inside the ancient quadrangle, quietly holding anti-war placards aloft and shivering slightly in the crisp autumn morning. Their presence was predictable, but peaceful, an opportunistic bid to piggyback on the publicity generated by the main attraction that day: the arrival of Prince William as he embarked on undergraduate life. William composed himself and fixed his trademark toothy grin. After stepping smartly from the car, he strode, hand outstretched, towards the university principal, Dr Brian Lang. Dr Lang stood slightly in front of a host of other academics and university dignitaries, keen to meet their VIP student who, despite his princely status, had been assured he would be treated no differently from any other fresher. This would be William's base for the next four years.

If William was nervous about what lay ahead of him, he did his best not to show it. In the weeks prior to the prince's arrival, Dr Lang had sounded a note of caution. He implored the media to respect the wishes of the prince and other students and allow them to get on with their respective courses without constant intrusion and pestering. However, behind closed oak-panelled doors, Lang must have quietly rejoiced at how good for business William's choice of alma mater was. St Andrew's was hardly an unknown backwater to start with. It is Scotland's oldest university. Steeped in history and myth, it dominates the small town and overlooks a sweep of sandy beach and the world-famous, wind-buffeted golf course. Applications for courses had risen by 44 per cent in the wake of William's decision to attend, and some fanciful reports claimed that female students had been ordering wedding dresses in anticipation of his arrival.

He looked every inch the student prince, but, as a student, he was determined not to stand out. It was this that lay behind his decision to study at St Andrew's. He longed for a sense of normalcy. He had been irritated by reports that his choice had been opposed within the royal family. William instructed palace aides to deny reports that the senior royals had really wanted him to attend one of the colleges at Oxford or Cambridge. The family, the officials insisted, were 'thrilled' by William's departure from tradition, not least because his choice underpinned the monarchy's firm ties with Scotland.

William made all the right noises, but he touched, too, on the underlying and inevitable tension that would be a feature of his student life. For most students, the fun of freshers' week is offset by the sorts of indignities best forgotten. If a few compromising pictures are taken or a few ill-advised liaisons forged, then the worst the fledgling intellectual might face is some common-room ribbing or the wrath of the dean. But how could the future king, however normal he wanted to be, fall out of student bars and into student beds without generating the sort of moral outrage and public debate reserved for wayward cabinet ministers? Where other students worried what their peers might think or sweated over whether college authorities might notify their parents, William had to concern himself seriously with what the nation might make of him should student high jinks get out of hand. He would have to be discreet, and he would have to choose his friends wisely. William had already stated in his pre-university interview that he was confident in his own ability to gauge the sincerity of strangers. 'People who try to take advantage of me and get a piece of me, I spot it quickly and soon go off them. I'm not stupid,' he said.[50] No doubt he felt the same certainty when it came to women.

Prince Charles had faced similar issues when he went to Trinity College, Cambridge. He even joked about 'going gay' to avoid the pressure of finding a suitable royal bride before his marriage to Diana. He made the quip at Trinity College. He recalled a newspaper article featuring several 'potential brides' for the bachelor prince that prompted Charles to crack the joke. His Cambridge contemporary Broderick Munro-Wilson said, 'We were all reading it together and I thought, poor sod, I'm not sure I'd go for any of those. He said to me, "Brod, shall I go gay?" That is a fact. We all roared with laughter and moved on. I think the market was so narrow … and of course she had to be a virgin.' When responding to a remark that there were few around, Munro-Wilson said, 'There were probably none, and I think it was a tricky one for him.'[51]

The girls William tended to hang out with tended to be tall, like him, slim, leggy, blue-eyed and usually blondes with trust funds more substantial than their frames, and double-barrelled, sometimes triple-barrelled, surnames. It wasn't that he made a beeline for that type, it was just that they happened to be in the circles he mixed in. They might not have presented him with any profound connection, but they were fun. He had been romantically linked to several girls before his arrival at St Andrew's, but none was deemed truly special.

In his twenty-first-birthday interview, William said that he did not have a steady girlfriend, but said that if the right girl came along, he would ask her out. Echoing his father's comments at the same age, William was concerned about the impact that dating a future king would have on these girls. 'There's been a lot of speculation about every single girl I'm with, and it actually does quite irritate me after a while, more so because it's a complete pain for the girls,' he said. 'These poor girls, you know, who I've either just met and get photographed with, or they're friends of mine, suddenly get thrown into the limelight and their parents get rung up and so on. I think it's a little unfair on them really. I'm used to it because it happens quite a lot now, but it's very difficult for them and I don't like that at all.'

He wouldn't be drawn on media speculation about specific friendships with girls. 'I don't have a steady girlfriend. If I fancy a girl and I really like her and she fancies me back, which is rare, I ask her out. At the same time, I don't want to put them in an awkward situation because a lot of people don't quite understand what comes with knowing me, for one; and secondly, if they were my girlfriend, the excitement it would probably cause.'

He soon struck up a close friendship with a fellow St Andrew's undergraduate, Carly Massy-Birch, from Devon. There was an instant mutual attraction. Her natural aloofness and charm intrigued William and she won his heart in the first term. He pursued her, and she became his first proper girlfriend. They dated for a few weeks, but then the couple agreed to cool things, and the split came at the end of the first term in October 2001. For all the normality, after he and Carly parted, it added to William's feelings of insecurity. He became increasingly unhappy. Perhaps uncertainty and a touch of homesickness and disenchantment were the flip side of normal student life, which he had failed to anticipate.

Catherine Elizabeth Middleton had been part of William's circle for a while, but it was at around this time that they began to grow closer. 'We just spent more time with each other, had a good giggle, had lots of fun and realised we shared the same interests and just had a really good time,' William said in his engagement interview.[52] Catherine added, 'Well, I actually think I went bright red when I met you and sort of scuttled off, feeling very shy about meeting you. William wasn't there for quite a bit of the time initially, he wasn't there for freshers' week, so it did take a bit of time for us to get to know each other, but we did become very close friends from quite early on.' William explained later that his courting didn't always go to plan. 'When I was trying to impress Kate, I was trying to cook these amazing, fancy dinners and what would happen was I would burn something, something would overspill, something would catch on fire and she would be sitting in the background just trying to help, and basically taking control of the whole situation, so I was quite glad she was there at the time.'

She first caught William's eye wearing that famous transparent dress as she strutted down a catwalk at a student charity fashion show. Neither William nor Catherine were single that night. Catherine's date was handsome fourth-year-law student Rupert Finch, and William's first love, Carly Massy-Birch, was also there, though their relationship was cooling. William first met Marlborough College-educated Catherine at St Salvator's Hall, their hall of residence. William paid £200 to sit in the front row at the 'Don't Walk' show on 27 March 2002. Catherine modelled a risqué black-lace dress over a bandeau bra and black bikini bottoms by designer Catherine Todd. As she sashayed down the catwalk in the St Andrew's Bay Hotel, William turned to his friend Fergus Boyd and said, 'Wow, Fergus, Kate's hot.'

Ten days later, Catherine entered public consciousness as the lithe, brunette, catwalk model watched by a clearly mesmerised William. A fellow student tipped off the *Mail on Sunday* and on 7 April 2002 the story ran under the headline 'WILLIAM AND HIS UNDIE-GRADUATE FRIEND KATE TO SHARE A STUDENT FLAT'. That same month, the first reports began to emerge that all was not well with the prince. He was apparently dissatisfied with his course and bored by his environs. He was seriously considering a change of scene. Perhaps, he wondered, Edinburgh University with its city attractions and bustle might have been a better move after all. William was unsettled and began to feel that he might have made the wrong choice of college. He discussed the matter with his father, spelling out his desire to abandon the four-year course altogether. Charles was sympathetic at first, but understandably concerned about the wider implications. He asked his private office to devise a strategy that would enable William to withdraw from the university should it prove necessary, but they were horrified at the prospect and the bad fall-out that would follow. 'It would be a major setback for William in terms of his public image – he would be seen as a quitter – and it would be an even bigger disaster for the monarchy, particularly in Scotland,' a royal aide confided. Charles then went back and strongly advised his son to 'stick with it' as first-year wobbles were normal, and it took most students time to settle. It was good advice.

When William later reflected on how he wrestled with the idea of quitting university, he recalled, 'I think the rumour that I was unhappy got slightly out of control. I don't think I was homesick. I was more daunted.' He conceded there had been a problem and that his father had been a big help. 'We chatted a lot and in the end we both realised – I definitely realised – that I had to come back.'[53] On his return, he switched courses to major in geography and immediately felt happier and more confident. His social life began to look up, too, and Catherine – who at that stage he still called Kate – became a much more important fixture in his young life. Years later, he reflected, 'We obviously met at university, at St Andrew's we were friends for over a year first and it just sort of blossomed from then on. We just spent more time with each other, had a good giggle, had lots of fun and realised we shared the same interests and just had a really good time.'

By their second year, the couple were close enough to share a £400,000 maisonette in the centre of the town, the Upper Flat, 13a Hope Street, which they rented for £400 a week (£100 each) with two friends, Fergus Boyd, an old Eton classmate of William, who would also meet his future wife, Sandrine Jane, at St Andrew's, and Olivia 'Livvie' Bleasdale. The students kept a low profile, walking or cycling to lectures, shopping at Safeway (now Morrisons), and spending the evenings at home, listening to William's R&B music or Fergus's jazz thumping from their stereos. They rarely ventured out during the week – unless they were attending lectures or visiting the university library – apart from on Wednesday afternoons when they played sport. Both William, who had by now been voted the university's water polo captain, and Fergus trained for two hours on Thursday nights in the pool of St Leonards girls' school.

The couple's cosy lifestyle inevitably increased speculation about the true nature of their relationship. Were these good friends really lovers? Could she be the one? The newspapers kept hinting. One university contemporary said, 'There was a bit of a buzz about them living together. But they were so careful in public you would never have guessed they were an item in the early days. They had the whole thing off pat. Obviously Fergus Boyd [their flatmate] knew, but at first they were seen as just friends.' Perhaps, at least at the outset, they were. In May 2003, Catherine's father felt compelled to issue a good-natured rebuttal of a report that William and his daughter were an item. 'I spoke to her just a few days ago and can categorically confirm they are no more than just good friends. They are together all the time because they are the best of pals and, yes, cameramen are going to get photos of them together. But there's nothing more to it than that. We're very amused at the thought of being in-laws to Prince William, but I don't think it's going to happen.' Nevertheless, despite her father's denials, Catherine had by now become an integral a part of William's circle.

Whether Catherine kept Michael Middleton in the dark about the intimate nature of their friendship is unclear. The media were not, either way, deterred by his denial. They were convinced that they had the right girl. Barely a month after Mr Middleton's statement, Catherine turned twenty-one and her parents threw a lavish party in the grounds of their large family home. Old school friends turned out in force as well as her new crowd from St Andrew's University. There was a champagne reception followed by a sit-down dinner in a marquee with everybody dressed, at Catherine's personal request, in fashions of the twenties. Among those in the happy throng was William, who slipped into the marquee unannounced.

The prince told Catherine she looked stunning, which she did. She smiled her acknowledgement, and they began talking and relaxing into each other's company. It was clear to everyone there that they had a special chemistry even at this stage of their friendship. William left soon after dinner with the party still in full swing. Discretion has always been crucial to William. Perhaps Mr Middleton, a charming and honourable man, was telling the truth, but there was no doubt Catherine was special to William. He was, of course, though, still very young.

William was still single in the autumn of 2003 and when he was back in London, he was a regular at the hedonistic Purple nightclub, based in the grounds of Chelsea Football Club, a favourite with the local Sloane Rangers and owned by respected Fulham businessman Brian Mason and run by his son, James. The successful club, which is now closed, had been a haunt of Prince Harry, too. They were heady times. Buoyed by his new-found freedom and emotionally unrestrained, William was enjoying spreading his wings. In March the following year, he was back at Purple where a stunning blonde from Chigwell, Essex, cheekily chatted him up. They were locked in deep conversation and William, then twenty-one, happily gave his email and mobile numbers to her. The *Sunday People* was tipped off and reported, 'By the way William was staring into the girl's eyes they could have been the only people in the club. At 2 a.m. he asked his bodyguard for a pen, and he took the blonde's number. The girl could hardly stop the grin spreading straight across her face, especially when he gave her his email address and mobile number. The other posh girls were green with envy.'

William's exuberance, however, got him into trouble that summer and back onto the front pages. In June 2003, Charles was forced to apologise on behalf of his elder son to an English aristocrat who slammed William for 'driving like some yob in a beat-up car'[54] during a weekend break from university. The seventy-six-year-old Lord Bathurst caused a security scare in a bizarre road-rage incident when he chased the prince, who had overtaken him on a private road on the Earl's estate in Gloucestershire. It was an extraordinary drama, occurring just a month shy of William's twenty-first birthday, which again showed his readiness to take risks. It came after William had played in a polo match at Cirencester with his father. Ignoring the unofficial speed limit on the estate, William was pursued by a furious Lord Bathurst in his Land Rover, blasting his horn, and flashing his lights at the prince's vehicle. William's police bodyguards intervened. Despite the apology, the aristocrat blasted William's behaviour. He said, 'I don't care who it is, royalty or not – speeding is not allowed on my estate. The limit is twenty miles an hour. If I were to drive like that in Windsor Park, I'd end up in the Tower. I thought he was some young yob in a beat-up car.' When he was unable to give the speeding prince a telling off, the earl turned on the prince's personal protection officers, whom he described as 'looking like a pair of yobs'. Charles's officials played down the encounter as 'a very minor incident in which no one was injured'. However, it did demonstrate William's more reckless nature.

It is understood that at this time whilst still at university, William and Catherine split for the first time. They were asked about their brief separation during their engagement interview with ITV's Tom Bradby in 2010. William responded, 'We were both very young. It was at university, we were sort of both finding ourselves as such and being different characters and stuff, it was very much trying to find our own way and we were growing up.' It is unclear exactly when this cooling off period was, but by the following August, William and Catherine's romance was going strong. Four months after the Christmas ball, in April 2004, *The Sun* published pictures of the two of them together on holiday in Klosters, the ski resort in the Swiss Alps, that caused an undeserved backlash from Clarence House. The newspaper had already speculated about the nature of the relationship, reporting that it had flourished thanks to a series of trips to the Balmoral bolt-hole cottage (see below).

Just over a week before the April trip to Klosters, the couple had travelled from St Andrew's to join a group of his friends riding with the coincidentally named Middleton Hunt in North Yorkshire. Even there, they were at pains not to show the extent of their attachment to each other. One observer noted, 'They were not touchy-feely. They were really so very careful, and afterwards, when everyone else went for a meal, they'd disappeared.' It was no bad thing for Catherine to be publicly associated with William. With her by his side, the sometimes irritable prince was notably more at ease. During that holiday in Klosters, she was one of the royal ski party of seven who had flown from Heathrow to Zurich airport. The group included Harry Legge-Bourke (younger brother to William's unofficial nanny, Tiggy), Guy Pelly, William van Cutsem, son of Charles's old Norfolk landowning friend Hugh, and van Cutsem's girlfriend, Katie James.

Catherine had already been a guest at Highgrove at least three times, as well as at Sandringham, the Queen's Norfolk estate. William had taken her for weekends to a Highlands bolt-hole, the cottage of *Tom-Na-Gaidh*, Birkhall, Ballater, on the eastern edge of the Balmoral estate, by the River Muick, given to him and Harry by the Queen and renovated at a cost of £150,000. It was inconceivable that she would escape notice. She was, after all, his first publicly acknowledged serious girlfriend. In Klosters, she was part of a lively, wealthy bunch that, every night, after an energetic day on the slopes, set out to enjoy the après-ski. One evening, the now remarkably carefree William, with his girl by his side, took to the microphone for a rousing shot at the karaoke bar. Catherine sat at a table with Charles, there with his old pals Charlie and Patty Palmer-Tomkinson. Laughing at William's attempts at karaoke, totally at ease in such elevated company, Catherine was a picture. William did not attempt to deny that Catherine was his girlfriend after pictures appeared in *The Sun*. The issue now, one on which royal observers including myself were divided, was: just how important was Kate? For their final two years, the group moved away from the centre of the town into a £750,000 eighteenth-century farmhouse on the Strathyrum estate. The cottage, set in rolling grounds brimming with orchids and fuschia bushes, was an idyllic venue for the young lovers. Not only was the house discreet, but it was also totally secure: a neighbouring cottage was chosen as the centre of a security operation, and squads of officers were drafted in to keep twenty-four-hour surveillance on the farmhouse. The cottage was also bombproofed, and CCTV cameras and panic buttons installed, linked to both local police stations and Buckingham Palace in case of an emergency.

During their time at the university, the couple immersed themselves in student life. They were often to be spotted drinking and chatting at Ma Bells, the bar in the basement of the St Andrew's Golf Hotel (now the Hotel du Vin), which is close to the university and overlooks the seafront. Known as 'Yah Yah Bells' because of its reputation as a hangout for the university's Sloane Rangers, it was often heaving in the evenings with students dancing to the resident DJ. Another favourite venue was the West Port Bar, where William and Fergus retired after playing rugby sevens. One of their annual outings was the May Ball, which was held in the Byre, a converted barn in the grounds of Kinkell Farm – the royal couple had VIP passes so they could avoid the riffraff.

The move to the farm marked a sea-change in William's approach to life, which some ascribe simply to growing up, but others put down to Catherine's influence. 'I do all my own shopping. I go out, get takeaways, rent videos, go to the cinema, just basically anything I want to really,' William said, acknowledging that the deal struck with the media was working. Some evenings he would stay in and cook. Discussing his prowess in the kitchen, he said later, 'I've done a bit at university when I had to feed my flatmates, which was quite hard work because a couple of them ate quite a lot.'

★★★

It had been a long night in Casa Antica, a nightclub in the Swiss Alps and a popular venue for the Klosters après-ski crowd and one of William's favourite hangouts. On 30 March 2005, he was there amid the smoke and throbbing music, holding court at a table in a dimly lit and sectioned-off room at the back of the club. Sitting next to his brother Harry, whose face was flushed red due to drink, William did something completely out of character. He spotted a tabloid reporter chatting with one of his Scotland Yard protection officers and spontaneously invited him over for a chat. The reporter, Duncan Larcombe, just a few years older than the prince, had arrived at the club just after midnight on a hunch that the princes and their friends would be there. He had wisely informed the protection team of his presence and offered to leave if they felt his presence was a problem.

At that precise moment, Guy Pelly, William's eccentric but often hilarious friend, burst out of a side room wearing nothing but a pair of brown silk boxer shorts. Inexplicably, he sat on the reporter's lap, perhaps assuming the journalist was a new royal protection officer and began talking to the officers. Much to William's amusement, Pelly disappeared almost as quickly as he had arrived when one of the officers introduced the chap on whose lap he was sitting as *The Sun's* new royal reporter.[55]

Sensing an embarrassing headline in the newspaper, the next day, William told his minders he would like a chat with the hack, and proceeded to give him an interview, at no stage saying his comments were off the record – although the next morning a flustered Paddy Harverson, Charles's communication director and media minder for the boys on the ski trip, insisted that the conversation had been private and not for publication. The editor of *The Sun*, Rebekah Wade, by now reading the copy back in the newspaper's headquarters in Wapping, London, rightly stood her ground and ran the story anyway.

The previous year, *The Sun* had been banned for publishing paparazzi pictures of William and Catherine. This year, however, William was totally relaxed about the photographs being taken, although he appeared genuinely surprised as to why there was such frenzied interest in them. The reporter suggested it was because there had been speculation that this relationship could lead to marriage, and that an engagement could be on the cards. Perhaps, gaining in confidence, the journalist did not expect a response, but it was certainly worth a punt. He had thrown the talk of marriage into the conversation, almost in jest, never seriously anticipating that William would take it on. The prince's forthright remark gave him quite a story: 'Look, I'm only twenty-two, for God's sake. I'm too young to marry at my age. I don't want to get married until I'm at least twenty-eight or maybe thirty.'

With those few words, William had given the tabloid a notable exclusive. The next morning, over five pages and in what was billed as a world exclusive, the paper ran the details of the extraordinary moment in which the young prince 'opened his heart' to one of its reporters. Catherine, after all, had been in the same room as he was when he chatted informally to the reporter, but at no stage had William thought of making an introduction. If Catherine had serious feelings and hopes for her relationship with William at that point, such a public dismissal of the prospect of a proposal any time soon might naturally have upset her. After all, she was standing close to William when he uttered his surprisingly frank words.

William's candour, however, did little to dampen Catherine's spirits, to her great credit. Far from appearing subdued, she joined wholeheartedly in the drunken rough and tumble of the evening. Good-natured horseplay ensued, resulting in the beaded bracelet that Prince Harry was wearing, a gift from girlfriend Chelsy, being grabbed and broken. As he scrabbled around the club floor trying to retrieve the beads, his whooping sibling, Catherine, and friends swooped on the intoxicated royal, threatening to pull down his trousers and underwear. Lost in peals of laughter, glowing and hot with the night's excesses, Catherine was hardly the image of a girl who had just witnessed the man she loved inform a relative stranger that, romantically speaking, he was still up for grabs. William is media-savvy. There were many in his circle of friends who suspected that the world exclusive, the denial of any serious thoughts of marriage, blurted out so apparently carelessly, was, in fact, a smokescreen designed to cool the media frenzy about William's steady girlfriend.

The royal press corps bowed to the scoop but weren't surprised by it. It was simply another case of William trying to have it both ways. He had seen what had happened to his mother and what had happened to his father. His father let the woman he loved, Camilla, slip through his fingers thirty years previously and was miserable for years. On the other hand, his mother, Diana, married far too young, and he was adamant that he would not make the same mistake.

The prince, echoing his father's view, often joked with friends that the media 'never let the truth get in the way of a good story'. But William and his advisers knew very well that in recent years the press had largely got it right far too often for the royal family's liking. Fleet Street legends, such as the late, great James Whitaker and urbane Richard Kay, had been working the royal beat and breaking stories with relentless accuracy for many years. This was no mean feat when their enquiries are often met with a stream of lies, half-truths and denials from Palace officials and even from the mouths of members of the royal family themselves. Like his late mother, Princess Diana, and despite his relative youth, William knows how to play the media. Would it really be so surprising if, to put the press off the scent and give his relationship with Catherine time to develop, William had embarked on a little late-night subterfuge in the Swiss Alps when he poured scorn on talk of marriage?

One senior official, who was on that same skiing holiday, revealed, 'The prince knew exactly what he was doing; he would not open his heart about his private life to a reporter he barely knows, no matter how much drink had been taken, without thinking about it first. It was for show, a way of dampening down speculation about him and Catherine, a way of protecting her from the press.'[56]

Catherine's obvious lack of concern as she partied with her boyfriend showed just how close the couple had become. She, like others who know William intimately, knew that whatever he said was with her best interests – rather than the next morning's headlines – in mind. William has a protective instinct towards all his friends when it comes to the press. He has inherited a style from his supremely loyal father. It is understandable, given his position and past. Emotionally scarred by the death of his beloved mother, he still believes, like Diana's embittered brother Earl Spencer, that the paparazzi had hounded the princess to her death. From that night on, Paddy Harverson placed himself in charge of William's press during his Klosters holiday. He took it upon himself to be William's chaperone, inhabiting a sort of awkward no-man's-land between laddish companion and maiden aunt on all the princes' subsequent visits to nightclubs. As is so often the case, though, the spin doctor was resolutely slamming the stable door shut long after the horse had bolted.

Unbeknown to Mr Harverson, undercover reporters had been working in the resort for more than a week, observing the young royals' drunken antics in all their glory, including Harry's bid to turn the tables on some members of the press by snatching up a camera and pursuing them as he snapped pictures and howled with laughter. The royals' relationship with the press – especially the tabloids – has always been a protracted game of cat and mouse. In addition, that royal 'stag' trip, as it was dubbed, was the last holiday Charles would enjoy with his sons before his wedding to Camilla in April 2005.

Within days, I heard a markedly different story from a reliable – perhaps in this instance more reliable – source than the prince himself did. A senior royal courtier let slip during conversation that the relationship between William and Catherine was very serious and developing at a fast pace. It rang true with me, even at such an early stage. 'The relationship is very much ongoing. Just because the two of them choose to keep things private and play their cards close to their chest does not mean it is waning. Far from it: in fact, it is quite the opposite,' a senior aide said to the *Evening Standard*. The following morning, the newspaper front-page splash carried the banner headline 'SERIOUSLY IN LOVE'. Beneath were the words: 'Wills and Kate romance moving at a rapid pace, say royal sources'. A photograph of a smiling William looking lovingly into his girlfriend's eyes accompanied the report. The look of love certainly seemed to me to betray something of the besotted prince's true emotions, even if his own words had not. Perhaps, however, it was just the sort of headline the intensely private prince didn't want to see; perhaps it was overboard.

★★★

In May 2005, William was putting down his pen after his last geography exam. Unlike William's university contemporaries, whether he got first-class honours, a 2:1 or scraped through with a third was irrelevant as far as his career path to kingship was concerned. Sandhurst, a commission with the Blues and Royals and then the fast-track into royal duties would follow, but William, a proud and intelligent young man, was desperate to perform well. He had prepared himself diligently for these exams and, as he finished, he recalled letting out an audible sigh of relief. Ahead of him were three weeks of festivities and fun, culminating in a lavish graduation ball at the university.

William had relished the relative anonymity that full-time education had afforded him, but whatever he did now, the reality and expectations of impending royal duties could no longer be ignored. A few weeks earlier, he had expressed some anxiety, admitting that he was wary of taking on public duties. 'I don't want to start too early and then be stuck doing that for the rest of my life,' he said.

On 23 June 2005, William graduated in front of his father, stepmother, and royal grandparents, as well as several hundred other equally proud parents. Looking nervous and biting his bottom lip, William waited his turn along with thirty fellow geography students. They hovered by the side of the stage in Younger Hall. William dressed in white bow-tie and black silk academic gown with cherry-red lining. As the dean of arts, Professor Christopher Smith, called out the name 'William Wales' from the lectern, the prince stepped forward to prolonged applause and the flashes of numerous cameras. William issued a statement that read, 'I have thoroughly enjoyed my time at St Andrew's, and I shall be very sad to leave. I just want to say a big thank you to everyone who has made my time here so enjoyable.' He added significantly, 'I have been able to lead as normal a student life as I could have hoped for and I am very grateful to everyone, particularly the locals, who have helped make this happen.'

Seated five rows in front of the prince, and graduating eighty people ahead of him, was the young woman who, more than anything or anyone, had shaped William's student life. Wearing high heels and a black skirt beneath her gown, she was called to the stage as Catherine Middleton. She smiled broadly as she returned to her seat, catching William's eye as he flashed back a proud smile. 'Today is a very special day,' William said after the ceremony. 'I am delighted I can share it with my family, particularly my grandmother, who has made such an effort to come, having been under the weather.' It was a predictably stiff summation of events. Far more natural was the affection with which the Queen patted her grandson's shoulder as he kissed her on both cheeks before she departed. Revealingly, far more natural was the smile on Catherine's face as, at William's urging, she introduced her parents to the monarch. It seemed the most normal thing in the world for her to do, but it marked another milestone for Catherine. The couple had taken a momentous step toward adulthood together that day and she was now well and truly part of the fold after her family had met the head of 'The Firm'.

'You will have made lifelong friends,' Dr Brian Lang, vice-chancellor of St Andrew's, told the new graduates in an address before they left Younger Hall that day. 'I say this every year to all new graduates: you may have met your husband or wife. Our title as 'Top Matchmaking University in Britain' signifies so much that is good about St Andrew's, so we can rely on you to go forth and multiply.' Dr Lang's words were met with laughter, of course, but there must have been a few couples in the auditorium that day who prickled slightly at his words and wondered if they referred to them – perhaps William and Catherine were among them?

Leaving the security of St Andrew's was always going to be a challenge, but during the run-up to their finals they had avoided the issue, and just focused on cramming for the exams. It is true that they had been through a few rocky patches during their student relationship, but the trials that lay ahead of them would test their commitment to one another to the limit.

In May 2021, William and Catherine, now the Duke and Duchess of Cambridge, sealed their return to their former university town by enjoying a quiet, romantic meal. They stayed overnight in St Andrew's before a day of royal events in the town, twenty years after the couple first met when students. When boyfriend and girlfriend they were known to enjoy Pizza Express, but on their return, they ate at fashionable Forgan's, a contemporary restaurant with a Scottish twist.

CHAPTER SEVEN

COLD FEET

'At the time I wasn't very happy about it, but actually it made me a stronger person'

Catherine Middleton, talking about her split from William

with ITV reporter Tom Bradby in 2010

As William and Catherine luxuriated on holiday on the terrace of the Maasai-owned Il Ngwesi Lodge, in the Mukogodo Hills of central Kenya, sipping cocktails in the evenings and dining al fresco, neither of them would have anticipated the dramas that lay ahead. As late summer gave way to autumn 2005, the uncomfortable process of trying to assimilate real life with royal life was, for Catherine, about to begin in earnest. In just a matter of weeks back home, the strain would begin to tell as Catherine's double life put pressure on her personally. It created tensions between the Palace and press and in turn took its toll on her relationship with William. How could it not? Hers became a surreal world. After all, one day, Catherine would be taking tea with the Queen at Windsor Castle, the next she was catching a ride on a London bus, seated next to a stranger who was oblivious to who she was.

William foresaw it would be a challenge; he knew too that he could not postpone forever either duties or big decisions about his future role. Catherine was an intelligent, determined, capable young woman and she had already invested much in her relationship with William. That said, he would be wrong to assume that she would hang around indefinitely without proper commitment. As for William, he was a young man still struggling to carve out his role in life and horribly conscious that the constitutional clock was ticking. 'I have so many things I want to do, I'm scared, really scared, that I won't have time,' he said.

When she was by William's side, Catherine was treated accordingly, afforded every courtesy and even the security normally reserved for a member of the royal family itself, even though all protection officers on duty with William are responsible chiefly for his safety and not that of his friends. She was taken to the best restaurants and the trendiest clubs, whisked through the VIP entrance, embraced by the phalanx of armed Scotland Yard security men. The privilege, and the glamour, would be enough to turn many a young girl's head. But, fortunately, not Catherine's. She had been raised wisely and brought up to keep her feet firmly on the ground. However, while her sensible nature may have helped steady her, the turbulence of this strangely conflicting life was still difficult to deal with – especially since her relationship with William was now considered to be moving to a new stage.

In September 2005, it seemed the relationship had moved on to a new level. Catherine, it emerged, had had a series of private, informal and friendly meetings with the Queen. Accompanied by William, the two women had enjoyed at least two dinners in recent months and the Queen had developed a warm and relaxed relationship with her grandson's girlfriend. One of the dinners took place at Windsor Castle, the Queen's favourite royal residence and the one that she truly regards as home. Catherine was ticking all the right boxes.

In the world of royal reporting, the story does not stand still for long. It soon gets 'legs' as they say. Outside castle walls, Catherine continued to act like an ordinary girl, independent, and possessing a certain degree of class, but not so very different from swathes of smart young women. She was often spotted browsing in shops on the fashionable King's Road, Chelsea, sometimes alone, sometimes with her mother, Carole, or friends, before heading back to the Chelsea flat where she was now living. There was no armed guard by her side. She always had to keep her wits about her. By autumn of 2005, she was hovering, half in, half out of the royal family and, despite the uneasiness of the situation, Catherine, for the most part, coped remarkably well with the ever-shifting sands.

William and Catherine tried to stick to a routine. After all, whatever William's status, they were like any couple trying to figure out what their relationship meant in the real world beyond the university gates. At its core was a need for secrecy and a continued game of cat and mouse with the pursuing paparazzi. William began to stay overnight with Catherine at her white stucco-fronted apartment opposite a bus stop in Chelsea. They would do what any young couple might. Sometimes they would head out to nearby clubs, such as Boujis or Purple, drink vodka and cranberry and enjoy the release of a throbbing dance floor and a mindless night of fun with friends. At other times, they would relax at a local restaurant. The Pig's Ear, a discreet and classy gastropub known for its good food and Chelsea-bohemian clientele, was one of Catherine's favourites, and William's, too. He was often seen there sipping his Breton cider. On other occasions, they would stay in; William would cook as he often had at their St Andrew's house, or they would order in pizza, watch a movie and try to emulate the simple bliss of their university 'marriage'.

It was all a far cry from the privilege and attention that the prince would receive when staying at the home of his father or grandmother, but, after four years of freedom, this was how he liked it. His double life was one of choice; Catherine's was foisted upon her, and she just had to get on with it. There was one significant difference from their carefree university days: the press, or particularly the press's attitude towards covering the story of the couple. As far as freelance photographers were concerned, the gloves were off. William – and by extension Catherine – was no longer shielded by agreements fixed by the Palace and newspaper editors.

Indeed, Fleet Street editors, for so long restrained in their royal coverage, were now ready to test the water and see just how far they could go, and just how much the circulation of their newspapers would increase by in the process. At university, the press had stuck by the gentlemen's agreement with the Palace and kept their distance. They had allowed William to go about his daily business free in the knowledge that he and his companions were not being followed. Now the paparazzi were out in force and Catherine, for the first time, would learn just what it really meant to be the beautiful girlfriend of a prince. Her Chelsea flat and its environs may have been vetted by William's Scotland Yard security officers, but nothing stops a paparazzo on a mission, as Catherine would find out to her dismay shortly after the wedding. Up to five such astute photographers had tracked her down to her home, having trailed doggedly through the town. They sometimes worked as a team, thus reducing the risk of missing a picture – but it meant having to share the spoils if successful.

They would pitch up outside in the early hours of the morning, sitting quietly in their cars, sometimes with blacked-out windows, engines off, patiently waiting and watching. As soon as the couple emerged, they would act – snapping a few frames from a distance. If Catherine was on her own, they would invariably follow her. A photograph of Catherine now earned something of a premium – not as much as the royal family and their advisers might estimate, but enough to make securing and selling it a worthwhile venture. Glossy magazines and newspapers had woken up to what was now newsworthy. Their readers wanted to know more about her: what she was wearing, where she shopped for her clothes, where she had her hair and make-up done. It all became part of an almost daily news diet.

Photographs of Catherine began to appear alongside snaps of footballers' wives and girlfriends or the latest girl-band member or pop sensation in glossy magazines and newspapers. At first, the pair said nothing. William understood the media attention went with the job. When he and Catherine were together it was also relatively easy to handle. There was always a waiting car and a royal-protection officer to deal with any eventuality. Pictures of William and Catherine climbing into a car after a night out together had rapidly become a staple of the picture editors' lists for morning news schedules.

It was more difficult for Catherine when her protective boyfriend and his security entourage were not there to assist her. Photographers began to follow her regularly, and it unnerved her.

William had had enough of his girlfriend being pursued, so a story was leaked to a friendly broadsheet, the *Sunday Telegraph*, that he had consulted royal lawyers in a bid to ensure she could pursue a normal life and career away from the prying lenses of the paparazzi. The newspaper broke the story saying it had learned that the prince, 'has mastered complex privacy laws and may ask lawyers to go to the European Court of Human Rights if the situation worsens. According to his friends, Prince William feels that Miss Middleton's future happiness and the survival of the relationship depend on protecting her from overly intrusive photographers.' It was a clear warning to Fleet Street's emboldened tabloid editors to consider themselves put on notice – if they continued to publish images of his girlfriend, William and the Palace would use the courts to act.

William's concerns may have been understandable, but they also proved a source of slight tension between him and his father. Charles sympathised with Catherine's lot, but he felt recourse to the European Court of Human Rights was ill-advised and could open a whole new can of worms for the royal family, who, after all, depended upon positive publicity for their existence as a privileged, expensive and unelected institution. Besides, Charles has never been a great fan of laws that he views as all too often abused by the undeserving at a cost to the greater good, and to the detriment of his country's sovereign laws. Much to the relief of all, it seemed that, as Christmas approached, the problem was abating; reporters and their editors did seem suitably chastened. But, weeks later, a story in the *Evening Standard* put privacy issues back in the spotlight and set alarm bells ringing at SO14, Scotland Yard's then elite Royalty and Diplomatic Protection Department before it was restructured to become Protection Command.

William had demanded to know how photographs pinpointing the location of his girlfriend's London home had come to be printed in a downmarket German magazine. The pictures showed William leaving the apartment following a night spent there with Catherine, and crudely indicated the exact location of the flat with a big red arrow and the caption '*Das Liebesnest*' – 'the love nest'. Senior protection sources condemned the story, printed in the Hamburg-based *Das Neue*, as 'grossly irresponsible' and the episode prompted an immediate review of the prince's security. William was furious at what he regarded as the magazine's stupidity in publishing such personal information at a time when security fears in the capital were at their peak in the aftermath of the city's bloody 7/7 terrorist bombings in 2005.

The couple had been back in the real world barely five months and already it seemed to be closing in on them and threatening their relationship. William knew that his father was uncomfortable with his proactive approach to the press, and it was a source of some friction between them. But it was not the only element of

William's life that seemed out of kilter. This period of adjustment was proving tense and uncertain as far as his continued relationship with Catherine was concerned. It was only a matter of time, it seemed, before the marriage was mentioned in the press. When it was, it came in the form of a snippet in the *Mail on Sunday*'s gossip column. 'Prince William's turbulent relationship with Kate Middleton is more gripping than any soap opera. Whether they will stay together is the question on everyone's lips,' the gossip columnist and royal writer Katie Nichol penned, before claiming that senior courtiers at Buckingham Palace had started discussing the prospect of a marriage and that 'contingency plans' for a wedding had been put in place. She allowed herself the safety net of pointing out that the Palace plans for all eventualities (preparations for the Queen Mother's funeral began in 1969), before going on to suggest that an announcement was being readied for spring 2006, with a wedding in the autumn. It had the impact of heaping more pressure on William.

However keen William was to maintain Catherine's privacy, by the end of the year, even the broadsheet newspapers – known for their comparative restraint – were publishing profile articles about 'Miss Middleton'. *The Independent on Sunday* referred to her as 'Her Royal Shyness'. William, they claimed, frequently conveyed the impression that, if the monarchy could be persuaded to call it a day before it was his turn to lift the crown, he would happily step out of the aristocratic limelight. He was, they said, a commoner by instinct if not by birth. This seemed to me a theory too far. However much William was a product of both his mother's and father's opposing influences, he was a royal through and through. His desire for privacy and for his version of normality was, if anything, akin to wanting to have his cake and eat it too. His attraction to Catherine and his continued relationship with her was, perhaps, evidence of a certain fascination with 'normality', but he could hardly be the sort of 'republican prince' envisaged in the article. Still, it was clear that William felt irresistibly drawn to the daughter of decidedly middle-class, self-made entrepreneurs in a way that he was not when in the company of, say, some obscure Ruritanian princess with a triple-barrelled name and several shaky connections to the extended family tree.

Under King William, commentators mused, and possibly Queen Catherine, we might yet see a move away from the present, expensive, fake-ancient patronage and pageantry (much of which dates back no further than the nineteenth century and Queen Victoria's adoration of pomp and history, however faux). In its place, we could expect a move towards a more modern, Scandinavian-type monarch, but perhaps at the cost of being far less secure. Undeterred, *The Independent on Sunday*'s article ran, 'The People's Princess may be replaced, in Kate, by a real princess of the people: a non-blue-blood. For republicans who prefer to be citizens rather than subjects and who hoped, after Diana's death, that the demise of the monarchy was imminent it's not the happy-ever-after they envisaged. But it might yet be for William.'

As the newspapers devoted pages of newsprint to crowning Catherine, lauding her for her normalcy, it was this, not her proximity to royalty, on which she seemed determined to focus. Speaking of her plans to design her own range of children's wear with her parents, one friend revealed, 'She had this fashion idea and she's decided to see it through. She's always loved clothes and has a good eye for design. Working with her parents means she won't be spied on if she and William do stay together. Kate believes she can make good money as well.'

Catherine had William's backing, or so it seemed. 'He's determined she should be able to lead a normal life,' close sources told the journalists covering the royal beat. Yet this harping on about normality was beginning to irk some sectors of the press. Catherine's normalcy might appeal for now, but it would begin to pall quickly if she, or her boyfriend's emissaries, turned it into a weapon with which to jab back even the most well-intentioned of press enquiries.

In a matter of months, the Palace had fired a variety of warning shots across the bows of Fleet Street's finest and it seemed that they were playing a dangerous game in the process. In his desire to protect Catherine and to indulge her fantasy that it was possible to date the future king and still lead a life unaltered by that reality, was William really doing Catherine any favours? Former royal press secretary Dickie Arbiter said the harassment of her by photographers in 2006 and 2007 was akin to the treatment of William's mother. The sheltered university days were over. Their relationship was moving on to another level. Catherine might still cling to her identity as a private individual but her relationship, their relationship, was not a matter for them alone.

★★★

On 8 January 2006, the day before Catherine's twenty-fourth birthday, Prince William arrived with his father at Sandhurst Military Academy in Surrey, where all officers in the British Army are trained to take on the responsibility of leading their fellow soldiers, for the start of his forty-four-week officer training course. He was the most senior member of the royal family to train at the academy, and he was taking his first step towards accepting the future inheritance that would make him head of the British Armed Forces. For now, the twenty-three-year-old prince, one of 269 other officer cadets to enrol at the famous Surrey institution that day, was faced with the less grand ordeal of having his head shorn of hair, in the process exposing that other Windsor crown to be handed down by his father – his bald patch.

William was assigned to a company and platoon and banned from leaving the camp for the next five weeks. He underwent a gruelling schedule, which saw him living in the field, improving his fitness and polishing his boots until they gleamed. By the end of his first term, the second in line to the throne would be proficient in using a hand grenade, an SA80 5.56 mm rifle and a Browning 9 mm pistol. He would have absorbed lectures on first aid, tactics and war studies given by some of the country's most knowledgeable officers and more fearless taskmasters. Lieutenant Colonel Roy Parkinson, an instructor at Sandhurst, laid it on the line. He told the media who had gathered at the academy to witness the prince's arrival that William would get 'very little sleep' in the first few weeks of training. Officer Cadet Wales, as he would be known, would receive no special treatment and his drill sergeants would not go easy on him. 'We receive people from all backgrounds,' Parkinson explained, 'but background goes right out the window once training begins. It's a team effort here. If someone steps out of line, they're stamped on, whether they're a prince or not.'

In the next day's papers, one wag predictably joked that the prince's time at Sandhurst was going to be a 'battle of Wills'.

Ahead of him lay one of the toughest experiences of his young life, physically at least. Just six weeks into training, he faced one of the most grim and notorious exercises, the 'Long Reach' – a twenty-four-hour march in sleet and snow on the Welsh hills. Carrying a pack as heavy as himself, deprived of sleep and on minimal rations, William was testing to the limit his resolve and physical and mental reserves. Pictures appeared of him, his body bowed against the icy wind as he and his platoon struggled through awful conditions. However, there was never any question of following his uncle Edward's lacklustre performance while training and failing to be a Royal Marine.

The army's motto is 'Be the Best', and William had to prove himself equal to that challenge. He had once flirted with quitting university, but he now knew that however tough the task, quitting for a royal of his rank was not an option. After almost a day and night slogging through the bitterly cold Black Mountains of Wales, pale, exhausted, and surviving on bites of chocolate and precious little else, there was a real determination about the young prince. He had inner strength and he wanted to prove to himself, and to his fellow cadets, that he had what it takes.

At one point, close to collapse during one steep climb, he sank to his haunches to gather his breath. Typically, he urged on his fellow cadets before gathering himself up and getting back on track. This was, after all, a team-building pursuit during which the young cadets marched more than 65 km (40 miles), navigating between nine checkpoints and sleeping, when they could, under the stars. Such are the demands of the exercise that up to a third of the 269 cadets who started, failed. William was not among them.

Whilst William threw himself into military training, Catherine had her own battle on her hands. Her position in his life was still, officially, rather up in the air. William had his route pretty much mapped out. She did not. Catherine was in love with him, of course, but she could not sit around waiting for William to come home and sweep her off her feet. She had already toyed with and rejected the idea of working in an art gallery; this after all was a girl with a degree in art history from one of the most respected universities in the country. She was no fool, happy to while away the hours dreaming about her prince. She resurrected her idea of setting up a business venture of her own, working in the meantime with her parents at their business, Party Pieces. She still had to contend with the life of contradictions presented by her strange, uncomfortable status of middle-class-royal-in-waiting. 'She is not, and never has been, somebody who would rest on her laurels,' one source close to the couple admitted at the time. 'But it's fair to say that this was a difficult period for them both.'

As Catherine was by now well aware, the smallest detail could be spun into a story, however throwaway it might seem. The salon where she had her hair and nails done was now news. It provided a light-hearted moment when, out with her mother in London's Sloane Square, she found herself accidentally and somewhat prematurely ascending a throne of sorts. At Richard Ward's up-market hair-and-beauty emporium, a favourite salon of Prince Edward's wife, Sophie, Countess of Wessex, and Prince Marie Chantal of Greece, the spa treatments involve sitting on a raised 'throne' while having a manicure. The gossip columnists thought it hilarious when this detail emerged about the young woman who, as far as they were concerned, was destined to be the future queen. Even Catherine must have seen the humour in the moment. 'Catherine drops in with her mother Carole,' said an inside source at the salon. 'She's very down to earth. You wouldn't say she was a preener by any means, but she always looks great.' It was true. Catherine always seemed to hit the mark. She was just glamorous enough. Her association with royalty lent her a certain sparkle, but in her own right she possessed that tantalising blend of understated style and a glint of self-confidence that turns a pretty girl into a sexy young woman. She never looked as if she was trying too hard. But she was never caught on camera looking anything other than great.

William's decision to join the army had marked a compromise on his part and an acknowledgement of his royal duty. He had resisted pressure to join the Royal Navy, a move that would require months at sea, away from his 'adorable Kate'. Joining the army had been a victory of sorts for William. But he still had many personal bridges to cross as he faced gruelling training, miles away from Catherine. Each mud-soaked step, each teeth-chattering night in the wilds, each barked order obeyed, served to remind him that this was not the life he would have chosen, but one forced upon him by birth. William let it be known from a very early stage that if he were to enter the army his aim was to join the Army Air Corps as a helicopter pilot. He was not interested in taking the more traditional route of serving in a Guards regiment, as his younger brother Harry had done when he joined the Blues and Royals.

In fact, it was Harry, rather than William, who proved himself to be a natural soldier and leader of men. This came as a surprise to critics who always failed to give Harry due credit. He had long since been regarded as the feckless younger brother, with no real job, no real responsibility and absolutely no qualms about capitalising on the fact. But, at Sandhurst, Harry knuckled down and bloomed. He impressed his superiors and proved popular with his peers, though he was far from a saint. 'He can be a lazy little shit,' one senior officer admitted. Yet, for all that, Harry's time at Sandhurst passed in the sort of uneventful fashion that must have had Clarence House aides offering prayers of thanks on a nightly basis.

As the brothers endured their personal trials at Sandhurst, Catherine's profile was about to rocket with one picture that underlined just how much she was a part of the royal firmament, with or without the presence of her royal boyfriend. The moment came on 17 March 2006 at the Cheltenham Gold Cup races. Camilla was due to present the winner's trophy and so the engagement was down in her and Charles's diaries as an official event. Catherine had arrived for the famous Friday race day with a girlfriend and her girlfriend's parents, entering through the punters' entrance and mingling with the rest of the day's spectators. She was particularly smartly dressed and looked stunning. Veteran royal photographer Mark Stewart spotted her in the crowds and mentioned her presence to Amanda Neville (now Amanda Foster), a friendly long-serving member of Prince Charles's press team. According to Stewart, Amanda looked a little surprised by the news that Catherine was at the races as well as her royal boss.

By the second race, Catherine, much to the photographers' surprise, had appeared on the balcony of the royal box, where Lord Vestey, a friend of the prince, was hosting a lunch for Charles and Camilla. Camilla's daughter Laura and Laura's then fiancé, Harry Lopes, were there, as were Tom Parker Bowles and his wife Sara, Zac Goldsmith, Ben Elliot and Thomas van Straubenzee, one of William's best friends, who was locked in conversation with Catherine. It was the first time that Catherine had been invited to adopt such an elevated position on her own. She had arrived. It was Camilla's most high-profile social engagement yet, but she did not seem bothered by the presence of the younger woman who threatened to steal her limelight. Quite the opposite: she appeared warm and welcoming. If anybody could understand the nerves that Catherine might have been experiencing, it was Camilla. She was a past master – or rather mistress – when it came to hovering publicly on the edges of royalty.

The pictures from that day, with Catherine in full view, were the first to present a 'new' royal family of sorts. It was fresh and surprisingly attractive, more representative in its blended nature of the social realities of its subjects. Here was a rag-tag group, each member with a tale to tell: some of marital strife and infidelity, some of young love, some of privilege squandered but recovered. Here was a new cast, or at least assorted members of the old cast, playing new roles: the mistress as wife, the petulant prince as doting stepfather, husband and, perhaps, father-in-law-to-be.

'It was astonishing to see how relaxed and comfortable Catherine was around the heir to the throne,' said Mark Stewart. 'It just goes to prove how serious her relationship with William is. It also shows how fond Camilla is of her, too. After all, it was Camilla's first year of presenting the Gold Cup, but she didn't appear to be remotely put out at being overshadowed by Kate's presence.'[57] Unsurprisingly, her impromptu appearance in the royal box sparked a betting frenzy, with at least one bookmaker forced to slash the odds on Catherine and William getting engaged before the following year's festival from 40–1 to 25–1.

It is easy to forget it with Prince Harry for a brother, but there is a rebel that lurks in William, too. On 14 and 15 April 2006, it was William and not, for once, his younger brother whose partying thrust him onto the front pages of the morning tabloids. It should have been all about Harry. Friday 14 April was, after all, the day that Prince Harry passed out at Sandhurst, the day that Officer Cadet Wales became Second Lieutenant Wales of the Blues and Royals and paraded in front of the sovereign – or 'Granny', as Harry called her. There had been the predictable, good-natured jokes at the young royal's expense: 'A red-faced Harry passes out; no, it's not what you think' – that sort of thing. In fact, after completing his forty-four-week training, Harry deserved his moment of self-pride and recognition and he deserved it to be unsullied by bad behaviour or scandal. It was a shame he did not receive it. The Queen gave a speech to the cadets in which she described the parade as a 'great occasion'. 'This day marks the beginning of what I hope will be highly successful careers,' she said. 'My prayers and my trust go with you all.' She then presented the prestigious Sword of Honour to the best cadet and handed out the Overseas Medal and the Queen's Medal, before addressing the newly commissioned officers. It was the first time in fifteen years that she had attended a parade, and there were no prizes for guessing why she had chosen to present the awards at this one.

The passing-out parade was Harry's graduation moment; the revelry that followed was his graduation ball. It is, of course, a well-rehearsed tradition at Sandhurst, and the day began well enough with the ceremonial Sovereign's Parade. Harry had, in accordance with custom, invited a party of ten family and friends to join him. His girlfriend, Chelsy Davy, was not among the elite group who watched Harry march, as she was spending the afternoon at the hairdresser in anticipation of the lavish black-tie event that evening. But Prince Charles was there, along with Camilla, Harry's former nanny Tiggy Pettifer (née Legge-Bourke), family friends Hugh and Emilie van Cutsem and Prince Philip. William was there, of course, along with the rest of the officer cadets, standing to attention and beaming with pride as his brother passed out. Catherine had been invited to the afternoon's events but, much to the surprise of many there, she did not turn up.

'Everybody was expecting Kate to be there but she did not show. In fact, she was still expected at about 5 p.m. that evening but, to be honest, I think there was a little bit of relief among the top brass that she did not come because the thinking was that, if Kate did not go, William would not and it would be less of a nightmare in terms of security later on. It made sense that William and Kate would not want to upstage Harry and Chelsy either, as it was Harry's day,' said a source close to William at the time. If the desire not to overshadow her royal boyfriend's younger sibling had been behind her decision not to go to the ball that evening, then her sacrifice was in vain. Once the passing-out ceremony was over, Harry and his fellow new officers changed into the mess suits that, until then, they had not been entitled to wear. Dressed in the tight-fitting trousers, stiff waistcoat and bright-red dress jacket, Harry looked every inch the officer as he chatted happily with the men of his platoon at the drinks that preceded the evening's party. His grandparents had expressed their pride and left early, as did the rest of his personal party of guests, except Chelsy.

After drinks in their individual platoon houses, the cadets and their guests headed across to the college's gymnasium, where the real party was waiting to happen. It may sound rather low-rent, the equivalent of a school disco held in a gym, but the building had been transformed into a breathtakingly lavish venue. A series of covered walkways connected the network of themed rooms that had been plotted throughout the vast space to cater for every taste and mood. In one area, a live band played in front of a chequered dance floor, surrounded by high tables, up-lit in red. In another, there was jazz. Elsewhere, the partygoers could play roulette or blackjack in the casino, drink vodka from an ice bar or eat chocolate from a chocolate fountain. Outside, the discipline of military life had been turned over in favour of an amusement park, complete with roller-coaster thrill rides and a hamburger van. It was an extravagant setting, but Harry had eyes only for Chelsy. She was dressed in a sheath of turquoise satin that clung to her curves, scooped low at the back to show off her flawless tanned skin, and flowed, mermaid-like, out and down to the floor. Her make-up was minimal and her earrings simple. She had flown into the country the previous afternoon, landing at Heathrow, and was met by the sort of security usually reserved for members of royalty, heads of state or – for that matter – wanted criminals. It had been weeks since she and Harry had been in each other's company, so there was little wonder that they seemed reluctant to take their eyes, or hands, off each other.

'Harry's protection officers stood around him as he and Chelsy danced and kissed. They were snogging, hugging and holding hands, massively and openly affectionate,' one partygoer recalled. 'I suppose he's used to that by now, but it did seem odd. He was joking with other cadets and is obviously very popular. He was happy to talk to anybody who approached him, although he did seem keener to talk to the girls.' He posed happily for pictures when asked by pretty guests and laughed good-naturedly when one girl, the worse for wear for drink and urged on by her friends, cheekily took a pinch at his bum. 'Instead of being annoyed,' one girl said, 'Harry just pinched her bum back and she ran off giggling.'

At midnight, the party moved outside, where a vast display of fireworks lit up the night sky and the new officers ripped the velvet strips that had been covering the officers' pips on their suits. It was a traditional rite of passage and a moment of whooping celebration amid an increasingly chaotic party, as some cadets and their guests were by now showing signs of flagging.

Among the stragglers, to the dismay of his senior officers, was Prince William. Harry was drinking and smoking and partying with the best of them. But he was, those who witnessed it maintained, a perfect gentleman throughout. He was not brash, or loud, or inappropriate. He was focused on Chelsy. He was proud of his achievement and that of his brothers-in-arms. The same could not be said of William and some of his civilian friends who had pitched up to join the fun. One college source recalled, 'One of William's civvy pals impersonated a brigadier all evening and tried ordering people about. He and the royal gang thought it very funny. Another found it highly hilarious to brag about a stag-night encounter with a prostitute and losing his wallet. Nobody else found them funny.'

Their behaviour was found so distinctly unfunny that, as 2 a.m. approached, William was advised by a senior officer that it would be best for him to call it a night. It was a humiliating rap on the knuckles for William and worse was to come. Hours later, Sandhurst's commandant, General Andrew Ritchie, rang Clarence House and apparently demanded an explanation for the raucous behaviour of the previous night. Pictures appeared in a morning tabloid of William, apparently the worse for drink, having a go on one of the thrill rides. Reports about 'upper-class twits' and the older prince's behaviour soon began seeping out. Harry had, by all accounts, been 'as good as gold' and had played by the rules. William had not.

Twenty-four hours later, William and Harry, joined by Catherine and Chelsy, were continuing the party back in London, and were pictured having a boozy night out at their favoured club, Boujis, in South Kensington. William was seen leaving with Chelsy, not Kate. Harry, it seemed, had sneaked out of a back door. It was the princes' way of playing with the waiting paparazzi, throwing them off their guard. Harry had something to celebrate: Sandhurst was over, and he and Chelsy would soon head off on holiday together. But for William, things were different. For once, he was the brother who seemed selfish, thoughtless, and downright badly behaved. He had gone too far the night before and here he was carrying on as if he could do whatever he pleased without fear of criticism. It may sound harsh, and some would argue that William was still just a high-spirited young man approaching his twenty-fourth birthday, having fun with his brother and their girlfriends. Possibly, but he was not beyond reproach either. With his lack of self-control and his inability to rein in his friends, William had spoiled Harry's moment of glory. He had turned the story away from his brother in the most negative fashion. Significantly, Catherine had not been by his side when it had happened. Would William have been in the same position had she gone to the ball? It seemed unlikely.

Suddenly and subtly, it became clear that the balance of their relationship had changed. Once, Catherine's glamour and image had been dependent on William's presence. But the night of Harry's passing-out suggested that this had begun to work both ways. The public liked her, and they had a limited tolerance for playboy princes, whatever their parentage. Catherine was now irrevocably linked with William as far as press and public were concerned. Could it be that we all liked William a little bit more with her by his side? William was always very keen to stress his youth when it came to talk of marriage and his royal duties. He may cite the fact that the average age for marriage in Britain is thirty-two and claim that, at twenty-four, he had many years of bachelorhood to look forward to. But there was nothing average about William or his position. This is something that William – like his late mother – does not want to hear. Diana famously parted company with William's first nanny, Barbara Barnes, when she pointed out that in trying to raise William as a 'normal' little boy Diana was fighting the forces of nature. Diana had a clear idea of how she wanted her sons to be raised. Barnes, a traditionalist, protested, 'The princes need to be treated differently because they are different.' She may have been speaking out of turn, but she was speaking the truth: William was not, and never would be, 'normal'.

In the summer of 2006, nearly four years into their relationship, any photograph of Catherine that appeared in a newspaper or magazine would do so under the caption 'princess-in-waiting'. For the media, it was only a matter of time before Kate Middleton would be William's bride. One pillar of William's year at Sandhurst had been his regular Friday-night escapes to Bucklebury, where he could collapse and be mothered by Carole and fathered by the quiet and affectionate Michael.

Speculation had grown further about a possible royal engagement after Catherine attended the wedding of Camilla's daughter, then twenty-seven-year-old Laura, to her boyfriend of eight years: aristocrat, model-turned-accountant, Harry Lopes, on 6 May 2006 at the sixteenth-century St Cyriac's Church, in Lacock, Wiltshire. For her to be at such a high-profile event, attended by the Prince of Wales, Prince William, Prince Harry and Princess Margaret's daughter, Lady Sarah Chatto, convinced some newspaper editors that the marriage of William and Catherine was a done deal. Later that year, when she looked on as William graduated from Sandhurst – an event also attended by Queen Elizabeth, Prince Charles and the Duchess of Cornwall, as well as her parents – the speculation reached fever pitch. For some in the press, it was just a matter of counting the days.

William was a dedicated cadet, but he was never in the running to qualify for Sandhurst's top honour, the coveted Sword of Honour given to the military academy's best cadet each year. To achieve that, he would have had to have reached the rank of junior under officer, which he didn't, although sixteen cadets in his year did. In the end, the Sword of Honour was awarded to a female cadet. But William had proved a competent and intelligent cadet and was placed in the top third of his year. After graduating, he was commissioned as an army officer in December 2006, becoming a lieutenant in the Blues and Royals Regiment. It was perhaps the most important date so far in the life of the girl now very publicly acknowledged as William's princess-in-waiting, a fact that Catherine Middleton must surely have recognised.

The official business of that crisp, clear day, 15 December 2006, dictated that it was William's proud hour, as he passed out at the Royal Military Academy, Sandhurst. However, the future king was not the only one seen to make the grade, for this was the first time that Catherine, then almost twenty-five, would attend a public engagement alongside the Queen and the rest of the senior royals. The apparent significance of this 'joining the Firm' did not pass unnoticed, and even the most hard-nosed of hacks allowed themselves a moment of romantic indulgence: the *Daily Mail*, for instance, in a rare moment of whimsy, observed that Catherine's scarlet coat echoed the sash worn by William that day. The synchronicity of her wardrobe and the simple fact that she was there on such a significant day in her royal lover's life was, it asserted, 'the strongest sign yet that she and Prince William could marry'.

Until that day, William's hugely protective attitude towards his girlfriend had ensured that, given the intensity of the relationship, they were seen out in public together comparatively rarely – save for the occasional night out or trip to the polo. But that December day William extended his most public invitation to Catherine; little wonder, then, that many people read so much into the move. She arrived with her parents, Michael and Carole, and the prince's private secretary, Jamie Lowther-Pinkerton, moments before the Windsor party. Although the Middletons did not sit next to the royal party – including the Duke of Edinburgh, Charles and Camilla – there was a certain pomp to her arrival. All the other guests were already seated as Catherine was ushered into her place in the front row accompanied by William's best friend, Thomas van Straubenzee, and two of his godfathers, King Constantine of Greece and Lord Romsey. Catherine and, tellingly, her family were in lofty company indeed. In truth, the arrival of the glamorous, assured young woman dressed in vibrant red completely overshadowed the royals, even the Queen.

So too did her assessment of her boyfriend's appearance in his smart passing-out uniform, when she chatted with a friend after the ceremony. It seemed there was no limit to what the media – and not just the press – would do to get a story. Britain's ITV network hired lip-reading experts who discerned that Catherine had apparently declared, 'I love the uniform, it's so sexy.' Whether this is what she really said, it showed that, like Diana before her, Catherine was more than capable of stealing the show – even when all the royal family's star performers were out in force. It was something that not only members of the family but also the Palace courtiers noted with some trepidation. William, now twenty-four, was among 233 cadets commissioned at the Royal Military Academy marked by the Sovereign's Parade. Like his younger brother, Harry, he was destined for a commission in the Household Cavalry's Blues and Royals regiment as a lieutenant where he would train to become a troop leader in charge of armoured reconnaissance vehicles. Unlike Harry, who was due to deploy to Iraq in 2007, William, as second in line to the throne, is barred from going to any frontline war zones. However sincere William's devotion to his military training, it is always destined to amount to a flirtation never consummated in warfare. Instead, he was expected to serve little more than a year in the army before moving on to the Royal Air Force and Royal Navy as part of his wider training as future head of the armed forces.

For all that, as he stood in the bright winter sun that day, William looked every inch the soldier prince. Standing six-feet three-inches tall, he was placed at the end of his platoon as an 'escort' to the banner, as well as acting as marker to ensure his colleagues marched in a straight line. Like his fellow cadets, he wore a smart blue uniform, cap and white gloves, but carried a rifle instead of a sword and wore a scarlet sash. He also wore the blue-and-white Jubilee medal given to him by his grandmother to mark her fiftieth anniversary on the throne. Reviewing the young soldiers lined up before her, the Queen paused briefly as she walked past her grandson and whispered a 'hello' that left William beaming.

Significantly, Clarence House sources indicated that, after the parade ended, Catherine and her parents joined the royal party for a family lunch for the first time. It was something Buckingham Palace later strenuously denied. Amid a row over snobbery by the royals towards the Middleton family, the palace would seek to claim that the Queen had never actually met Carole – a claim that dumbfounded the press, given that, at the time, the royal family's spin machine was happy for the story of that convivial lunch to be written.

To mark his passing-out, Clarence House released photographs and footage of the prince taken on his last major exercise at Sandhurst. They also arranged for interviews with fellow cadets to be released to the press in which he was described as a 'normal guy'. Junior Under Officer Angela Laycock, twenty-four, who was in William's Blenheim platoon, told how he fitted in with other cadets. She said, 'I've not really noticed anything different to be honest. The first loaded march, we had a bit of a detour to avoid some photographers. He's just a normal guy and gets stuck in like everybody else.' Describing how William joined in training with the other cadets, she added, 'On a riot-training exercise he was grabbing potatoes and lobbing them at the force protection people just like the rest of us.'

Of course, he is not a 'normal' guy at all, and at that moment his girlfriend was far from just a 'normal' girl. For the focus of the national newspapers was not on the royals, but on Catherine. It seemed they had found their new princess. That night, she and William partied at the traditional passing-out ball, as Harry and Chelsy had done in such style earlier in the year, at his own graduation from Sandhurst. As they sipped champagne and celebrated, there was nothing to suggest that this romance was any less perfect than it appeared. The *Daily Mail* best summed up the mood of the moment with its headline, 'ON WILLIAM'S BIG DAY KATE MAKES THE GRADE, TOO'. Perhaps it was inevitable, but, as the outcome of the relationship between William and Catherine seemed such a certainty, his passing-out parade was also the day that the focus began to shift from Catherine and the royal family she seemed about to join to Catherine and the family she was bringing with her. However uneasily the notion of class and breeding sits with modern sensibilities, it is fated never to pass without comment, especially where issues of Crown and State are concerned. And so, the backlash of soft, deft blows began.

Carole Middleton, it was observed, was chewing gum as she watched her possible future son-in-law passing out. The veteran royal commentator, the late James Whitaker, for one, suggested it was 'common'. Others pointed to the fact that Carole was trying not to smoke and, therefore, as she was probably chewing nicotine gum, she should be praised rather than criticised for the lapse in social niceties. Others still viewed the whole discussion as ludicrous and peripheral. William and Catherine were, after all, very much in love – weren't they? Just a few weeks after her starring role at Sandhurst, the *Daily Mirror* quoted senior sources as saying William felt he had to decide one way or the other. 'In frank discussions between the prince, his private secretary Jamie Lowther-Pinkerton and other key aides,' a source said, 'William has been presented with two clear scenarios: he could announce an engagement in the New Year, or cool his romance with Kate during his military service with the Household Cavalry at Bovington Camp, Dorset.' It was to prove prophetic and apparently prompted a heart-to-heart between Catherine and her mother. When William failed to show at the Middletons' family gathering in December, the chill thought must surely have seeped into Catherine's heart that perhaps he was not as serious about her as she had once thought, or indeed as he had once so genuinely appeared. Perhaps he was having cold feet. Perhaps Catherine's heart was about to be broken. Carole Middleton, an astute, down-to-earth woman, realised she would have to have a long, hard talk with her beloved eldest daughter. Carole has the reputation of being nobody's fool. She is worldly wise, having travelled widely during her career as a flight attendant.

Around this time, William seemed to panic. He had cold feet but didn't really know what to do. As 2006 came to an end, William and Catherine's four-year relationship suffered a setback when Catherine's family invited William to come and stay with them for New Year. The Middletons had booked Jordanstone House set in snowy countryside on the outskirts of Alyth, north of Dundee. William had originally intended to come, but then changed his mind, which upset Catherine. They hadn't seen each other over the festive season, as William always spent Christmas with the Queen and the rest of his family at Sandringham. Although certain things were changing with the times within the royal family, Christmas at Sandringham was still strictly a royal affair. It meant they would not be able to spend Christmas Day together unless they were married. Unfortunately, the trend of their spending time apart continued into the new year. The day before Catherine's twenty-fifth birthday, William left to join his first regiment, the Blues and Royals, stationed with the Household Cavalry at Bovington Barracks in Dorset. He would be away for much of the following months, and the three-hour drive meant that he wouldn't necessarily be returning to London every weekend.

In 2007, many had been predicting a royal wedding, and presumptuously Woolworths were already stocking wedding paraphernalia. Just before Catherine's birthday, Diana's former private secretary Patrick Jephson wrote a feature for *The Spectator* called 'The Next People's Princess' about how she would be a glamorous and much-needed addition to the royal family. When Catherine went to work on the morning of her birthday, she was pursued by more aggressive paparazzi than ever before.

Interest in her had now crossed over into harassment, and the following day, William requested that his press secretary release a statement, reading, 'He wants more than anything for it to stop. Miss Middleton should, like any other private individual, be able to go about her everyday business without this kind of intrusion. The situation is proving unbearable for all those concerned.' The following month, William gave Catherine a pre-Valentine's present of a green enamel Van Cleef & Arpels diamond-framed make-up compact, featuring a polo player about to hit a pearl. Gestures were one thing, but the couple weren't spending any time together and cracks were beginning to show, and then to deepen.

William being stationed away meant that the couple spent significant amounts of time apart over the next few months. They were also still young, and both figuring out what they wanted from life, but Catherine felt like she had less of a say in their relationship and their future. Although she had her job at Jigsaw, the Kew-based high-street store run by John and Belle Robinson, she wasn't sure it was what she wanted to do long-term. Four years before exchanging vows in a fairy-tale wedding at London's Westminster Abbey, the college sweethearts ended their relationship. With William being stationed outside of London with the Household Cavalry, on top of mounting media pressure, the young couple had grown apart.

Carole had already made it clear to her daughter that if William did not want to commit, it was not wise for her to drift along in the relationship indefinitely, perhaps preparing her for the fall. Later, much would be made of Carole's 'social ambitions', with the suggestion that it was her fierce desire to climb the social ladder that guided her actions when it came to Catherine. This is unfair. No mother likes to see her daughter taken for granted and not receiving the respect and consideration she deserves. Catherine, after all, was an intelligent girl who had put her life on hold for the sake of William and her willingness to make their relationship work.

Catherine's Monday-to-Thursday job as an accessory buyer for Jigsaw was hardly a challenging role, and one that she had taken primarily for the freedom it afforded her to visit her boyfriend near his Dorset barracks. As 2006 turned to 2007, it must have been a difficult period of renegotiation between Catherine and William, as both nursed their own trepidations over just how significant their romance was and exactly where it was going. However, they had been down this rocky road before and always pulled back from the brink of breaking up. They still loved each other and, despite his reservations concerning commitment, William did not want to lose Catherine. She was simply too precious to him. They had a shared history. They understood each other. He needed her.

At the beginning of the year, at least, these private reservations did not deter the media, and everybody hoped for a successful conclusion. The speculation intensified and rumours of a possible imminent engagement led to increased paparazzi attention outside Catherine's apartment. It reached fever pitch on the day of her twenty-fifth birthday on 9 January 2007, with more than fifty paparazzi and TV cameramen positioned at the door of her Chelsea flat as she walked to her car to leave for work that morning. It was a birthday surprise that alarmed Catherine. She tried hard to accept it with her trademark smile. The 'cult of Catherine' had never been so visible or so palpable and for the first time she was elevated from 'girl next door' to commercial trendsetter. The £40 Topshop dress she wore that morning sold out within days, proving she had a following all of her own. The scenes outside her flat prompted William, fearful that his girlfriend was being forced to endure the same media pressure experienced by his late mother, to express his concern at the 'harassment' of his girlfriend. He issued a statement saying he wanted 'more than anything' for her to be left alone. Her family had already employed law firm Harbottle & Lewis to urge the media, both in Britain and abroad, to use restraint. This time, however, there were not just a few freelancers on Catherine's doorstep, but representatives of newspapers and those from respected agencies such as Associated Press and the Press Association. There were also at least five TV crews, including a team from ITN, which produces news bulletins for ITV and Channel 4. The BBC did not send a camera crew but used footage supplied by the agency APTN. Sky News also used footage in its bulletins. The Palace sat up and took notice. Her lawyers were in close contact with the Press Complaints Commission and stopped short of making an official representation on her behalf. Sources said they hoped to use 'persuasion' rather than legal action to protect her. The similarities with the problems faced by William's mother were clear.

The ugly scenes on Catherine's birthday prompted the late princess's aides to speak out in a chorus of disapproval and a call for action. Inspector Ken Wharfe, the retired former bodyguard to Princess Diana, was in no doubt that the number of photographers pursuing Catherine, coupled with the lack of any control, put her in danger of becoming the victim of a Diana-style tragedy. He said at the time, 'History appears to be repeating itself, despite claims that lessons have been learned after the loss of Diana. As far as I can see, the warnings have not been heeded.' He said it was imperative for Prince Charles to employ former royal protection officers to guard Catherine until she became engaged to William and full-time official Scotland Yard security became available. After their brief split, Mr Wharfe wrote to Carole offering to protect Catherine until the furore died down. Patrick Jephson, Diana's former private secretary, echoed Wharfe's views: 'I think that any reasonable person would be horrified about the situation and what Miss Middleton has to endure. I think the attempts to use legal, regulatory, and informal methods to deal with the situation will help. Nothing is more effective than proper control on the ground. That is the lesson of the Diana experience, including her death. That level of control on the ground is the only method which will work effectively for Catherine.'

Unusually, Charles's office at Clarence House took the decision to comment on the move to back off Catherine. An official spokesperson said, 'We are pleased that News International has agreed to stop using the paparazzi pictures. What Prince William wants more than anything is for the paparazzi to stop harassing her.' There was even speculation that Catherine's situation was being manipulated in a test case involving harassment laws, to protect her privacy and curtail the activities of photographers. In the inevitable dissection of these events, many royal commentators rallied protectively round Catherine. The issue of privacy and press intrusion became the focus of the House of Commons' Culture, Media and Sport Select Committee for its investigation of media invasion of privacy on 6 March 2007, during which leading media figures were called to give evidence. One of those was veteran royal photographer Arthur Edwards MBE – the contributor of photographs to this book in return for a donation to his favourite charity – who was recently honoured with a lifetime achievement award by his peers. During the proceedings, Edwards, whose astute reading of the nuances of the royal story in the previous thirty years is second to none, was met with somewhat condescending titters by committee members when he said William had told him he intended to marry Catherine. As ever, he was right.

'She is a private citizen, and she is in love with Prince William, and I am sure that one day they will get married. I have talked to him about this. He has made it clear that he wants to get married and I believe what he says, and they should be left alone,' he said. He added that he had heard from Catherine's friends about her distress at media intrusion and said photographers had followed her shopping, and even climbed onto buses to photograph her. But by this time there was pandemonium. Moreover, as he tried to clarify his comments – saying the prince had said it would not happen until he was at least twenty-eight years old – the political reporters had already left the room to file his comments to the news wires.

There was something missing in all this well-meaning attention and earnest endeavour to get it right this time, in terms of coverage and acceptable levels of interest. I was not alone in thinking that, as she left her flat that morning, Catherine seemed curiously isolated, miles from her barracks-bound boyfriend. Yes, William had swept in to make his statement and attempt to redress the balance, pull the press up short and remind them that this girl was very special to him. But there were some who felt this 'chivalrous' gesture was rather too little, too late. Might she have felt so too?

There are also those who believed that Catherine was enigmatic at best, boring at worst. 'What are her interests?' asked a newspaper editor. 'All she seems to do is go to the gym and go to either Boujis or Mahiki [at that time, the favourite nightclubs for wealthy twenty-somethings in London]. She does not have a job. She does not go to the theatre. We don't really have any idea of who she really is, and what we do see is rather shallow.' Then came another signal that perhaps she was positioning herself for a change in status. In May, it emerged that Kate had asked people to call her 'Catherine'. The press was quick to point out the obvious: 'Catherine' is a far more regal name than 'Kate'. A defensive Paddy Harverson, Prince Charles's communications secretary, strenuously denied all these reports. Nonetheless, *Sunday Express* columnist Adam Helliker, who wrote the 'Catherine' story, insisted he had heard about – but had not seen – a 'gentle' email sent by Catherine to her friends, saying she was reverting to the name she had had until she was in her mid-teens. Helliker said, 'It was just a very jokey thing.' He defiantly stood by his story. Another, potentially more damaging, report emerged soon afterwards and claimed that Catherine's lack of industry was causing the Queen some irritation. The report stated that the Queen wanted Catherine to get a full-time job. In fact, she was quietly working, as her lawyer Gerrard Tyrrell had already confirmed: getting up each morning in Bucklebury, driving to the Party Pieces office in Reading and putting together the catalogues for her parents' company. She also took a technology course to learn how to make digital catalogues. Under the circumstances, it was probably about the only job Catherine, as a princess-in-waiting, felt safe doing.

'She's been offered every job under the sun,' I was told. Everyone from Russian oligarchs to top fashion designers wanted her. But Catherine understood taking such positions could open her up to accusations of using her association with William for financial gain, an accusation that could come back to haunt her. Until William formalised their relationship, she was left in an awkward spot. She was not officially entitled to any royal benefits paid for by the taxpayers, such as security, yet she, perhaps more than some of the minor royals, was exposed. She had no spokesperson or official guidance on what to wear or how to conduct herself in royal circles. Yet, because of her boyfriend, she was already a celebrity, having to cope with the difficulties that fame brings. Her main lifeline was the media lawyer Gerrard Tyrrell, whose clients included British model Kate Moss and Roman Abramovich, the then owner of Chelsea Football Club. Any time Catherine felt harassed, as she claims she did on her twenty-fifth birthday, it was to Tyrrell that she turned. His response was

Prince William at play in the garden of Kensington Palace, London, in June 1984, the year in which he celebrated his second birthday, on 21 June. The official photocall was arranged by his parents, the Prince and Princess of Wales.
(All photographs © Arthur Edwards MBE)

Prince William poses on a bench with his parents at Kensington Palace in 1984. Princess Diana was months away from giving birth to Prince Harry, who was born on 15 September that year.

Prince William throws a tantrum as his nanny Olga Powell tries to calm him down. She was nanny to the princes for fifteen years, at their sides as their parents divorced and she was there to comfort them after their mother, Princess Diana, died in a car crash in Paris in 1997. She continued to be a part of their lives, invited to William's twenty-first birthday party at Windsor Castle and his passing-out parade at Sandhurst in 2006. When Olga died, aged eighty-two, in 2012, William cancelled his engagements to be at her funeral in Harlow, Essex.

Princess Diana was unhappy about the close relationship Prince William had with his nanny Barbara Barnes (pictured) and she was later axed.

Diana, Princess of Wales, accompanies her sons, Prince William and Prince Harry, to their first day at Wetherby School in London on 12 September 1989. They are greeted by headmistress, Frederika Blair-Turner.

Prince William has a special affection for Wales. His first public engagement was at Llandaff Cathedral in Cardiff on St David's Day on 1 March 1991, at the side of his mother, Diana, Princess of Wales. Diana's Scotland Yard personal protection officer Inspector Ken Wharfe MVO is in the background, with a daffodil in his lapel.

Prince William, then fifteen, and Prince Harry, then twelve, put on a brave face as they look at the flowers laid in tribute to their mother Diana outside Kensington Palace. Diana died in a car crash in Paris with her lover Dodi Fayed and their driver Henri Paul on 31 August 1997. William later said of his mother, 'She really enjoyed laughter and fun.'

The Queen Mother in 2001, aged 101, with her grandson, the Prince of Wales, and great-grandsons, Prince William and Prince Harry.

In December 2006, Prince William became a commissioned officer in the British Army after graduating from Sandhurst. The Queen, Prince Charles and William's then girlfriend Catherine Middleton attended the parade marking the end of his training at the royal military academy. William, who was described by fellow trainee officers as 'a normal guy', became a second lieutenant in the Household Cavalry's Blues and Royals.

Prince William and Prince Harry on 18 June 2009 when they lived together on base at RAF Shawbury in Shropshire, England, as they learned to fly helicopters. William, then twenty-six, was learning to become an RAF search-and-rescue pilot, while Prince Harry, twenty-four, was six months into a course to become an Army helicopter pilot.

The newly married Duke and Duchess of Cambridge seal their love with a kiss on the Buckingham Palace balcony, on 29 April 2011. As Catherine stepped out onto the balcony with her new husband, the sight of the crowds filling The Mall prompted from her an involuntary, 'Oh, wow!'

Swaying in time to the music, the Duke and Duchess of Cambridge became true South Pacific royalty during their visit to Tuvalu, in September 2012, when they donned colourful skirts and danced at a gathering of island chiefs. William and Catherine joined six island communities at a *fatele*. Half of the island's population of 10,000 residents came out to see the couple.

The Duke and Duchess of Cambridge and Prince George bid farewell to Australia after their overseas tour in April 2014. Prince George, who was dubbed 'The Republican Slayer' by those who want to get rid of the monarchy in Australia, won over hearts and minds Down Under.

After the birth of Princess Charlotte, on 2 May 2015, at the private Lindo Wing of St Mary's Hospital, London, Prince William and Prince George greeted photographers together outside the hospital.

Princess Charlotte makes her Buckingham Palace balcony debut. The stylish tot, whose mother, Catherine, described her as 'cute but feisty', was joined by big brother Prince George, then three, and parents William and Catherine, for the annual Trooping the Colour celebration in June 2016. They are with the Prince of Wales, Her Majesty the Queen and Prince Philip, Duke of Edinburgh. Prince Harry and his cousin Peter Phillips are behind.

Before the split: Best Man Prince William and Prince Harry, Duke of Sussex, on his wedding day, 19 May 2018, wearing their Blues and Royals frock coats. William's coat bears a golden, braided aiguillette on the right of his uniform because he was made an aide-de-camp to the Queen in 2013.

The Prince of Wales leads the so-called 'Fab Four'— William, Catherine, Meghan Markle and Harry – before they fell out, as they walk to St Mary Magdalene Church, Sandringham, Norfolk, on Christmas Day 2018.

William and Catherine in Joe's Ice Cream Parlour in the Mumbles, Wales, in February 2020, where they stopped by to sample the chocolate and vanilla flavours and to meet local parents.

Like his mother, Diana, Prince William, has a warmth that connects him with his future subjects when he is meeting people on walkabouts.

The Duke and Duchess of Cambridge worked tirelessly throughout the Covid-19 pandemic, from March 2020 onwards, to help boost the morale of the British people and to thank front-line workers.

often swift, sending letters to newspaper editors warning them that Catherine was a 'private' citizen and as such had a right to privacy. One of Prince Charles's former aides said he was a very 'laissez-faire father' to his two sons. 'He likes Kate a lot, but she won't be getting any 'training' or guidance as to how to behave.'

In March, around the time William started army training in Dorset, the couple attended the Cheltenham Gold Cup races in traditional tweed suits. The press covered their attendance ironically, noting how much like Charles and Camilla – nicknamed 'Fred and Gladys' – the pair looked in their old-fashioned clothes. William was said not to be amused. A few days later, Catherine, looking far more youthful and modern in a warm coat and Russian-style fur hat, went to the races on her own. Lord Vestey, a friend of Prince Charles, was hosting a lunch for Charles, Camilla, Camilla's children, Tom and Laura, as well as Zac Goldsmith and Camilla's nephew Ben Elliot, among others. When the royal party heard Kate was there, she was invited to join them in the royal box.

Unlike Diana, Catherine was hardly ever rattled by the cameras. Photographer Niraj Tanna revealed, 'Even in the early hours of the morning, when William and her pals look a little worse for wear through drink or just tiredness as they leave their favourite nightclubs, she always looked immaculate.'[58] She would never let herself go. She would drink cautiously, and carefully touch up in the women's toilet before facing the cameras that would inevitably be waiting for her. In July, her boss at Jigsaw, Belle Robinson, gave an interview about Catherine, portraying her as down-to-earth, even though she had asked for a job with 'an element of flexibility to continue the relationship with a very high-profile man and a life she can't dictate'. Yet the older woman liked her part-time employee. 'She sat in the kitchen at lunchtime and chatted with everyone from the van drivers to the accounts girls,' Robinson told the *Evening Standard*. 'She wasn't precious. Many people have distorted it to say we're friends with her parents, but I've only met them four times. I have to say I was so impressed by her. There were days when there were TV crews at the end of the drive. We would say, 'Listen, do you want to go out the back way?' And she'd say, 'To be honest, they're going to hound us until they've got the picture. So why don't I just go, get the picture done, and then they'll leave us alone.'

Throughout 2006, Catherine and William had tried to keep their heads down about the media. They were tracked down and photographed mostly on holiday, leaving nightclubs or on the polo field. Harry, too, was caught, having been out partying perhaps a little too often. These images increasingly began to leave a somewhat negative impression – the British media referred to the young princes as 'boys' or, even worse, as playboys. It did not sit well. The future hopes of the British royal family were being openly mocked in lots of circles as just a pair of prize silly Sloane Rangers spending oodles of cash celebrating on cocktails. For young men purporting to be serious soldiers, they appeared to spend an awful lot of time in nightclubs. Interestingly, of the tight-knit royal clique who hit the clubs with increasing frequency, perhaps the most aware of the bad impression they were creating was the media-astute Catherine. On holiday in 2006, Prince William and Guy Pelly, an old friend in the group, often simplistically referred to as the 'court jester', were racing around on mopeds at the villa of Kate's uncle, Gary Goldsmith, in Ibiza. She came out of the house and, matron-like, told them to stop. Anyone, after all, could be watching. Like chided schoolchildren, they did what they were told. William may not have liked it, but he could not fault her judgement.

Catherine's confidence in her role as the royal girlfriend steadily grew. She was more self-assured – buoyed by the confidence her mother had instilled in her. She met the Queen, who liked her, as did Charles and Camilla. Harry, according to one friend, took longer to warm to her. Catherine, with her demure outfits, fitted jackets over a dress, drop pearl earrings and self-control, was the opposite of Harry's blonde Zimbabwean girlfriend, the wealthy Chelsy Davy, who dressed in a far more provocative style. Chelsy never shied from photographers, with a glass in one hand, a cigarette in the other. At times, she may have looked like an unmade bed, but she has raw, earthy sex appeal – something Catherine, perhaps, lacks. The passionate attraction between Harry and Chelsy fizzled, but in public, at least, the same could not be said of William and Catherine.

The last time William and Catherine went out together before they split was with their friends Hugh and Rose van Cutsem, whose wedding they had attended two years earlier. At the end of March, the four had a quiet night out in the Van Cutsems' local, The King's Head pub at Bledington in the Cotswolds. By the time Catherine flew to Ireland with her mother on 3 April, her four-year relationship with William was over. She was devastated, but instead of crying at home, she kept herself busy. Mother and daughter had gone to Dublin to support one of Carole's friends, an artist who was having a private exhibition. They saw the paintings, attended the champagne reception and then completed a cultural day with a tour of the National Gallery of Ireland.

William decided to celebrate the end of his relationship rather differently – with a trip to Mahiki nightclub in central London. The news of their split was not yet public, but those around him had more than a clue of what was going on when he leaped onto a table, shouting, 'I'm free!' He then slipped into his version of the robot dance – made famous by England footballer Peter Crouch – and suggested to his friends that they drink the menu. News of their split broke in public the following day.

William's behaviour at clubs did little to help the pair's strained relationship and ultimately, the inevitable happened and they broke up in April that year. Rather than staying at home and mourning the end of her romance with the UK's most eligible bachelor, Catherine hit the social circuit, prioritising herself instead of William for a change. It would seem the future duchess was showing the prince what he was missing, and he eventually realised it, too. In June, Catherine attended a themed party at William's barracks, and by the end of the night, the pair were back together for good. Three years later, the golden couple announced their royal engagement. For some it is fate, for others, chance. Anyone who has experienced a lengthy courtship will understand how easy it is, in moments of uncertainty, to walk away. In just such a moment, Catherine could have lost her prince. That she and William loved each other was never questioned. They 'fitted' so well, friends said. But when William was hit by doubts and they split for three months, the story of their relationship could easily have ended very differently.

It is intriguing that Catherine had the strength of character to win back her prince by doing all the things that his circle had urged her not to do. She went out partying in thigh-skimming skirts; she went roller-skating (and was photographed spreadeagled on the floor after falling over in a most unladylike fashion). In fact, she and her sister Pippa partied so hard they were nicknamed the 'sizzler sisters'. In the wake of this, the Queen was privately said to consider Miss Middleton 'something of a show-off' and courtiers were 'appalled' at such a display. So, what was she up to? She was taking the biggest gamble of her life. Weeks before, she had asked William for reassurance that she was the only woman in his life – particularly since he had been photographed in a nightclub with his arm around a pretty young woman, his hand apparently cupping her right breast.

'She felt that William was making her look a fool,' recalls one of her oldest friends. 'What she wanted was a clarification of where she stood, and what was going on. She wasn't looking for an engagement ring, she just wanted to know that he was committed to her, and only to her.' Faced with what he saw as demand for his long-term commitment, especially his fidelity, the prince declined to give in. And on that sad and uneasy note, the romance was terminated. Catherine could have slipped away into oblivion, but instead she risked her reputation for quiet modesty to show William just what he was missing. It wasn't easy.

Interestingly, it wasn't the first time Prince William had broken up with Catherine. As mentioned previously, the two had split previously in 2004, albeit briefly, while they were both studying at St Andrew's University. Although a lot of couples get together in college and stay together, Prince William and Kate were not one of these. William said the 2004 break-up was because they 'were both very young' and therefore decided to break up. It seems this was his reasoning for the second break-up too: he had met the right girl, but just too soon.

Yet it wasn't long before William was having second thoughts. Mindful, perhaps, of the decision his father had made when he was in his twenties and had failed to marry his early love Camilla, William did not want to make the same mistake. Catherine, however, needed some convincing. She wasn't going to be a pushover. He had broken her heart and she wanted to make sure that if they did get back together it would be for the right reasons, and that things would change. In the meantime, she got busy. She signed up for a charity challenge with an all-female dragon boat racing crew called the Sisterhood, who billed themselves, A-Team style, as: 'An elite group of female athletes, talented in many ways, toned to perfection with killer looks, on a mission to keep boldly going where no girl has gone before.'

William spent the summer at his barracks, fulfilling royal duties, playing polo and enjoying a few nights out with friends. Catherine, meanwhile, said 'yes' to a slew of invitations and, in public at least, appeared more vibrant and sociable than she had been for some time. She was soon joined in London by her sister Pippa, who had just finished university and moved into Catherine's Chelsea flat. Spray-tanned and blow-dried, the two appeared together at a series of upmarket social events. Still only twenty-five, a single girl with the world at her feet – and a taxi waiting outside. Although she was heartbroken, she wasn't going to show it. Her dresses grew shorter, her tops lower. April and May saw numerous nights out to hot spots where she had been a regular with William, and she was frequently photographed – her swirl of brunette hair, bronzed limbs carefully folded – getting out of taxis in the West End. She attended diverse events, including a reception at luxury jeweller Asprey for the launch of *Young Stalin* by Simon Sebag Montefiore and, on another night, attended a party to promote the film *Rabbit Fever*, which was about women obsessed with a brand of sex toy. Gone were the frumpy tweeds of two months earlier; now Kate wore a slinky off-the-shoulder top and silky skirt with a bare midriff and caramel tan. Once inside the party she put on a pair of pink silk bunny ears and proceeded, as one partygoer put it, to 'tease all the boys'.

The tenth anniversary of their mother's death provided a distraction for the princes. Harry and William decided, as the controversy over the manner of Diana's death still raged, that they should at least take charge of her legacy. Whilst others, notably Mohamed Al-Fayed, the father of Diana's last lover, Dodi, who had died alongside her, peddled conspiracy theories that would ultimately be dismissed by an inquest jury in 2008, the princess's sons wanted their mother to be remembered for the good she had achieved in her life. They decided on a two-pronged memorial. First, they organised a charity pop concert in her memory at the new £800-million Wembley Stadium. It was followed by a service of thanksgiving. They also agreed to a series of interviews in which they would talk openly about her. During a walkabout ahead of the concert, William joked that his brother was 'the ginger Bob Geldof', a reference to the organiser of the Live Aid concert staged at the old Wembley Stadium and attended by their late mother more than twenty years before, and Harry admitted in an interview with the BBC's Fearne Cotton, 'If it goes wrong, it'll be very nerve-racking.'

It had been reported that a few weeks earlier William had finally won back the love of his life. While William was notoriously the instigator of the couple's break in April, he was also the one who fought the hardest for them to get back together. He knew after a few weeks that he had made a mistake and implored Catherine to give him a final chance. But when he told her of the mistake, that wasn't enough for Catherine, she wanted to know how their future would map out. The watershed moment came in June, just before the concert, when William invited Catherine to a fancy-dress party at Bovington barracks in Dorset. The theme was 'Freakin' Naughty' and Catherine went dressed as a sexy nurse. As soon as he set eyes on her he was besotted. They danced the night away and enjoyed a public kiss at midnight before disappearing. 'They couldn't keep their hands off each other,' said an onlooker. William didn't care who knew, he just wanted the love of his life back in his life. 'His friends were joking that they should get a room,' said the partygoer, which they did. They were officially back together by the end of the party and have been an inseparable team ever since.[59]

Despite the reports of a reconciliation, William and Catherine played it cool at the 'Concert For Diana'. Whilst she joined the prince in the royal box, she sat two rows behind him with her sister Pippa, while he took a place next to long-time pal Thomas van Straubenzee and his brother Harry. But there could be no doubt that the poignancy of Take That's song 'Back For Good' did not go unnoted by the former lovebirds, who were seen swaying to the hit tune. It was reported that Catherine's car had been spotted the previous night at Clarence House, reinforcing reports that the couple were back on. They more than likely decided to keep their distance at the Wembley Stadium gig to keep the focus away from them and on the evening in memory of the princes' mother.

Harry, on the other hand, was all too happy to be seen with his Zimbabwean love Chelsy Davy, who cut a stunning figure in a low-cut black dress. At one point, the pair even shared a passionate kiss. Also in the royal box were Princesses Beatrice and Eugenie, Zara

Phillips with her rugby beau Mike Tindall, and Diana's siblings Earl Spencer, Lady Sarah McCorquodale and Lady Jane Fellowes. While both the princes admitted to pre-concert nerves, the duo had no trouble getting into the groove once it kicked off – at one point joining in a Mexican wave and showing off their dance moves. As they stepped onto the stage in front of the 63,000-strong crowd to open the musical extravaganza, they received a standing ovation which Harry responded to with a typical rock star greeting, calling out, 'Hello Wembley!' The boys had previously said the event, which coincided with what should have been their mother's forty-sixth birthday, had to be the best birthday present their mother could ever have. And there was no doubting they achieved their aim. 'This event is about all that our mother loved in life, her music, her dancing, her charities and her family and friends,' said William.

Sir Elton John opened the six-hour-long evening with 'Your Song', taking to the piano in front of a huge image of Diana by famed photographer Mario Testino. Acts ranging from Rod Stewart and Status Quo to Nelly Furtado and P. Diddy – who reprised his hit 'I'll Be Missing You' in honour of Diana – made it a night to remember. A host of stars were also on presenting duties to help introduce the performances, including actress Sienna Miller and actor Kiefer Sutherland. There were words of praise from music mogul Simon Cowell, who said: 'Prince William and Prince Harry, you have put on one heck of a show. Congratulations. If you ever get tired of running this country, you can come and work for me producing TV shows.'

A few weeks later, both Diana's 'boys' publicly showed how far they had come since that awful day when they walked behind her coffin. On 31 August, marking a decade since her death, they paid a fitting tribute to her at a memorial service at the Guards' Chapel. On that special day of remembrance, her second son, Harry, was a boy no longer. He emerged from it as a confident, strapping young man ready to defend his mother's memory and his family honour from all those he and his brother felt had hijacked it.

Unfazed by the enormity of the moment, Harry spoke from the heart and with real passion of his mother's 'unrivalled love of life, laughter, fun and folly'. He said, 'She was our guardian, friend and protector,' as his older brother, with whom he had organised the service, looked on. 'She never once allowed her unfaltering love for us to go unspoken or undemonstrated.' This was a clear attempt by Diana's sons – William assisted with the writing of the speech – to show the world that they had learned to smile through the pain and were now intent on celebrating their mother's remarkable life.

CHAPTER EIGHT

A TRUE ROMANTIC

'It was very romantic. There's a true romantic in there. I really didn't expect it.
It was a total shock … and very exciting'
Catherine Middleton, when asked about Prince William's marriage proposal[60]

William took the lead, gently guiding his bride-to-be through her first outing before the press. Catherine knew her every move and nuance was being scrutinised, her every word reported around the globe to millions of television viewers who, until now, had seen her image only in glossy magazines and newspapers. The Prince of Wales had earlier released a statement saying, 'The Prince of Wales is delighted to announce the engagement of Prince William to Miss Catherine Middleton.'

The press and the people were thrilled. At last, the marathon courtship of the second in line to the throne, more than eight years in all, was over. Life for this handsome young couple, both twenty-eight, would never be the same again. 'It's obviously nerve-racking,' Catherine said, and revealed that the Queen had been 'welcoming', as too was her prospective father-in-law the Prince of Wales. Now, with the late Princess of Wales's eighteen-carat oval sapphire ring on her finger, she had realised her destiny.

Holding the arm of the only man she had ever truly loved, Catherine tried her best to maintain her poise. With a beaming smile, she leant gently on her royal prince – Royal Air Force Flight Lieutenant William Wales – and they looked like a couple deeply in love, completely at ease with each other.

William pointed out significantly, 'It was my mother's engagement ring, so I thought it was quite nice because obviously she's not going to be around to share any of the fun and excitement of it all – this was my way of keeping her close to it all,' he said. It was a touching gesture that had taken Catherine's breath away when William produced it from his rucksack out of the blue while they holidayed together in Kenya. 'It's beautiful. I just hope I look after it. It's very, very special,' she told him.[61]

The proposal had been truly romantic. It was exactly out of the textbook for princes on white chargers sweeping their chosen damsels off their feet. His mother, whose step-grandmother, Dame Barbara Cartland, made a fortune peddling such stories in slushy romantic novels, would have been proud. William revealed in his engagement interview, 'It was about three weeks ago on holiday in Kenya. We had been talking about marriage for a while, so it wasn't a massively big surprise. I took her up somewhere nice in Kenya and I proposed.'

Tom Bradby asked Catherine, 'And he produced a ring there and then?'

She replied with a beaming smile, 'Yes.'

William explained, 'I'd been carrying it around with me in my rucksack for about three weeks before that and I literally would not let it go. Everywhere I went I was keeping hold of it because I knew this thing, if it disappeared, I would be in a lot of trouble; and, because I'd planned it, it went fine. You hear a lot of horror stories about proposing and things going horribly wrong. It went really, really well and I was really pleased she said yes.'

But why had he waited so long to propose? 'I wanted to give her a chance to see in and to back out if she needed to before it all got too much. I'm trying to learn from lessons done in the past and I just wanted to give her the best chance to settle in and to see what happens on the other side,' he said.

In fact, his proposal plan had been truly adventurous and wildly romantic. He had selected a remote spot beside a shimmering lake in Kenya to ask the most important question of his life. Just five miles from the equator and 11,500 feet above sea level, Kenya's peaceful Lake Alice is so far from civilisation that only a handful of sightseers witness its astounding beauty each year. The lake has stunning turquoise waters and is surrounded by lush green hills, against the backdrop of a snowy Mount Kenya. It is not difficult to see why the prince had selected this destination to propose to his future wife.

Helicopters usually land on a rough shingle beach at Lake Alice's southern tip. Once the rotor blades have stopped spinning, passengers are treated to the kind of silence that can almost be heard. With no other humans for several miles in any direction, the only sounds that are made are those of nature – a rare passing bird or the splash of a fish or frog. Meanwhile, the lake's waters bob with unusual floating rocks – lightweight black stones serving as a reminder of its volcanic origins. With a blazing blue sky and a brisk mountain breeze, William and Catherine used borrowed rods for fly-fishing from the pebbly beach before the prince plucked up the courage to ask for her hand in marriage.

Most who go to Lake Alice fall in love with the place on sight. The peace is breathtaking. It is a unique place where one feels as if nobody else has ever been there. It takes so much effort to reach Lake Alice that it feels virtually untouched by humankind. It is a hundred per cent seclusion and a hundred per cent romantic. William had spent weeks planning his trip to Kenya, where the couple stayed in a romantic log cabin. Without air transport, Lake Alice is at least a four-hour journey from the nearest tarmac road – twenty miles on slimy dirt roads accessible only by four-wheel-drive cars, before a gruelling two-hour uphill trek.

But the prince decided instead to arrive in style and flew in in a chartered helicopter, carrying his mother's sapphire engagement ring in his rucksack, as mentioned earlier. It was, as Catherine said, truly romantic.

Lying in the top of a long-extinct volcano, Lake Alice is now surrounded on all four sides by a ring of ridges, which protect it from the icy high-altitude winds. Poking out from behind one of the nearby peaks is Mount Kenya – the second-highest mountain in Africa – whose snowy summits are famously difficult to reach. William enlisted the help of family friend, Ian Craig, who owns the nearby Lewa game reserve, where the couple spent most of their holiday, and who arranged for their helicopter ride. Details of William's romantic proposal came as the staff at a secluded Kenyan lodge where the couple stayed revealed how they spent their final romantic day before the prince popped the question.

Stunned staff at the isolated Rutundu lodge said they had no idea they were hosting the heir to the throne when William arrived with his future bride and were amazed when they found out afterwards.

This was just hours before he asked Catherine to marry him. The peaceful lodge consists of just two simple wooden cottages nestled high in the Mount Kenya range, around three miles from Lake Alice, and is permanently staffed by three local workers, who live on site to greet the guests and tend to their every need.

But the royal couple were undemanding. William and Catherine asked for virtually nothing as they enjoyed a back-to-basics stay, during which they tucked into a simple supper home-cooked by the future king. Jackson Kimutai, twenty-eight, one of the members of staff, said the pair's only request was to be taken fishing for trout from the back of a rickety rowing boat. And he added that the team believed William and Catherine were just another ordinary young couple when they arrived at around 3 p.m. on 20 October in a rented Toyota Land Cruiser. The prince was dressed in a casual shirt and chinos, while Kate wore a summer dress. Jackson said it was, as Catherine herself said, truly romantic.

He said, 'Some people fish from the jetty or the banks, but William was keen to go out in the boat, so we rowed them out to the middle of the lake. It is a small boat, but it works very well.

'They sat at the back facing the water so they could flick their rods for fly fishing. We were at the front and rowing for them. They were having a great time. It is only fly fishing which is allowed and he spent some time showing her how to do it. Sometimes she was flicking her rod wrong and he helped her to do it better. You could tell they were very close and happy to be together. She kept looking at him and smiling and he was happy too,' he added.[62]

The couple spent around an hour on the water before eventually heading back to shore empty-handed. Jackson went on, 'Sadly, they didn't manage to catch anything. We went back after an hour and they hadn't had a single bite, but some days it is like that. We told them it is hard to catch a fish in Lake Rutundu and they laughed. After that they went back to their cottage to relax.'

The peaceful lodge's staff are well versed in their evening procedures to keep guests warm despite the biting mountain breeze and lack of electricity. At sunset each day, they leap into action – lighting a fire underneath an external water tank for hot water and burning lamps to flood the cottage with romantic light.

'We always get hot water for the guests and light two fires inside – one in the main room and one in the bedroom,' Jackson added.

'The only light is by paraffin hurricane lamps, but people seem to like them. Although we are not cooks, we always offer to help the guests with their meals.'

As darkness fell, William and Catherine ran themselves a hot bath and snuggled up beside the front room's roaring fire. The prince cooked them up a simple meal which they tucked into using the cottage's off-white plates and tarnished, well-used cutlery. Meanwhile, the staff said the couple didn't even have any wine – choosing instead to sip mugs of tea made from hot water left for them by the workers in a battered vacuum flask.

'He was very happy to cook,' Jackson said. 'They had brought their own supplies, although we did not see what. We usually ask people to leave their dirty plates and things in the sink so we can wash up for them, but they hardly left any mess. Sometimes there are also lots of empty bottles of wine or beer but we didn't see any sign of any alcohol from these guys. We think they just drank the tea we left them and enjoyed themselves by the fire.'

Later, the couple retired to the bedroom, where a rustic, wooden four-poster stands alongside a set of bunk-beds for families with children. At night, the cottage is enveloped by total silence, broken occasionally only by the flapping of nocturnal birds or a wandering buffalo or antelope. Lying at the heart of the Mount Kenya National Park, Rutundu is protected by three permanent rangers, who watch for intruders or poachers and use a radio link to summon armed colleagues when required. The site's blissful tranquillity is ensured, as the nearest mobile signal is receivable only from a rocky outcrop about a thirty-minute walk away through the bush. But by night, the presence of deadly animals means guests are warned not to attempt the journey and advised instead to stay tucked up inside their cottage.

The next morning, William and Catherine emerged, blinking, into the African sunlight before enjoying a simple breakfast on the terrace prepared by the prince. The staff said they took the couple for a second, shorter, fishing trip before they left – in time for the 10 a.m. checkout.

Jackson said, 'They had obviously had a really lovely time and had burned a lot of wood for the fire. We took them down to the lake again and then they left. Willy was joking that they had heard a tapping on their window when they woke up. He pulled back the curtains to see who it was, and it was a weaver bird banging at the glass. They are bright yellow and often come up to meet the guests. Willy said after that it went around to all the other windows and tapped on the glass there, too. The whole time the couple were here they were chatty with us, and very friendly. He was joking about the weather because he said he had been here before and got cold. Although it's usually sunny, it's very high here so it does get cold – especially at night. This time he said he had brought two jumpers and she also had some clothes for the evening with her.'

The trip to Rutundu was one of several excursions planned by the prince during their holiday at the nearby Lewa wildlife park, where William had spent a month working during his gap year before he met Catherine at university. Ian Craig, the owner of the reserve, is believed to have put the royal couple up for part of the time in his personal house on the 55,000-acre site, which is home to dozens of animal species, including lions, giraffes, zebra and antelope. William and Catherine also spent several nights at the spectacular Sirikoi game lodge, where they shared a romantic tented room in the wilderness. Happy locals have told of their joy that the prince chose Kenya to confirm his commitment to the future princess. David Kamau, twenty-three, works at a craft stall in the Lewa reserve and said he was delighted when William came in to buy hand-crafted local decorations for the couple's Christmas tree.

He said, 'Everyone is so pleased that they came to Kenya to get engaged. To have a prince and princess staying was wonderful. I met William when he came to my shop. He chatted to us for ages and then bought a pack of ten wire angels and a pack of ten beaded Christmas trees. It is great that we know they got engaged in our place – and even better to know our work will be decorating their Christmas tree.'

Both wrote in a visitors' book after their romantic trip to the log-cabin hideaway. Catherine wrote, 'I had a wonderful twenty-four hours. Sadly, no fish to be found but we had great fun trying. I love the warm fires and candle lights – so romantic! Hope to be back again soon.' William's note dated 20–21 October 2010, said, 'Such fun to be back! Brought more clothes this time! Looked after so well. Thank you, guys! Look forward to the next time, soon I hope.' He signed it,

'William'; she signed hers, 'Catherine Middleton'. Now, of course, she has a different name and title, as she has joined the House of Windsor.

What followed was an extraordinary attempt by the couple to keep their engagement a closely guarded secret. Even the Queen was kept in the dark for over two weeks. 'We're like sort of ducks,' said William. 'Very calm on the surface with little feet going under the water. It's been really exciting because we've been talking about it for a long time, so for us it's a real relief and it's really nice to be able to tell everybody. Especially for the last two or three weeks – it's been quite difficult not telling anyone, keeping it to ourselves. I was torn between asking Kate's dad first and then the realisation that he might say no dawned upon me. So, I thought if I ask Kate first, then he can't really say no.'

William even kept his big news a secret from the Queen as he and Catherine excitedly made their plans for a future together. He was determined to do it his way, and protocol went out of the window. It also gives us an insight into how the new-look House of Windsor will be led from the front by William when he becomes king. One senior member of the royal household told me, 'He did not tell his family until the last minute because he knows once it was official there was a danger he would lose control of it all. William is determined his wedding to Catherine is going to be their day as well as one of public celebration.

'He knows it is a public event, but it is also going to be their special private moment, too, and they don't want that to be forgotten by the courtiers charged with the organisation.'

The happy couple were all smiles for the cameras when they arrived for their pal Harry Meade's wedding. They were already secretly engaged as they boldly strolled through past the front of the church before a battery of waiting photographers. But Catherine, of course, was not wearing Princess Diana's sapphire engagement ring.

A week later, on 30 October, William invited Catherine's parents to Birkhall on the Queen's Balmoral estate in the Scottish Highlands. It was there, in the Queen Mother's favourite old royal retreat, that William – knowing his bride-to-be had accepted his proposal – asked her father Michael for his daughter's hand in marriage. They were preparing to announce the news on Wednesday, 3 November, once he had told the rest of his family. Just four days later, on 7 November

2010, I penned an article in the *News of the World* breaking the story. The headline read, 'WE WILLS WED NEXT SUMMER', with a strapline deck below that read: 'Royal engagement to be announced Xmas'. The opening line of the story could not have been clearer. It read: 'Prince William and his patient girlfriend Kate Middleton will announce their engagement before Christmas, the *News of the World* can reveal.' Nine days later, I was to be proved right. In the past, the dates and venues have been announced simultaneously, but, in typical William style, he wanted it his way.

Palace officials – who had still not been told of the arrangements – refused to confirm the story. The otherwise happy turn of events was not without tragedy, however, with the death of Catherine's ninety-year-old paternal grandfather, Peter, on 2 November, in his home in the village of Vernham Dean, Hampshire. Catherine and the rest of her family were devastated by his loss, and all focus was switched from her big day to the preparations for the funeral on 12 November. A close source said about the engagement, 'It's not clear at this point if [Catherine's father] Mike had actually told [her mother] Carole, because William and Catherine had asked them not to say anything.' Kate even admitted that there was an interesting period when even she was not sure if her mother knew. 'We had quite an awkward situation because I knew that William had asked my father, but I didn't know if my mother knew.' So, she came back from Scotland, where they had been photographed on the royal Balmoral estate on a shoot. Carole did not make it clear to her daughter whether she knew or not.

Then, on his last solo engagement before the big news broke, William flew to Afghanistan along with the Defence Secretary, Dr Liam Fox. In a surprise visit to Camp Bastion in Helmand Province, he joined about 2,500 servicemen in the remembrance ceremony, laying a wreath to remember his own friends and others who had lost their lives. He returned on Monday, 15 November, and that night he telephoned the Queen to tell her the good news. She was delighted. His father, too, was happy, although the Prince of Wales's comment that his son and future daughter-in-law had 'practised long enough' was a classic illustration of his emotional limitations. That, coupled with the timing of his comment that he did expect his wife the Duchess of Cornwall to be queen when he is king, raised eyebrows, and suggested possible future tensions between his and his son's rival courts. Happily, the Queen, in her Accession Day message issued by Buckingham Palace on 5 February 2022, the eve of the seventieth anniversary of her reign, made it public that her 'sincerest wish' is that when Charles is king, she would like his wife to be officially known as Queen Camilla.

On 23 November 2010, the Palace announced that the marriage would take place on Friday 29 April 2011 at Westminster Abbey. At a briefing, they were keen to stress that the royal family would pay for the wedding, but that Catherine's parents would be chipping in too. It was, they said, a precedent set by the marriages of the Prince and Princess of Wales in 1981 and Princess Elizabeth and Prince Philip in 1947. Jamie Lowther-Pinkerton, the sharp former SAS officer turned courtier, revealed it would be a 'classic' royal wedding with all the pomp and pageantry the world expected of the British. He said the couple, who were 'over the moon', were very much in charge of the arrangements. They wanted it to be their wedding and, even though it would take place at Westminster Abbey, the royal family's church, at the high altar it still had the feel of an English parish church. They wanted everyone to enjoy the day and welcomed Prime Minister David Cameron's suggestion that it should be a public holiday, allowing everyone to celebrate. 'This is their day,' Jamie said. 'They are calling the shots.'

Given that Prince Harry was in charge of organising William's stag do, one might have expected something a little wilder. Ahead of the wedding, William celebrated with a select group of twenty friends. They went clay-pigeon shooting and sipped on port before going surfing during a weekend at a Devon Mansion named Hartland Abbey. William didn't escape some classic bachelor party high jinks when he was forced to wear a chest wig and a hairpiece by his friends. He also had a sticker with the Queen's name on his head. But he took in all in good spirits. Harry was determined to hide details of the bash from the media and went about the planning with military precision. He insisted on such secrecy that he even instructed his pals to avoid setting foot in a nearby village in case they raised locals' suspicions.

On the eve of the wedding, William and his fiancée Catherine returned to the place where they had first met, St Andrew's University, for the 600th anniversary celebrations. It came a few days after they had carried out their first engagement as a couple, when they launched a lifeboat near their home on Anglesey. They were leaving their old life behind and forging a new royal partnership. 'It was such a special time for us. It was the start of our life together really,' Catherine remarked, perhaps reflecting on the peace and privacy she and William had enjoyed during their time on Anglesey whilst he was stationed at the RAF base as a search-and-rescue pilot. On another trip down memory lane, at St Andrew's, Catherine wore a bright red coat, perhaps forgetting it would be the same colour as the gowns worn by the undergraduate students. The sun was shining and 3,000 people turned out to greet them both on the street outside. Her royal career was well and truly underway. 'This is a very special moment for Catherine and me,' William said, 'It feels like coming home.'

CHAPTER NINE

WEDDING OF THE CENTURY

'I am so proud you're my wife'

Prince William

With two barely audible words, 'I will', Catherine Middleton, in an ivory-and-white satin dress with lace sleeves and shoulders, designed by Sarah Burton, sent cheers ringing around the country, not to mention the far-flung parts of the world where people still held the British monarchy close to their hearts. Catherine did not vow to obey her husband during their wedding ceremony; nor had Diana, Princess of Wales, in her marriage to Prince Charles. And, with that, the one-time commoner, Catherine, stepped into the magical world of royalty – destined to be the future queen consort of sixteen countries. Together, William and Catherine erased the sadness of the recent royal past and evoked memories of happier times when the public still wanted to believe in fairy-tale royal marriages.

It was one of the most anticipated and most watched events in Britain's long national history, and, indeed, perhaps in world history, given the reach of our truly global media. It finally eclipsed the terrible sadness of William's late mother Diana's funeral on 6 September 1997, which had played out on the same stage of Westminster Abbey. At last, in the same place, on 29 April 2011, the royal family could move on from the tragedy of her death, and, finally, the icon Diana, Princess of Wales, could rest in peace.

Indeed, it was the crowning moment of the first grand act in the theatre of royalty in the twenty-first century, pomp and pageantry at its finest. Crowds had cheered as William's car drove him the short distance from Clarence House to the abbey and roared even louder as the newly-weds rode in an open carriage from the abbey to Buckingham Palace after the ceremony. In all, a million people lined the wedding route. Bells pealed over central London and flag-waving crowds roared in excitement.

It was a resplendent symbol of British national pride and unity, played out on the perfect stage, Westminster Abbey, a setting for 1,000 years of royal history. Prince William, destined to be King of England, the forty-third monarch since another William, the Conqueror, had been crowned there on Christmas Day, 1066. William looked regal to the core, wearing the red tunic of a colonel of the Irish Guards, fitted by Kashket & Partners. It had a distinctive arrangement of buttons in groups of four, featuring the Harp of Ireland surmounted by the Crown Imperial. The arrangement of buttons on the uniform denotes the Irish Guards' position in the Order of Battle as the Fourth Regiment of Foot Guards. He also wore the Garter Sash with the Wings of the Royal Air Force, the Garter Star, and the Golden Jubilee Medal. His forage cap displayed the regiment's motto: 'Quis Serabit?', which translates as: 'Who shall separate us?' William had been appointed to the honorary rank two months earlier. On the day, he also wore the star emblem with St George's cross indicating that he is a Knight of the Most Noble Order of the Garter.

Prince Harry, who wore a Blues and Royals officer's uniform in Dismounted Review Order, with a Forage Cap, aiguillettes, a cross-belt and gold, waist belt with sword slings, but no sword, along with the Wings of the Army Air Corps and Golden Jubilee and Afghanistan Campaign medals. If Prince Harry appeared to be walking with a bit of a limp, it's because he was. At 3 a.m., just eight hours before the wedding ceremony was to begin, Harry exited the nuptials-eve festivities taking place at the Goring Hotel by jumping off one of the hotel's balconies. Reports claimed he landed awkwardly on his ankle and injured himself, meaning he had to have it strapped on the day.

Non-royal guests were instructed to arrive as early as 8.15 a.m. for the 11 a.m. ceremony, and no exceptions were made. The result was the abbey packed with their friends, family, old colleagues, school friends and people who had supported them over the years, including John Haley, the landlord of the Middleton family's local pub, The Old

Boot. Celebrities in the congregation included Sir Elton John, who had famously sung 'Goodbye England's Rose' an adaptation of his hit song 'Candle in the Wind' at Diana's funeral, David and Victoria Beckham, Mr Bean actor Rowan Atkinson and singer Joss Stone. They had also invited eighty representatives from charities close to the couple's hearts, including the CEO of homeless charity Centrepoint, Seyi Obakin.

Catherine had decided against riding in the Glass Coach, the royal carriage that had traditionally been used to transport brides to the ceremony, including Diana, Princess of Wales, as well as Queen Elizabeth II. Her choice was a 1997 Rolls-Royce Phantom VI. She looked incredible. Catherine wore a tiara designed by Cartier, known as the 'Halo Tiara' or the 'Scroll Tiara'. The tiara, which was loaned to her by Queen Elizabeth, was originally given to Elizabeth on her eighteenth birthday by her mother. Her mother had received it as a gift from her husband, King George VI, in 1936.

For the ceremony, the bride carried a bouquet of lily-of-the-valley, Sweet William, ivy, myrtle and hyacinth. Two of those flowers had special significance: one, Sweet William, for obvious reasons; the other, myrtle, has been a royal wedding tradition since the wedding of Princess Vicky, the eldest daughter of Queen Victoria and Prince Albert. Myrtle, which represents love, fertility and innocence, has been grown on royal grounds since 1845 when Prince Albert's grandmother gave Queen Victoria her first myrtle plant.

The royal family's official website tells a touching story of how in 1923, the Queen Mother laid down her bouquet at the Tomb of the Unknown Soldier in Westminster Abbey before she walked down the aisle, bouquet-less, to marry her husband, Bertie, later, King George VI. 'The gesture was in remembrance of her own brother, Fergus, who died at the Battle of Loos in 1915 and to pay tribute to the millions of others killed and injured in World War I.' No other royal bride has walked down the aisle bouquet-less since, but many, including Catherine, have left their bouquet on the tomb too.

Following royal tradition, the wedding ring Prince William placed on Catherine's finger during the ceremony had been fashioned from a nugget of Welsh gold. It was not, however, made of the same nugget of Welsh gold from which the Queen's own wedding band and those of her mother, sister, and daughter, as well as Diana, Princess of Wales was made. There wasn't enough left of that nugget to make a ring for the Duchess of Cambridge.

The palace publicity machine could not have asked for anything better during the royal couple's first public appearance as man and wife. On the famous balcony, the prince, wearing the red tunic of a colonel of the Irish Guards with a blue sash, looked at his beautiful wife and asked, 'Are you ready? OK, let's ...' He then drew her close and they kissed, not once, but twice, to the delight of the huge crowd tightly packed along The Mall opposite the palace. Minutes later, World War II fighter planes roared overhead in the fly-past. It was all timed to military precision. But this was not just a kiss for the cameras; this was true love, and everyone watching, including the estimated two billion glued to their televisions around the world, knew it. Everyone present could feel something special was beginning.

It was a very good day for both royalists and for the House of Windsor, created by George V out of necessity nearly a century earlier. Catherine, with her ancestry that included working-class miners, was the perfect recruit to 'the Firm', as the royal family is sometimes referred to. There was a natural nobility and grace about her. The couple had seemed unflappable as they delivered their vows to each other and as William placed the band of Welsh gold on her finger. The Queen concurred. 'It was amazing,' she said as she left the abbey. 'Are you happy?' Catherine asked her husband as she climbed into the open-topped 1902 State Landau to return to the palace. 'It was amazing, amazing,' replied William, the newly ennobled Duke of Cambridge. 'I am so proud you're my wife.' They were totally at one with each other.

Although Catherine had chosen not to ride in the Glass Coach to the ceremony, the Duke and Duchess of Cambridge travelled to Buckingham Palace for the Queen's luncheon reception in the horse-drawn carriage that transported Charles and Diana during their 1981 wedding. Originally built for King Edward VII in 1902 for his coronation, it is often used by the Queen to meet foreign heads of state.

Five horse-drawn carriages transported the wedding party to Buckingham Palace, accompanied by numerous well-rehearsed riders on horseback. That didn't stop one of the horses from getting spooked and throwing his rider to the ground while the Cambridge newly-weds looked on in shock. Thankfully, no one was injured.

Royal Air Force jets then flew over the crowd and the palace in formation, the official climax of the wedding celebration. The prince and Catherine went inside to a lunchtime reception for 650 people, hosted by Queen Elizabeth II, which featured an eight-tier wedding cake. They left about two hours later in an open-topped, dark-blue Aston Martin DB6 with a licence plate reading 'Just Wed', with William at the wheel. The car is one that the Prince of Wales has owned since 1969 and had converted in 2008 to run on biofuel made from English wine wastage.

William, who had his father's permission to use the classic convertible sports car, wasn't used to driving it and left the handbrake on as he drove his new bride to Clarence House. He got off to a shaky start and the car struggled, appearing to lurch forward and not run smoothly. Photographer Arthur Edwards revealed, 'I was talking to Prince Charles about that. I said: "Did you mind him borrowing your car?" Because he loves that car. It was a birthday present from his mother on his twenty-first birthday. He said: "Oh, no. He asked me if he could use it."' But when Edwards pointed out to the prince that there seemed to be a problem with the sports car, Charles told him, 'Yes. Because he didn't take the handbrake off.' A search-and-rescue helicopter flew past as the newly-weds left the palace, a nod to William's RAF role. Fortunately, no great damage was done to Charles's beloved car.

Tradition dictates that senior royal men receive a title on their wedding day. Although William has never been a stickler for tradition, he happily accepted the royal dukedom from the Queen. When William first set eyes on Catherine at St Andrew's University in September 2001, he said he instantly knew there was something special about her. They had become friends first before falling in love, now she was a royal duchess. She ticked all the right boxes for a future queen consort. But she was no fawning subject desperate to marry into royalty.

As mentioned earlier, the wedding day was sealed with a kiss on the palace balcony, not one kiss but two, which was greeted by enthusiastic cheers from the huge crowds outside the palace and along The Mall. Photographer Arthur Edwards said that William had kindly made sure that he had been able to get a shot of the couple's special kiss on the balcony, despite the photographer's original press pass giving him a spot outside Westminster Abbey. William had ensured he got a prime spot at the palace for him because the couple wanted copies of his photos for themselves. 'That was a pleasure to do that,' he said.[63]

Inside, the wedding party gathered in the Centre Room (East Front) before emerging onto the palace balcony overlooking the palace forecourt and The Mall to greet the massive crowd and a wall of noise. The shots perhaps encapsulated even more memorable moments for those watching on television, thanks to the expression of one of the young bridesmaids, Grace van Cutsem, Prince William's three-year-old goddaughter, who was clearly not amused by the noise and showed this, by scowling and covering her ears.

Inside, official photographer Hugo Burnand had his own bridesmaid issues as Eliza Lopes, the granddaughter of Camilla Parker Bowles, the Duchess of Cornwall, refused to relinquish a bright pink, fuzzy, worm-like toy, even for the official photos.

Camilla later revealed that she had been 'terribly worried' in advance of the big day that the wedding would be overwhelming for Eliza and the other young children in the wedding party. Harry came prepared and when Eliza appeared to be frightened by the roar of the crowds outside Westminster Abbey, he pulled the toy out of his pocket to distract the young girl. The trouble was Eliza liked the toy so much, that she couldn't be persuaded to put it down, not even for the photos.

The next day, the newly-weds dressed casually before flying off in a helicopter on the shortest of breaks. Their honeymoon was put on hold as William had to return to RAF duties as a search-and-rescue pilot just a few days later. The couple sent a message of thanks to the nation for their support on the 'most wonderful day of our lives' and the new Duchess of Cambridge said, with characteristic humility, of their glittering wedding: 'I am glad the weather held off. We had a great day.' Just twenty-four hours later, the pair, who used to use the pseudonym Mr and Mrs Smith whenever they checked into a hotel as students, looked just like any other young couple going on a weekend away. Walking together, holding each other's hands, in the garden of Buckingham Palace they posed and smiled for the cameras before boarding the helicopter. In an instant, they were gone, but the whirlwind of goodwill they had created was not forgotten. Together, William and Catherine were the royal family's new golden couple ready to take the world by storm.

'Beforehand, I had a lot of time to think about it,' William said in an interview for the 2017 documentary *Diana, Our Mother, Her Life and Legacy*, when he reflected on his mother's absence in the run-up to his 2011 wedding. 'When it came to the wedding, I did really feel that she was there. There's times when you look to someone or something for strength, and I very much felt she was there for me.'

For the evening reception, Catherine changed into a second dress, which she wore with a bolero, also designed by Burton for McQueen. It, too, was white, but with a strapless neckline and shorter train, better suited to the more relaxed atmosphere of the evening festivities. William's best man, his brother Harry, was on fine form. In his speech, he said his mother Diana would have been 'proud' to witness the marriage of her son to the 'beautiful' Catherine. His words were heartfelt as he had grown to love Catherine like a sister. Harry went down the kind and affectionate route with the address, calling William the 'perfect brother'. Wisely, he opted to drop a reference to Catherine's killer legs, on the advice of his then girlfriend Chelsy Davy, who said it was inappropriate. Instead, Harry referred to William as 'dude' several times at the Buckingham Palace reception.[64]

When the time came to let their hair down at the after-party, the couple went all out best-of-British, choosing Sir Elton John's 'Your Song' as their first dance, performed by one of their favourite artists, Ellie Goulding. 'I did their first dance and like, talk about scary,' said Ellie, 'I was so nervous, my hands were shaking.' She went on to perform several tracks, including her hit single 'Starry Eyed' from her debut album. Ellie and her band also played a cover of The Killers' 'Mr. Brightside', another on the royal couple's playlist.

The newly-weds had something special for a finale. They stood holding hands in the middle of the dance floor grinning, then suddenly the opening bars of the song 'You're the One That I Want' from the musical *Grease* came booming out. William and Catherine then began dancing around, pointing at each other, and mouthing the words with the style of the lead characters Danny and Sandy. It brought the house down. Guests were transported home from the party at 3 a.m., leaving the newly-weds as the only guests at the palace.

Looking remarkably fresh, the young couple emerged at the back of the palace. She was wearing a knee-length blue dress, dark jacket and summery wedged shoes, while William wore a navy blazer over a finely striped shirt, chinos and brown shoes. They waved and smiled for the cameras before leaving the palace grounds by helicopter, but it was announced that they would not be going on their honeymoon immediately. Instead, they spent a weekend privately in the UK. The couple would take their honeymoon overseas later. A few weeks later, it emerged that the two had slipped away ten days after the wedding to an exclusive location, the North Island resort in the Seychelles, with a price tag of £5,000 a night.

★★★

If Catherine had felt any pre-tour nerves, she did not show any. She may have been the new (royal) kid on the block, but the newly ennobled Duchess of Cambridge seemed to take to the job of roving royal ambassador alongside her husband in her stride. She looked every inch the picture-perfect princess and did not put a foot wrong while accompanying her husband on their first joint tour to Canada. If the far-flung Commonwealth realms were to continue their long-term loyalty to and affiliation with the monarchy, the people had to believe in them. With that in mind, the young husband and wife had something of a mission to fulfil: to take Canada by storm in July 2011.

Canada is a well-trodden path for members of the royal family. In 1939, the Queen Mother, then Queen Consort, toured the vast and beautiful country from coast to coast with the king. She immediately fell in love with the place. The tour, then, was designed to bolster trans-Atlantic support in the event of war and to reaffirm Canada's status as a self-governing kingdom, albeit with a British monarch at its head. During a walkabout, a Boer-War veteran asked the Queen Consort, 'Are you Scots or are you English?' to which she replied, as quick as a flash, 'I am a Canadian.'

Catherine knew she would have to learn quickly if she was to follow in the esteemed footsteps of the last so-called 'Commoner Queen' (despite her aristocratic roots, the Queen Mother was technically a commoner because she was not of royal blood), whose quick wit and consummate PR skills were legendary.

William and Catherine worked the huge and excitable crowds who gathered to see them with aplomb. In an opinion poll taken just before they touched down, almost half of Canada's citizens thought the monarchy was 'a relic of a colonial past that has no place in Canada'. If that was truly the case, then that half must have stayed at home. Thousands turned out just to try to catch a glimpse of their future king and queen when they arrived on 30 June 2011. Further crowds lined the route up to the residence of the Governor-General, Rideau Hall, fervently waving their Canadian flag hours before the couple had even arrived. Some had travelled for many hours across the enormous country to be there to welcome the royal couple.

Canadians seemed more than happy to continue their association with the monarchy, perhaps more so than any other Commonwealth realms. Victoria Doherty and Olivia Dale, both thirteen, and Jasmine Starks, fourteen, drove with their families for six hours from Waterloo, Ontario. Jasmine said, 'We love Kate. She's so down to earth and very beautiful. We got up at four in the morning to watch the royal wedding. I can't wait to see what she's wearing as it's what everyone will be talking about.'

Pat Cook, sixty-four, from Hamilton, Ontario, said, 'I think William and Kate have really renewed interest in the monarchy in Canada. They seem very in love and Kate has so much self-confidence and will fit right in with the royals. We've been here since nine this morning to get a good spot.'

Just before they arrived, the 300 VIP guests, made up of military families and people who worked for charities close to the couple's hearts, took their seats, and the guard of honour did some last-minute rehearsing. The official car drew up alongside the red carpet and waiting to greet them was Canada's Prime Minister Stephen Harper and his wife Laureen. Around 10,000 people cheered wildly as William and Catherine stepped out. A tanned and healthy Catherine looked particularly delighted at the warm reception and waved shyly. The four of them then approached the Tomb of the Unknown Soldier and stood in quiet contemplation as a solo trumpeter played the Last Post. William carefully placed a large wreath on the monument, while his wife leaned forwards to put down a small posy of flowers. She warmly greeted the woman who had handed it to her, Mabel Girouard, who had been chosen by the Canadian Legion as their Memorial Silver Cross Mother after her son Bobby, forty-six, was killed by a suicide bomber in Afghanistan.

The royal couple left the memorial and began to undertake the first of many joint walkabouts. At first, Catherine looked apprehensive – with a fixed smile on her face, she stepped forward to work the crowd under the watchful eye of the private secretary Jamie Lowther-Pinkerton and her protection team. Before long, though, she had sent the crowd into a frenzy of excitement, although there were just as many screams for William. Kate visibly began to relax after a few minutes as she grew into her role and was handed armfuls of flowers and gifts. Each time, she said, 'Thank you so much. We are so delighted to be here.' As if she was seeking reassurance, she occasionally looked over to catch William's eye on the other side of the crowd, perhaps to make sure she was moving quickly enough, but there was no doubt that she was performing admirably. William himself smiled as one woman told him, 'Canada is so happy you are here,' to which he replied, 'Thank you. That is so kind.'

As she waited for the prince to finish, Catherine chatted with the prime minister and his wife, telling them, 'That was so amazing, there were so many people there … How many do you think? We have been on the go since 7.30 this morning, so it's been a long day.' As the couple got into their official car, her first test over, Catherine leaned into her husband's shoulder and grinned broadly.

The next stop, by State Landau, was to Parliament Hill. The cheers subsided for a few seconds and a woman, five yards from the carriage, shouted out, 'Happy Birthday, Diana,' adding, 'We love you, Will and Kate.' The day, of course, would have been Princess Diana's fiftieth birthday. Just as her late mother-in-law had done so many times on her travels with the clothes she selected, Catherine embraced Canada's birthday celebrations by wearing a stylish outfit in the country's national colours.

Catherine was wearing an elegant cream Reiss dress – the same one that was worn for her official engagement pictures by photographer

Mario Testino – and a red hat by Lock & Company's Sylvia Fletcher that appeared to feature a maple leaf, worn in honour of Canada Day in Ottawa. She matched the hundreds of people who were also dressed in the national colours that had turned out for her first engagement with her husband, a citizenship ceremony. The duchess finished off her look with a maple leaf diamond brooch, which the Queen loaned her for the tour and that had first been worn by the Queen on her visit to Canada in 1951. As with all royal tours, the pace was relentless. At one point, she appeared to wilt in the heat and her make-up began to melt. She gestured towards her cheeks and told Prime Minister Stephen Harper's wife Laureen, 'I'm just so hot. It's incredible.'

The Canadian Museum of Civilisation in Gatineau was the next stop. There they were serenaded by a tune that had been penned by a Canadian piper, designed to remind them of their days as a courting couple. As they came down an escalator into the attraction's Great Hall, Pipe Major Bethany Bisaillion's great highland bagpipe wheezed into life as she began her piece, entitled St Andrew's Courtship. Ms Bisaillion, forty-four, from the Sons of Scotland Pipe Band – who had played for the Queen in the past – said after the performance, 'It's a lively march in honour of their time at university – it is uplifting and fun. I play at many citizenship ceremonies and I thought it would be a great way to mark their visit by creating something unique.'

The couple then joined Governor-General David Johnston and his wife, Sharon, on stage as twenty-five new citizens, surrounded by their families and friends, swore allegiance to the Queen and, poignantly, her 'heirs and successors'. As they were called forward, William gave the new Canadians a large national flag, while Catherine presented them with a small hand-held one. After the ceremony, the couple posed with the group and the prince made them laugh when, told by an official he was standing on the wrong step, he turned to those behind him and said, with great humility, 'Sorry.'

Royal aides were keen to pace the duchess on her first ever tour, so they ensured that the couple would enjoy some private time as well. For a few hours, William and his new bride were alone. He rowed her across a stunning lake to an island where they spent hours together in a romantic log cabin, complete with a packed picnic.

They had even managed to ditch their Scotland Yard bodyguards, who gave them radios and kept a discreet distance so that the young couple could wander off into dense woodland completely alone. 'They took food and drink with them and just disappeared together,' a senior source said. The secret hideaway was on Harrington Lake Estate near Lake Meech, where Canadian Prime Minister Stephen Harper has a private retreat – his version of Chequers – thirty-five miles from Canada's capital Ottawa. The cabin – built in the 1920s as a hideaway for a lumber baron, which has its own bedroom, bathroom and kitchenette – is nestled in an area known as Gatineau Park, amidst the Gatineau Hills, and is complete with the most breathtaking views. It is a royal favourite and has been used by people ranging from the Queen to a multitude of Canadian prime ministers as a quiet place to go fishing and, simply, to chill out. The couple, who had only just wed in April, watched by two billion globally on television, looked rejuvenated after this much-needed mini-break.

Later, the duchess, at an open-air pop concert on Parliament Hill, Ottawa, wore a purple Issa jersey dress and thrilled the ecstatic 100,000 crowd as she arrived with William, dressed casually in an open-necked shirt. Catherine, seen by now as a natural royal performer, looked relaxed and happy as the royal couple took their seats in the VIP section. As they sat down, Canadian singer Alan Doyle, of local favourite band the Great Big Sea, shouted to the crowd, 'Put your hands up. We're in the presence of royalty for God's sake.'

As the TV panned onto them, showing the couple on the big screen for the crowd, the show host, CBC radio star Jian Ghomeshi, joked, 'We have to keep introducing you because we like having you here.' Throughout the concert, William and Catherine were tactile – chatting lovingly to each to each other as the Canadian bands entertained them.

They completed their trip to Ottawa, with Catherine by now dubbed 'Catherine the Great' by the Canadian media, by visiting veterans at the Canadian War Museum. After planting a tree at Rideau Hall, they paid their respects at the headstone of the Unknown Soldier. Inside, they mingled with 150 veterans of World War II, the Korean War and Afghanistan, together with their families. They listened to harrowing stories of heroism and injury and were informed of how rehabilitation programmes help Canadian veterans.

Everywhere she went, Catherine drew comparisons with Princess Diana – most notably when she visited sick children and babies at the Sainte-Justine University Hospital in Montreal, the largest mother-child centre in Canada. She appeared, understandably, slightly unnerved by the experience. William, with a tender stroke on her back, stood by her side as the two of them met gravely ill children in the hospital cancer unit, and he was able to reassure her. They first spent an emotional hour privately visiting babies in the hospital's premature-baby unit, and then the couple spent at least twenty minutes with six children, taking care to spend time showing each child individual attention. There was a particularly touching moment when William gently reached out to his wife as the pair spoke to a shy Jak Kilow, a two-year-old, in the playroom of the hospital.

The couple, just like William's late mother, sat at the children's level on small chairs, leaning in to ask questions. One patient, Laurence Yelle, fourteen, who was diagnosed with a brain tumour and was wearing a headscarf after having lost her hair through gruelling chemotherapy, said, 'Kate was so lovely, she spent a lot longer talking to me than I thought she would. She asked me questions about the artwork I was doing and about my illness. It was easier than I thought to talk to her, she was the most normal person.'[65]

The fast pace of their first tour continued relentlessly. It was almost like a military operation. The royal entourage, too, had a very masculine and military feel to it. The aides all had military backgrounds; Jamie Lowther-Pinkerton, a former major in the SAS, who had served with distinction in Colombia, ran the show. But even the press supremo, Miguel Head, had cut his teeth at the Ministry of Defence. What this meant was that there appeared to be a distinct lack of female support staff for Catherine. While her husband, a guardsman attached to the RAF as a search-and-rescue pilot, had a services background, it felt to me as though Catherine was being expected to keep up with their schedule, rather than have them adjust the tour pace to allow for her relative inexperience. She is fit and intelligent, but she needed stamina to run with this royal pack. Fortunately, she had it.

On 3 July, after spending the night aboard the Canadian frigate HMCS *Montreal*, in which they sailed up the St Lawrence from

Montreal to Quebec City, William and Catherine began their day by joining the ship's company of around 200 sailors for a Sunday-morning prayer service. It was predictably named a 'love boat' in the press, but it was hardly that – Catherine later admitted that she barely got a wink of sleep on the naval vessel. At City Hall in Quebec's picturesque old town, where the couple received the freedom of the city, they also witnessed their first anti-royal demonstrators on the trip. Only a handful turned out, though, and they were kept back behind a cordon. Besides, supporters of the royal family vastly outnumbered them.

Catherine teetered carefully down the ship's steps in her four-inch stilettos to meet a line-up of Quebec dignitaries, including the Grand Chief of the Huron-Wendat Nation, Konrad Sioui, who was wearing traditional dress. He said, 'Kate was very interested in my hat, and she wanted to know what feathers it's made of. I told her turkey feathers. I gave William a document that is the treaty that was signed between our two nations by our ancestors in 1760. It is a treaty to say we will live in peace and friendship as brothers.'

It was here that Catherine spoke publicly for the first time since her engagement interview with ITV correspondent Tom Bradby. Interestingly, she spoke of her hopes of starting a family after meeting the father of a 'beautiful' little girl. Perhaps as a sign of things soon to come, she appeared a little broody after being presented with a bouquet by Raffaela, the two-year-old daughter of British ex-pat David Cheater, aged twenty-eight, during a walkabout. The proud dad wished her luck on starting a family and Catherine thanked him saying, 'Yes, I hope to.'

The couple went on to visit the town's Province House, the venue for the Charlottetown Conference in 1864, where the idea for the nation of Canada was born. Taken on a brief tour of the building, which is where the Prince Edward Island's legislature met for the first time in 1847, and, in fact, still do today, they were shown the Confederation Chamber, where the Charlottetown Conference was held. On the other side of the building, in the Legislative Assembly, where the politicians sit, Speaker Kathleen Casey explained the history behind the building. When told there were only two opposition members, William joked that they were not 'doing very well'.

Outside, William made his first major speech of the trip. 'It is quite a moment for Catherine and me to be standing here in Atlantic Canada, in front of Province House, where the Canadian Federation was forged,' he said. 'Here, in the crucible of Canadian nationhood, we look forward to meeting many of you. We have both so looked forward to this day and discovering more about your beautiful island.' Following this, they set off by helicopter for the beautiful Summerside Harbour where there was a spectacular search-and-rescue demonstration, made extra-special by having William at the controls. The backdrop was straight out of one of Catherine's favourite childhood books, *Anne of Green Gables*, which is set there, in 1870. While her husband showed off his flying skills, Catherine remained on land, chatting with Captain Josh Willemsen. On one occasion, William brought the helicopter around in front of the watching duchess – perhaps trying to impress his young bride – banked slightly so that she had a good view into the cockpit and flew off.

In what would become a feature of their future royal-tour style, the couple later rolled their sleeves up and gave the waiting photographers just what they had been waiting for. Each climbed into separate boats to join crews in a Dragon Boat race on Dalvay Lake. This was the new, young and vital royal family for all to see. Both gave it their all – William was given a position as a rower, while his wife was in charge of steering in her boat. The prince seemed delighted that, despite the wet and miserable conditions, his team emerged victorious. Heather Moyse, the Olympic bobsled gold medallist, shared a joke with the prince as she presented him with a bottle of champagne for winning the race. She said afterwards that he had said that the island should be named Prince William Island following his stunning performance, if he could arrange it with his uncle. She added, 'Both he and Kate are very competitive. As a female athlete, I would be really annoyed if someone let me win.'

This was a fast-paced, whistle-stop tour. They criss-crossed the vast nation, taking in Yellowknife, the sparsely populated capital of the Northwest Territories, where they were welcomed with traditional drumming by the Dene people at the Somba K'e Civic Plaza. Members of the Inuktitut and Chipewyan people were among the greeting party too. After a quick change out of formal wear and into casual clothes – Catherine wearing an olive fitted shirt, skin-tight jeans and cream-and-white deck shoes – they took a float-plane to Blachford Lake, a remote Ranger outpost in the vast wilderness of the north, situated right on the edge of the tundra. This was a fine example of the extraordinary life that Catherine had signed up for.

On 8 July, nine days into the tour, William and Catherine joined the colourful Calgary Stampede, complete with white Stetsons and the best country garb, including jeans and checked shirts. It was a spectacular triumph. William agreed. 'I can only say that the experience of this past seven days has exceeded all our expectations. We have been hugely struck by the diversity of this beautiful country, from Ottawa to Quebec, from Prince Edward Island to the Northwest Territories and now the excitement of Calgary. And what about these fantastic white hats!' Canada, he said, had far surpassed all that we were promised. 'Our promise to Canada is that we shall return.'

The visit was an unmitigated success. The next stop for the world's most famous couple would be another first for them. They were heading to the City of Angels, the capital of celebrity, Los Angeles. William and Catherine were the toast of Hollywood, their celebrity eclipsing all the wealthy stars who had made the city their home; they took America by storm. They were joined by 200 guests for drinks and canapés in the garden of the British Consul General, Dame Barbara Hay's residence in Los Angeles. Among them were England footballer David Beckham and actor and comedian Stephen Fry. Beckham, who was playing at the time for the local LA Galaxy team, told William, 'Victoria really wanted to come but she is just so tired at the moment. She sent you both lots of love. How was Canada? It looked amazing.'

The prince replied, 'Don't be silly, send her all our love and tell her good luck with it all. It's been an amazing few days – we've been so lucky with all the incredible places we've been able to see, and we've met so many fascinating people. It's been amazing, amazing.'

Beckham then spoke about the media frenzy surrounding the birth of his first daughter. 'I woke up on Wednesday to a ton of messages on my voicemail from our friends congratulating me on the birth of our daughter. I turned to Victoria and said, "Did I miss something?" Apparently, it's being reported every day that she's already been born.'[66]

One way or another, fingers crossed, she'll be with us in the next few days.'

William listened with interest – David thought the media intrigue surrounding his children was hard to deal with. The media storm that gathered ahead of William and Catherine's first child was to be on a whole different level. Sir Nigel Sheinwald, Britain's ambassador to the US, said, 'They have had a fantastically successful trip to Canada, and they will have a great welcome in California. They will meet a huge range of people, from the governor to people working in the projects of Skid Row. They will get a good snapshot of life in this part of California.'

He was right. There was near-hysterical screaming everywhere they went, from Los Angeles's Beverly Hilton Hotel, where they arrived for a new media summit, to a glitzy charity polo match to raise money for their charities. The highlight of the weekend trip came when they rubbed shoulders with the Hollywood acting elite at a BAFTA event. They arrived to deafening screams from crowds held behind crash barriers as they walked along the red carpet. Catherine looked stunning in a lavender-coloured dress by Alexander McQueen, and William was smart in his dinner jacket and black bow-tie.

William took to the stage to give a speech to the guests. He shared a joke with them to begin with, drawing on the huge success of *The King's Speech*. Speaking in a slightly husky voice, he made the audience laugh when he said, 'Before I start, I should just like to thank Colin Firth for my perfect opening line – "I have a voice".' He went on, 'As President of BAFTA, I am immensely proud of the success Brits have had in the fiercely competitive world of film, television and video games.' When William stepped down from the ballroom stage, one of the first groups the royal couple talked to were Jennifer Lopez, Tom Hanks and his wife Rita Wilson and Barbra Streisand – not an everyday occurrence for either the Hollywood A-listers or the royal couple.

The royal couple were a big hit. Nicole Kidman gave her verdict on William and Catherine as she arrived at the sparkling BAFTA bash. Asked what she thought of the royal newly-weds, she replied, 'I just think they're lovely. I was just on the phone to my mum, and she said, "It's so good you're going" because we're Australian. It just makes you smile.'

It had been their first joint American visit, and they had done extremely well. The couple finally boarded their British Airways flight back to London, posing for a few moments before entering the first-class cabin. Their relief was palpable, their mission certainly accomplished. They well and truly deserved a break.

CHAPTER TEN

NO CLOSER

'It was a grotesque and unjustifiable invasion of privacy'
The Duke and Duchess of Cambridge, reacting to the publication of topless
photographs of Catherine taken while they were on holiday

Wearing an ice-blue lace dress by designer Alice Temperley, her hair pulled back in a bun and held in place with pearl-headed pins, Catherine sipped tea and chatted to several guests, including shoe designer Jimmy Choo, a favourite with Princess Diana. Somehow, Kate managed to keep her composure, smiling and laughing her way through a Diamond Jubilee tea party at the British High Commission in Kuala Lumpur. Inside, however, Catherine was distraught, humiliated by the actions of the paparazzi. She had every right to be grim-faced after the French magazine *Closer* published intrusive topless pictures of her on holiday with Prince William. It was devastating, but she was not about to allow her tears of frustration to flow in public.

William did not look himself. He was not about to let it rest. Earlier, he and Catherine had been locked in private talks with aides who were travelling with them on the Far East Diamond Jubilee tour of Singapore, Malaysia and the Solomon Islands. They had been utterly shocked when private secretary Jamie Lowther-Pinkerton broke the news. Communications were immediately sent to the offices of both the Prince of Wales and the Queen, in London. William wanted decisive action. He called the photographs a 'grotesque breach of privacy' and said he and his wife felt 'violated' during a 'highly intimate moment during a scene of married life'.[67] He was simply not prepared to let the paparazzi hound his wife as they had his late mother.

Their Diamond Jubilee tour had started well enough. The couple had arrived in Singapore on 11 September and they had been greeted by large, animated crowds everywhere they went. In Kuala Lumpur, Catherine delivered her first overseas speech with aplomb at Hospice Malaysia. During it, she stressed the importance of palliative care in transforming the lives of sick children. Catherine – patron of East Anglia's Children's Hospices in the UK – also used her speech to announce a UK-Malaysian partnership between the two hospices, an announcement that won enthusiastic applause from her audience. 'Providing children and their families with a place of support, care and enhancement at a time of great need is simply life-changing,' she said. 'With effective palliative care, lives can be transformed. Treatment, support, care and advice can provide a lifeline to families at a time of great need.' Then, in an instant, the whole mood of the tour changed.

At first, the couple, guided by their aides, were not sure what action to take against the photographer (later identified as Valerie Suau, from the newspaper *La Provence*) and the magazine that first published the shots. But they were convinced of one thing; the pictures taken as the couple relaxed at Viscount Linley's retreat, Chateau d'Autet, in Provence a few days earlier were a complete violation of their privacy – privacy that they could reasonably expect.

William and Catherine's popularity was going from strength to strength. As they were thrust into the public spotlight, the love and friendship they had forged over many years stood them in good stead. They were undoubtedly a strong team, but that composure was about to be tested as they carried out a Diamond Jubilee tour of Singapore, Malaysia and the Solomon Islands on behalf of the Queen in 2012.

After consulting their legal team, the couple took the bold step of announcing on 14 September that they had launched legal proceedings against the publisher of the French magazine *Closer*. Once the matter was in the hands of their lawyers, they pressed on with the tour, a testament to the couple's togetherness, culminating in a colourful spectacle in the Solomon Islands, where Catherine was crowned with a headdress of fresh flowers.

While Catherine was able to look relaxed, in public at least, William was noticeably unsettled. He had, it seemed, the weight of the world on his shoulders. As they watched a traditional Malay tea-pouring ceremony before heading on to the next leg of their South-East Asia tour, they certainly looked distracted.

A few commentators questioned the wisdom of going to France and parading topless in a country where the paparazzi have perfected the 'fine art' of taking intrusive photographs. But, on the whole, the reaction was sympathetic. Away from the tea party, the young royals showed the strain of the day's revelations and appeared downcast as they left for the airport. This was the first big media test since they had married in a whirlwind of positive reaction. Their response had to be a fine balancing act – they wanted action, but they did not want it to overshadow the overseas Diamond Jubilee mission they had been sent on.

Logistics meant that the tiny press pack on that leg of the trip had to advance to the Danum Valley, usually reserved for university research students. The tour was to go ahead as planned. By now, the topless picture controversy was the story; what the couple planned to do in the jungle was becoming increasingly less newsworthy.

The jungle itself was a mystical place. As they crossed the rain-forest canopy bridge at dusk, they watched in awe as a giant flying squirrel, scientifically known as Pteromyini, leapt from tree to tree. Photographer Ken Goff had earlier photographed an adult orangutan as it had walked past him, just a few metres away. It was like stepping back in time to another age entirely.

As the royal couple received a briefing on conservation in the Danum Valley, the small press pool had a briefing of our own from the couple's advisers. We were left in no doubt whatsoever about the anger that the two of them felt. William's spokesman said he felt strongly about privacy and harassment and told us that if necessary he was prepared to pursue a criminal prosecution against those who had snooped on his wife. 'It's part of a very long-standing and heartfelt position by the Duke and Prince Harry, given their past, to do everything they can to protect themselves. They've always said they don't have an issue with the mainstream media just doing their job, but they have always had an issue with paparazzi whose work intrudes on their privacy.'

The Borneo jungle seemed a symbolically fitting backdrop to their troubles. No one could have guessed though, from watching them in public, that the previous twenty-four hours had left the royal couple 'livid' and feeling 'violated'. As the scandal surrounding the photographs raged elsewhere – with more pictures being published in the Irish edition of the *Daily Star* – William and Catherine spent the day smiling and joking as they photographed orangutans and admired exotic flowers.

At one point, the young couple were fitted with special harnesses and helmets before being hoisted 138 feet up into a giant Parashorea tomentella tree using a counterweight pulley system, which had been set by technicians to their combined weight, believed to be about twenty-three stone. Having been winched high into the jungle canopy, William spotted the official photographer Ken Goff, who had been granted permission to perch in an adjacent tree. As they waited in their harnesses, the prince looked at his wife and quipped, 'Girls don't have the same wardrobe malfunctions as men do. I hope I don't have any wardrobe malfunctions.' To their great credit, even while they must surely have been seething with anger, the pair could make light of the events in front of the cameras.

Meanwhile, the royal lawyers went into battle to seek an injunction in a French court. At the same time, they also tried to halt the publication of what was being billed as a 'twenty-six-page photo special' in an Italian magazine. The female French photographer who took pictures of the Duchess sunbathing at the chateau – but not, she says, the topless ones – tried to distance herself from the affair. Valerie Suau's only work, which she insisted was 'decent', had been published in *La Provence* newspaper the previous Saturday with no complaint from the royal family. It was clearly a false trail from Valerie. Months later, she would face a French magistrate and would have to face the consequences of her actions.

Back home, the affair had become so far-reaching that even the Church had waded into the controversy. The Archbishop of York, Dr John Sentamu, said, 'It would be a very sad day when we are taken into the gutter of believing that every woman wants to flaunt her body for all to see. The only time we cannot escape revealing our nakedness is when we are born. Beyond that our culture has said that the only other time should be in the privacy of our homes.'

The Duke and Duchess of Cambridge welcomed a French court verdict that paparazzi photos of Catherine topless on holiday were an invasion of the royal couple's privacy. The court in Nanterre, west of Paris, awarded them €100,000 (£91,000) in damages and interest to be paid by the celebrity magazine *Closer* and two photographers. The magazine's editor and the CEO of its publisher were each fined a further €45,000 – the maximum allowed. The awards, while high for a French court, were considerably lower than the €1.5m that had been reported in the media.

Borneo had been, to an extent, a sanctuary from the excesses and intrusions of the outside world. It was also a testament to how impressive their control was in front of others that they were able to continue touring so professionally. They even wanted to stay the night, but their schedule prevented it. Because of the threat of bad weather causing them to miss their flight to the Solomon Islands, William and Catherine had to travel on, leaving the comparative peace of the jungle.

The next stop was the South Seas. When Catherine arrived on the Solomon Islands, she was immediately crowned with a headdress of fresh flowers. In an instant, the tension which had been building lifted. The couple seemed in a much brighter mood. They first headed for an overnight stay on a remote luxury resort for some much needed, and well-deserved, downtime, before leaving the next day for their trip to the tiny island of Tuvalu. There the couple, in grass skirts and flower crowns, tried hula dancing, Polynesian-style. The nine coral atolls that make up the tiny nation of Tuvalu, where the British Queen is still monarch, boast a population of just 10,000 – but that day it seemed as though most of them had come out to see their future king and queen.

The royal couple arrived by plane, where award-winning Arthur Edwards MBE was the only photographer to join them. He took, by his own admission, some of the best photographs of his long and illustrious career. William was carried through the streets on a 'carriage' with a thatched roof made of leaves, hoisted on the shoulders of twenty-five strapping young islanders. The prince greeted their hosts by saying, '*Talofa*,' a traditional Samoan greeting, and described Tuvalu as the highlight of their nine-day Diamond Jubilee tour, which came to an end that day. He told them the whole world remembered the warmth of their welcome for the Queen when she visited in 1982. It was one of the 'iconic images of her reign'. Then, in an unusually informal 'state dinner' hosted by the island chiefs, the couple threw themselves into the celebrations. With a shimmering shake of the hips, they seemed to put all the drama of the last few days behind them, and they danced their worries away. They had passed the first big test of their marriage, and now, thankfully, they were going home.

CHAPTER ELEVEN

LITTLE GRAPE

'Well, plenty more to come from here of course. None of it is news because
that will come from Buckingham Palace. But that won't stop us'

Simon McCoy, infamously irreverent BBC presenter on the media mayhem outside
the hospital where the Duchess of Cambridge was about to give birth

Almost from the moment William and Catherine wed, the next pressing question in the press was, 'When will Kate fall pregnant?' If recent royal history was anything to go by – the Queen and Diana both fell pregnant within a year of their wedding – the Palace would very soon be announcing a royal pregnancy, but the editors were to be disappointed. Their first anniversary came and went, and the newspapers seemed to back off. The royal pregnancy, or lack of it, became the great unsaid.

On 3 December 2012, William and Catherine capped what had been a wonderful Diamond Jubilee year by announcing that they were expecting their first child. The news apparently caught even the Queen and the Prince of Wales by surprise. William had wanted to keep it secret so badly that they had kept even their closest family members in the dark. Unforeseen circumstances meant they had no choice but to reveal their most cherished secret. William had to break the news to his grandmother, father and brother in hurried telephone calls just minutes before making the announcement to the world after his wife was taken to hospital suffering from acute morning sickness.

Not wanting to take any chances, he took his wife to London's King Edward VII's Hospital and spent several hours with her. Catherine was less than twelve weeks pregnant and was expected to stay for several days at least, being cared for by gynaecologist Sir Marcus Setchell, who had delivered the Countess of Wessex's two children. Whilst Catherine was being cared for in hospital, the wider world was thrilled by the news. Prince Charles seemed to capture the mood perfectly. When asked about the pregnancy as he was boarding HMS *Belfast* in London to cross over to the SA *Agulhas*, where he met Sir Ranulph Fiennes to wish him well on his latest Antarctic exhibition, he teased reporters, joking, 'How do you know I'm not a radio station?' before going on to say, 'I'm thrilled, marvellous. A very nice thought of grandfatherhood at my old age if I may say so. So that's splendid. And I'm very glad my daughter-in-law is getting better, thank goodness.'

The Archbishop of Canterbury, who married the couple, said, 'The whole nation will want to join in celebrating this wonderful news. We wish the Duchess the best of health and happiness in the months ahead.' As speculation swirled about the sex of the unborn baby, Catherine's royal apprenticeship was also gathering pace. With Prince William away, working as an RAF search-and-rescue pilot, Catherine was asked to support the Queen and the Duke of Edinburgh on engagements. Her Majesty had been taken ill, hospitalised after a bout of gastro-enteritis, but this was never going to derail her for long. For the Queen, the need to do her duty is elementary, almost part of her DNA. It was fitting, then, that she returned to work at Baker Street Tube Station – famed for links to Sherlock Holmes – to mark the 150th anniversary of the London Underground.

Catherine looked blooming as she walked a step or two behind to add that touch of glamour to the occasion. Right on time at 11.30 a.m., the royal party viewed a restored 1892 underground coach, and met staff and apprentices involved in the restoration project. All three royals then walked through a brand-new S7 train, before the Queen unveiled a plaque, naming the train *Queen Elizabeth II*. At the end of the visit, London Underground's chief operating officer Howard Collins presented Catherine with her 'Baby on Board!' badge, and Catherine said, 'Oh yes, I've seen this before – how do they work? … I will have to wear it at home.' At home, William and Catherine were mulling over names and they already had a nickname for him. He was known as 'little grape' by his parents until he was born.[68]

Britain was in the grip of a heatwave when the time came for the royal baby to enter the world. By mid-July, temperatures had soared to the high 80s Fahrenheit, and on a couple of days, hit 90°F (32°C). Understandably, Catherine flitted between her parents' Berkshire mansion and Kensington Palace whilst William packed in the hours in his day job as an RAF search-and-rescue pilot in north Wales. She didn't, it seemed, want him hovering around her. Instead, when he did have free time at the weekend, he played charity polo matches with his brother, Harry.

The first photographer's ladder – used to stake out and hold a position – had already been put up at the end of June outside the Lindo Wing, St Mary's Hospital, Paddington, in west London, where the royal baby would be born. No official due date had ever been given; all William and Catherine's private office at Kensington Palace had said about a due date was to repeat what the duchess herself had let slip during a public walkabout earlier in the year – that the baby was expected in 'mid-July'. The great 'Kate Wait', as it became known, had started in earnest.

By now, teams of television crews were arriving from all over the world. Tape was placed on the ground with the names of television networks on them, marking their spots, too. With so many journalists in town, and with very little to report until Catherine was inside the hospital, false alarms and wayward stories became the order of the day. Some TV broadcasters became so bored that they started interviewing each other. When the moment came it felt truly historic. William decided to delay the official announcement of the birth for four hours and ten minutes after the delivery. He also decided not to make what has become a traditional appearance on the hospital steps to tell the world about his new son and how happy he was.

At 7.14 p.m. on 23 July 2013, twenty-seven hours after the birth, an exhausted but beaming Duchess of Cambridge emerged through the door with her proud husband, William, who could hardly keep his eyes off his son and heir as he stood at her side. In her arms, Catherine showed off their 8 lb 6 oz bundle of joy amid tumultuous cheers from hundreds of well-wishers and hospital staff crammed into every vantage point. Simultaneously, television transmitted the picture-perfect image of our 'New Royal Family' to hundreds of millions of people watching live around the globe. William, standing protectively close to his wife and baby, added: 'It's very special.' Then, seeming to confirm that their son had been born after his due date – the topic of much media hype – the prince joked: 'I'll remind him of his tardiness. I know how long you've all been standing here [to the press] so hopefully the hospital and you guys can all go back to normal now and we can go and look after him.'

At this moment the baby born to be king was still only known as 'Baby Cambridge', for His Royal Highness Prince George of Cambridge's name had yet to be made public. Barely visible, a wisp of dark hair peeping from the £45 merino shawl made by Nottinghamshire firm G. H. Hurt & Son Ltd, he underwent his baptism into the mayhem of the demanding modern media world that will chronicle his life from the cradle to the grave. After just a few seconds, smiling as the cameras whirred, Catherine, wearing a bespoke cornflower-blue crêpe-de-Chine dress by Jenny Packham, carefully passed their baby boy to her husband, who was looking relaxed in an open-necked blue shirt with two buttons undone and casual trousers, before they walked forward to speak to a waiting press, who were hungry for more information about the little day-old prince. At this moment the baby, hardly awake, managed to free his hands. The auto-drive cameras clicked and clattered in unison. It was, the newspapers would record the following day on their front pages, as though he had perfected his first royal wave.

'He's got a good pair of lungs, that's for sure. He's a big boy, he's quite heavy,' the prince said, adding: 'We are still working on a name so we will have that as soon as we can. He's got her looks, thankfully,' he went on in his typically self-deprecating way. 'No, no, I'm not sure about that,' Catherine chipped in. Asked what colour the boy's hair was, the prince gazed adoringly at his firstborn, and the smattering of fair hair on the boy's head, before joking: 'He's got way more than me, thank God.' The Duchess revealed, too, that her husband was a hands-on father: 'He's done his first nappy already,' she said. When asked how he had got on, William said 'Good,' and his wife added, 'Very, very good.'

William, calm and confident, stood tall. He was a man, a loving husband and a proud father. The couple then returned to the hospital briefly before re-emerging with their son strapped into his first 'throne' – a £99.99 Britax baby car seat. As the Duchess got into the back of their black Range Rover, Prince William put the baby seat containing his son and heir into the car for the first time. He let out a mock sigh of relief that he had managed to do this without a hitch, since the cameras were ready to record any mistake. With only their Scotland Yard personal police protection officer accompanying them, William then drove his new family off to their temporary Kensington Palace home, the two-bedroomed Nottingham Cottage. It would be their secure sanctuary for the next couple of days, since their new home at the palace, Apartment 1A, was not yet ready. Now, safe behind the security gates, protected and hidden away from prying eyes, they could start bonding as a family.

Keen to stem the media circus surrounding the royal birth, William and Catherine would not keep the world's media waiting that long. As William prepared to drive his new family from the hospital, the BBC's unflappable royal correspondent, Peter Hunt, asked him whether he would name his son George, in line with the bookmakers' predictions. He laughed and said, 'Wait and see … We're still working on a name so we will have that as soon as we can.' First, however, the couple had to initiate a historic meeting between Her Majesty Queen Elizabeth II and her first great-grandson and third in line to the throne. It had been almost 120 years since a reigning monarch had met a future king three generations ahead, and she was 'thrilled' to meet the latest addition to her family. This time, however, there would be no cameras or television reporters shouting out questions. This after all was the sovereign, and such behaviour just would not do.

The Queen made the short journey from Buckingham Palace to Kensington Palace in a dark-green Bentley to meet her great-grandson for the first time. It was just after 11 a.m. on 24 July as she arrived and was photographed sitting in the back seat by Jeremy Selwyn, a veteran staff lensman with the *London Evening Standard*. Within minutes, my report, under the banner headline 'Queen Drops in on Great-Grandson' was splashed with Mr Selwyn's photograph across the front page of the respected 187-year-old newspaper. Meanwhile, inside the palace, William, Catherine and the baby were awaiting Her Majesty's arrival. Prince Harry, a proud uncle now pushed down the line of succession to fourth place due to the arrival of his nephew, waited too.

William and Kate already had a few names in mind. But given their little boy's status and what he represented, they wanted to be sure their choice met with the monarch's approval. She would not make suggestions – it is not her style – instead leaving the choice of name to the parents. But as many prime ministers and advisers had learned in the past, the slightest raising of an eyebrow from Her Majesty would be enough indication that the couple might like to think again. There are no formal rules when it comes to picking a royal name; like Britain's constitution, they are well understood but unwritten. Traditional names are considered good, especially for a child in the direct line of succession who will one day reign. After all, royal names come to define much more than an age, for they also stand for values – like the Victorians – or architecture, like the Georgians.

When Peter Hunt had pressed them about the name George, the royal couple had appeared to flash a knowing glance at each other and give a slight chuckle before William said that naming his son was still a 'work in progress'. Huge sums of money had been wagered at bookmakers on everything from the sex, weight and date of birth of the baby. Now, there was only one bet left: what would he be called? George was the bookmakers' favourite at odds of 7/4, ahead of James (4/1), Alexander (8/1), Henry (12/1) and Louis (12/1). It would be, after all, a name that would be a clear and touching tribute to the Queen's father, George VI – as, indeed, would Albert, for the late king's original names had been Albert Frederick Arthur George, and he had been known to his family as Bertie. George was also one of the seven names of Edward VIII, who abdicated the throne. He had been christened Edward Albert Christian George Andrew Patrick David, but was known to his family by the last of these. William's father, the Prince of Wales, had been christened Charles Philip Arthur George. Perhaps it is not surprising that his bride, Lady Diana Spencer, mixed them up while taking her wedding vows.

The Queen, who was due to travel to Balmoral for her traditional annual holiday two days later, stayed for thirty-four minutes. An hour-and-a-half after her departure the Cambridges left too. Less than twenty-four hours after returning to Kensington Palace from hospital they were on the move again, this time to stay with the Middletons at the family home in Berkshire. The new parents drove away in a Range Rover at 1 p.m., with Prince George in the back, strapped safely into his car seat. An hour later they arrived at the £4.8-million Georgian mansion recently bought by Kate's parents in the leafy village of Bucklebury, where Carole Middleton had been busy redecorating a 'nursery-style' room for her first grandchild. According to officials, the Duke and Duchess just wanted 'private time together, like any new family', adding, 'They just want to get to know their son.'

Yellow police cones showing 'no waiting' symbols lined both sides of the road every few yards for around a mile either side of the Middletons' majestic Bucklebury Manor, a substantial estate set in eighteen acres of land and boasting its own tennis court, swimming pool and library. A bright yellow notice stuck to a road sign confirmed an emergency three-week by-law prohibiting any form of waiting in the road, while a pair of police officers stood at both entrances to the Grade II-listed Georgian mansion and marked police cars swept past the entrances every couple of minutes. A large police horsebox marked 'Mounted Section' arrived in the picturesque village at lunchtime, and a small marquee surrounded by marked and unmarked police cars was visible in a nearby field. But still, no name had been announced.

Then, at 6.18 p.m. on 24 July, Kensington Palace issued its last royal baby statement. It was the final piece of the jigsaw. Under the headline 'The Duke and Duchess of Cambridge name their baby' it read: 'The Duke and Duchess of Cambridge are delighted to announce that they have named their son George Alexander Louis. The baby will be known as His Royal Highness Prince George of Cambridge.' There has been at least one 'HRH Prince of Cambridge' before: Prince George of Cambridge, born in 1819, grandson of King George III.

Prince Adolphus, seventh son and tenth child of King George III and Queen Charlotte, like William, was created Duke of Cambridge by the monarch. He married Princess Augusta of Hesse-Cassel in 1818 and they had three children: George (1819–1904), Augusta (1822–1916) and Mary Adelaide (1833–97). Mary Adelaide was in fact the Queen's great-grandmother. The Duke of Cambridge died in 1850 and was succeeded by his son, George, who became the Duke of Cambridge. His marriage was in contravention of the Royal Marriages Act, so his three sons and their male-line descendants used the surname FitzGeorge. The second Duke died in 1904, and his title reverted to the Crown. Not only was the royal baby not the first to be styled as 'of Cambridge', but he is also a direct descendant of Prince

Adolphus, Duke of Cambridge, through his youngest child, Princess Mary Adelaide of Cambridge.

No matter how much William and Catherine wanted their unborn child to have as ordinary an early life as possible, it was clear this baby was going to be special, very special.

The royal baby was toasted by celebrities on Twitter and George's birth was even marked in an episode of BBC soap opera *EastEnders* after show bosses ordered some last-minute filming to reflect the birth. A scene showing Dot Cotton (June Brown) and Abi Branning (Lorna Fitzgerald) discussing the happy news was filmed on Monday night and featured in the BBC soap. Kermit the Frog and Miss Piggy were among the stars offering their congratulations to the Duke and Duchess of Cambridge on the birth of their son. The Muppets stars – who were in London filming their new movie, *Muppets Most Wanted* – sent a video message to the royal couple, and Miss Piggy confessed she was starting to feel broody. She shrieked to Kermit: 'Isn't it exciting?! Kate is a mummy, Prince William is a daddy. It kind of makes you want to have a royal child of your own, doesn't it Kermit? Can't you just hear the patter of little tadpole feet.' Kermit shrugged: 'Not really … tadpoles don't have feet.'

On the following day, gun salutes sounded across London to mark the birth of the royal baby as the armed forces joined in the celebrations. The King's Troop, Royal Horse Artillery, and the Honourable Artillery Company carried out the ceremonial royal salutes that are fired for the birth of every prince or princess, no matter where their place is in the line of succession. The last royal salute had been for the birth of Prince William's cousin Princess Eugenie twenty-three years earlier. In full dress uniform, the King's Troop paraded past Buckingham Palace to Green Park, where they staged a forty-one-gun royal salute. They went from their forward mounting base in Wellington Barracks into Green Park, where seventy-one horses pulled six First World War-era thirteen-pounder field guns into position for the royal salute at 2 p.m. Each of the six guns fired blank artillery rounds at ten-second intervals until forty-one shots had been fired. The Honourable Artillery Company (HAC), the City of London's Army Reserve Regiment, also fired a salute from Gun Wharf at the Tower of London at 2 p.m. Uniquely, at the Tower of London, a royal residence, sixty-two rounds were fired as the salute includes an additional twenty-one rounds for the citizens of the City of London, to mark their loyalty to the monarch.

After Prince George had been introduced to the Queen, Her Majesty immediately afterwards headed to Scotland to start her delayed annual holiday at her Balmoral estate. The royal couple then stayed for the next few weeks with their baby at the Bucklebury mansion in Berkshire, with Catherine's parents. For the young couple, enduring sleepless nights with a newborn, assistance from the experienced hands-on grandparents was welcomed. The Palace only revealed the couple would be enjoying 'some private time together like any new family' adding, 'they just want to get to know their son'. After his paternity leave was up, William returned to work as an RAF search-and-rescue pilot in Anglesey, leaving Catherine and the new baby to stay on at the Middletons' estate for a few weeks as planned.

There is no doubt Diana would have been delighted by William's choice of bride. In Catherine he had found a woman he married for love who is also his best friend, confidante and lover. The idea of a loving family meant everything to the late Princess Diana. Sadly, she never experienced it, either as a child or as a wife. Helping William and Catherine to raise George would undoubtedly have been a great joy for her. Had she lived, Diana, a July baby herself, would have just turned fifty-two at the time of her grandson's birth. His arrival would have been one of the most fulfilling moments of her life.

She had championed her sons' right to live their lives freely and fully; her ambition had always been a simple one, to see them content, safe and happy. Like Diana, Prince George's star sign is Cancer. 'He will have the psychic imprint of Diana,' says her one-time astrologer, Penny Thornton. Diana's brother, Earl Spencer, spoke of his family's joy at the birth of baby George. 'We're all so pleased – it's wonderful news,' Lord Spencer said. 'My father always told us how Diana was born on just such a blisteringly hot day, at Sandringham, in July 1961. It's another very happy summer's day, half a century on.' If Diana had taught her elder son anything, it was to stand his ground. Yes, he had duties and obligations that came with his role, but this new father was not about to be pushed around by anyone. He had always made it clear that he would find his own path in life, and it is something the princess had tried to encourage in her eldest son. As a future king, like William, George's future has been mapped out. His parents chose from the outset, however, to avoid George being over-exposed in the media wherever possible.

William opened his heart about the joy of becoming a father a few weeks later in an interview on camera at Kensington Palace with CNN correspondent Max Foster on 19 August 2013. He said, laughing: 'I think more shock and daunting was the feeling I felt. I was on such a high anyway, and so was Catherine about George that really, we were happy to show him off to whoever wanted to see him. As any new parent knows, you're only too happy to show off your new child and, you know, proclaim that he is the best looking or the best everything.'

Max Foster asked whether the Duke was comfortable presenting his son to the waiting press and trying to adjust the car seat watched by millions on TV. He laughed again, before he replied, 'It's nice that people want to see George, so, you know – I'm just glad he wasn't screaming his head off the whole way through. Believe me, it wasn't my first time. And I know there's been speculation about that. I had to practise; I really did. I was terrified that I was going to do some, you know, it was going to fall off or it wasn't going to close properly. So, I had practised with that seat, but only once before.'

Foster then asked: 'And your decision to drive off, I remember that moment as well. That was the most nerve-racking thing for me, having my family in the car. But that was something that you were clearly determined to do.'

William replied: 'Where I can be, I am as independent as … as I want to be. And same as Catherine and Harry. We've all grown up, differently to other generations. And I very much feel if I can do it myself, I want to do it myself. And there are times where you can't do it yourself and the system takes over or it's appropriate to do things differently. I think driving your son and your wife away from hospital was really important to me. And I don't like fuss so it's much easier to just do it yourself. I didn't stall, well it's an automatic so it's all right.'

Foster asked: 'The interpretation of the imagery we saw there, which went around the world, was that this was a modern monarchy and a new way of monarchy, but was it that? Are we reading too much into it, is it just you doing it your way, you and your wife doing it your own way?'

William said, 'I think so, and I'm just doing it the way I know this, you know, if it's the right way then brilliant, if it's not, if it's the wrong way then I'll try to do it better. I'm reasonably headstrong about what I believe in, and what I go for, and I've got fantastic people around me who give me great support and advice. Well, yeah – he's a little bit of a rascal, put it that way. So he either reminds me of my brother or me when I was younger. I'm not sure. But he's doing very well at the moment. He does like to keep having his nappy changed, and I did the first nappy, yeah. A badge of honour, exactly. I wasn't allowed to get away with that. I had every midwife staring at me, saying, 'You do it. You do it.' He's growing quite quickly actually. But he's a little fighter. He kind of, he wriggles around quite a lot. And he doesn't want to go to sleep that much, which is a little bit of a problem.'

Asked how his wife was coping, William replied: 'Yes, very well, yeah. For me, Catherine, and now little George are my priorities. And Lupo [the couple's dog].' He added that their dog is 'coping all right, actually', adding, 'As a lot of people know who have got dogs and bringing a newborn back, they take a little bit of time to adapt, but, no he's been all right so far. He's been slobbering sort of around the house a bit, so he's perfectly happy.' He ended the warm and natural interview saying he is quite looking forward to returning to his job as an RAF search-and-rescue helicopter pilot based at Anglesey, where the couple had been living. 'I'm just hoping the first few shifts I go back I don't have any night jobs.'

Never one to miss an opportunity, the prince also used the interview, which he knew would generate widespread coverage, to highlight one of his great passions, saving endangered species in Africa, and spoke of how he wants his son to follow in his footsteps. William, patron of conservation charity Tusk, said he wants his son to experience the same Africa he saw as a boy and as a young man and give his son a passion for preserving the rarest animals as Prince Charles encouraged in him.

'At this rate I'll probably whisper sweet nothings in his ear. I'll have toy elephants and rhinos around the room. We'll cover it in sort of, you know, lots of bushes and things like that. Make him grow up as if he's in the bush. At the moment, the only legacy I want to pass on to him is to sleep more and maybe not have to change his nappy so many times. I think the last few weeks for me have been just a very different emotional experience.' Speaking about how becoming a father has forever changed him, he went on, 'Something I never thought I would feel myself. And I find, again it's only been a short period, but a lot of things affect me differently now.'

George's christening ceremony was relatively low key, given his status. Just three months after his birth, once Her Majesty had returned from her annual summer at Balmoral, the third in line to the throne was baptised at the Chapel Royal in St James's Palace by the Archbishop of Canterbury, Justin Welby. The intimate service on 23 October had a congregation of just twenty-two: the Queen and Prince Philip, Charles and Camilla, Harry, Catherine's parents, Michael and Carole, her brother James and sister Pippa and the seven godparents and their spouses. William's uncles, the Duke of York and the Earl of Wessex, and aunt, Princess Anne, were among those who had been left off the list. This meant the Cambridges could invite close friends instead. The size of the chapel meant that numbers on the guest list had to be kept down.

It was in stark contrast with William's own christening at Buckingham Palace in 1982. Then, a large crowd had gathered outside the palace and the Queen Mother appeared on the balcony before the ceremony. This time it was a closed event. Photographer Jason Bell was selected to take the historic photographs at Clarence House, including one of the three direct heirs, Princes Charles, William and George, the first time such a picture had been taken since 1899, when an eighty-year-old Queen Victoria posed with her direct successors, Edward VII, George V and Edward VIII. This time, the Queen, then eighty-seven, is pictured with her son the Prince of Wales, then sixty-four, grandson the Duke of Cambridge, then thirty-one, and three-month-old great-grandson Prince George.

George wore a replica of the christening gown worn by Queen Victoria's daughter created by the Queen's dresser Angela Kelly, who had been commissioned to make a new gown after the old one, which had been passed down for generations, had been deemed too fragile for further use. It took just forty-five minutes and the guests returned for tea at Clarence House, hosted by the proud grandfather, Charles. George's godparents comprised a mix of school friends, those from William and Catherine's childhood and others who had had a positive impact on their lives. William's long-time aide,

Jamie Lowther-Pinkerton, a former SAS officer, was named one of George's godfathers. Julia Samuel, who had been a close friend of William's mother, was named one of George's godmothers. She had founded the charity Child Bereavement UK, which helps youngsters struggling with the loss of a parent or loved one. The couple also turned to William's childhood friend William van Cutsem and their school friends Emilia Jardine-Patterson and Oliver Baker. Zara Tindall, Princess Anne's daughter and William's first cousin, was asked to be another of George's godmothers and Earl Grosvenor, another family friend, rounded off the list.

With their Kensington Palace renovations unlikely to be fully completed until mid-autumn, Catherine relied on her mother to help care for George as she adjusted to motherhood. The young couple had never employed a large domestic staff. Catherine did most of the cooking, although just prior to George's birth they hired Italian housekeeper Antonella Fresolone from Buckingham Palace, where she had spent thirteen years on the staff before applying for the post. The advertisement said the position needed somebody with 'discretion, loyalty and reliability'. It stressed 'attention to detail, together with a flexible and pro-active approach is essential'.

The couple had spent three years at their Anglesey home without domestic help. Catherine was often spotted shopping at local stores. But once George had arrived, she soon realised that her busy schedule meant she would need help as she juggled parenthood and public responsibilities.

The Palace said they would at first rely on their doting grandparents and loving families. 'They have both got families which will care hugely for this baby,' a statement said. A month after George's birth, they began making enquiries about part-time help. When they still couldn't find a suitable person, William reached out to his former nanny Jessie Webb, who was then seventy-one, to see if she would consider coming out of retirement for a short time. William believed Jessie, who had stayed in touch with the prince and attended the royal wedding, would provide the stability, and had the experience that was needed to help with the little prince.

The appointment was initially part-time to assist the Cambridges as they returned to royal duties, splitting their time between William's posting in Anglesey and Kensington Palace in London. She agreed, but stressed they must find somebody else for the long term. Six months later they had found the perfect candidate and hired Maria Teresa Turrion Borallo for the position. Maria, forty-three at the time, who wore a traditional uniform and bowler hat, was trained at the prestigious childcare institution Norland College in Bath. Trained in taekwondo, avoiding paparazzi, anti-terrorism techniques and driving in extreme weather among other practical skills during her time at the school, she had been born in Madrid and had worked for other high-profile families before joining the Cambridges. She soon developed a close relationship with her boss, Catherine. The arrangement meant that she would accompany them and care for George during their forthcoming overseas royal tour to New Zealand and Australia.

While William served out the remainder of his service as a search-and-rescue pilot before eventually bowing to the inevitable and quitting operational military service for good in September 2013, Catherine divided her days between her parents' Berkshire home and Kensington Palace. A nursery was established at the Middletons' estate so that their daughter could focus on the early days of motherhood, cushioned by her family.

Catherine wanted to replicate for her baby the loving environment she had experienced growing up. She wanted to ensure he had stability away from the media glare. She wanted him, and the children she hoped would follow, to do lots of arts and crafts and to revel in being outdoors. Speaking on the *Happy Mum, Happy Baby* podcast with host Giovanna Fletcher years later, in February 2021, Catherine spoke of her desire to create a 'happy home' for her young family. 'I had an amazing granny who devoted a lot of time to us – playing with us, doing arts and crafts and going to the greenhouse to do gardening, and cooking with us. And I try and incorporate a lot of the experiences that she gave us at the time into the experiences that I give my children now.' She went on, 'As children, we spent a lot of time outside and it's something I'm really passionate about. I think it's so great for physical and mental wellbeing and laying [developmental] foundations.'

Although called a 'commoner', Catherine is hardly a mismatch for William. Michael and Carole Middleton, her parents, are said to be worth in the region of £20 million, based on the value of their online party gift business Party Pieces and their new link to the royal family.

Carole, a former British Airways flight attendant, had started the business when pregnant with Catherine in 1981. She started making up children's party bags which she sold to friends and neighbours. Carole, who spent the first years of her life in a council flat in Southall, north-west London, then formalised her hobby as a business in 1987 with husband Michael. It is now a thriving enterprise, employing thirty people. Her parents earned enough from it to put their three children, Kate, Pippa and James, through the most expensive private schools – Marlborough College in Wiltshire in Catherine's case, which would have cost an estimated £250,000.

William's 'transitional year', as the Palace described it, would give him the chance to develop his role, to work out what causes he wanted to put his considerable celebrity and influence behind. Catherine did not have to over-complicate her role. The duchess, palace courtiers insisted, was still on maternity leave with no end date. With their London home, Apartment 1A Kensington Palace, now complete, Catherine would focus on being a wife and mother. For the time being, for Catherine, day-to-day royal duties would wait.

CHAPTER TWELVE

DOWN UNDER

'The best things in life are those that have stood the test of time'
Australia's Prime Minister, the Right Honourable Tony Abbott, commenting
on the monarchy after the Duke and Duchess of Cambridge's visit in 2014

It was billed as the most significant royal tour for a generation. The accredited media contingent from across the world for the New Zealand leg of the two-country tour Down Under in April 2014 alone was 450-strong. The numbers would swell even further when they reached Australia. New Zealand's canny Prime Minister John Key, a successful former banker, had worked out that the cost of the visit to his country, estimated at NZ$500,000, would be more than offset by the positive publicity his country would get in terms of branding and tourism. He was spot on. Television crews from US programmes such as ABC's *Good Morning America* and NBC's *The Today Show*, as well as teams from Japan, Germany and, of course, Australia, would be beaming images and reports of William and Catherine and baby George back to their huge audiences.

The royal party arrived on a rainswept military airport tarmac in New Zealand's capital, 'windy' Wellington, where they were officially welcomed by John Key. With his bare legs showing, the little prince was carried down the steps by Catherine as they alighted from the Royal New Zealand Air Force flight. She looked stunning, showing a hint of Jackie Kennedy's sixties style in a scarlet Catherine Walker coat and matching pillbox hat by Gina Foster, accessorised with a diamond brooch in the shape of New Zealand's national symbol, the silver fern, loaned to her by the Queen.

It was George's first public appearance since his christening in October and the local and international press couldn't get enough of him. Days later he was pictured taking his first public crawl at a baby group held in his honour at the official residence of his great-grandmother the Queen in New Zealand. William and Catherine watched as he played with ten other children at Government House, the Governor-General's Wellington home, an event that had been arranged by a parent support group, Plunket.

The babies who interacted with George were born within a few weeks of him. He was the star attraction. A tight media pool recorded the historic moment. The ten families, who included a single mother and a gay couple, were picked to meet the young prince, and William and Catherine spoke of their excitement. George, whose first two bottom teeth had recently popped through, happily played with the other babies, crawling on the blue patterned carpet of the Blandor Room, which was full of toys including building bricks and a xylophone. The next day he was dubbed 'Gorgeous George' by the local papers in New Zealand.

Dressed in blue dungaree shorts with a ship on the front, a white shirt and soft blue pre-walking shoes, he did not seem worried about taking toys from other children, as described later. 'Quite a bruiser,' one onlooker remarked, as George, one of the bigger children, relieved other children of their toys. Catherine, wearing a Tory Burch dress, occasionally wiped dribble from George's chin, as William chatted to some of the other parents.

'It's madness – there are babies everywhere!' William said. At one point the duchess pulled George to his feet and bounced him up and down.

The idea behind the event was to give William and Catherine the opportunity to introduce George to the world in a less formal way than usual. Kate Bainbridge, twenty-nine, a tax accountant whose daughter Sophie had been born on 11 July, said in advance of the meeting, 'I've had a few jealous looks from other parents when they found out we were meeting the Duke and Duchess. We're all first-time parents, like them, so it should be quite easy to chat to them.'

Also meeting the royal visitors were gay couple Jared Mullen and Ryan McRae and their daughter Isabella. Jared, from Oregon in the United States, and Ryan, from Australia, were chosen to represent the growing numbers of same-sex couples in New Zealand who use Plunket's parental-support service.

As the media were invited in, the Duchess was holding George on her hip as the teething prince pulled at her hair and put it in his mouth. He was a lively youngster, waving his arms and kicking his legs in excitement as he spotted the other children with their toys. Kate frequently shifted him from hip to hip, distributing his not inconsiderable weight on her slight frame. The future king then turned to a little girl called Paige, who was with her parents, Jenny Stevens, thirty-four, who is British, and New Zealand dad Mark, forty-three. George waved his arms to get her attention and touched Paige's face – before grabbing her toy wooden doll. Mother Jenny told the Duchess, 'Paige grabs toys; she's just started teething.' Catherine replied, 'George too.' Paige started crying after losing her doll to George and turned to her mother to be comforted, burying her face in her arms.

As George looked around, bored, waving his arms and indicating he wanted to be put down, Catherine gave him a blue plastic block, which George put in his mouth, but then threw to the floor. She eventually put him on the carpet and immediately George took off, taking a particular liking to a toy tambourine. Baby Eden, dressed in a floral dress and headband, got in George's way and he reached out to stroke her face. Then he reached a little too far and biffed Eden in the face with a flailing arm. She lost her headband in the mêlée, but seemed unconcerned. George grabbed at several other toys being held by other youngsters before Catherine encouraged him to crawl towards her and then pulled him to his feet.

Grant Collinge, thirty-eight, and Magda Gurbowicz, thirty-five, met the royal couple with baby Lucas. Grant said, 'We chatted to the Duke first and asked about how they and George coped with the jet lag. William said sleeping and distracting [the baby] was the best thing to get over jet lag and that's what they'd done with George. The Duchess said George was sleeping well through the night and that he's on solid food now, so that has really helped his sleeping.'

Some compared the photographs of George crawling to those taken of William thirty-one years earlier. There is a distinct difference, of course. The pictures of baby William were of him alone, with no interaction with other children. Access was restricted and there was not a member of the public in sight. Sending a clear message, William and Catherine highlighted that George will be a monarch of a very different time. If the institution of the British monarchy is to retain its relevance in a modern society, particularly in Commonwealth countries such as New Zealand and Australia, the principal players, such as William, Catherine and George must adapt to the demands of the modern world. George was unfazed by the media attention he received.

Then it was on to Australia, and George's cameo appearance in Sydney at its Taronga Zoo, where the royal couple went to officially unveil a new exhibit named in honour of the little prince, 'The Prince George Bilby Exhibit'. He even came up close to a reluctant bilby, a rabbit-like marsupial, that was named after him. Catherine and William warned keeper Paul Davies about their son's iron-like grip when he tried to grab one of the unfortunate creature's ears.

George loved the zoo. He looked on in wonder at the crowd surrounding the enclosure and wriggled his arms and legs in excitement, squealing and gurgling. Each parent took turns to hold George in their arms and then to support him as he stood up and held onto a low clear-plastic fence that surrounded the marsupial's pen. He was only interested in the real thing, and when Catherine gave him a stuffed-toy replica of a bilby, he threw it to the floor, to the delight of the crowds.

Local TV networks and commentators could not get enough of him; even the republicans were impressed. One, Shelly Horton, on Australia's top breakfast show, *Sunrise* on the 7 network, said live on air, 'I think he's a republican slayer. He's just so cute and William and Kate are such a lovely couple.' She certainly hit the mood of the country on the button, as Prince George seemed to put the case for ditching the monarchy in Australia back years. All the talk was about the impact of the 'Prince of Cuteness.' Geoff Gallop, of the Australian Republican Movement, admitted that the royal family have a 'pretty good' PR machine. This royal renaissance, however had nothing to do with spin.

The New Zealand and Australian visits gave William a chance to showcase his brand of royalty, a new style for a new generation. The huge crowds that came out to see the young family were testament to that. All the talk before the visit had been by way of comparisons with the Charles and Diana tour of 1983. Would Catherine live up to Diana and her style? Would the crowds be smaller? As soon as they had arrived in Sydney the comparisons just stopped. It was a watershed moment. This time, William carried George in his arms, as Catherine, in a stunning yellow dress giving a nod to Australia's national colours, was presented with a bouquet of flowers

After a brief welcome, the royal couple, without George, went to the Sydney Opera House where they received a rapturous welcome from a huge crowd. After stepping from their Jeep, William and Catherine walked up the steps to the opera house, admiring the amazing view of Sydney Harbour Bridge. The crowds called for the duchess to turn towards them, which prompted William to touch her hand to usher her to turn around and flash a winning smile.

William also spoke about his late mother's love for Australia. He said, 'My mother's deep affection for Australia – which you were so kind to reciprocate – needs no reminder.' He also spoke about his son: 'I don't think I could finish these brief words to you without mentioning one other family member, George, who is now busy forging his own link with Australia. Catherine and I were very grateful for the many kind messages and gifts from across the country that we received when George was born. I suspect George's first word might be 'bilby' – only because 'koala' is harder to say. We really look forward to our time here together as a family.'

He went on, 'Australia is an inspiring place, as this amazing opera house shows so vividly, and I know that a truly unforgettable few days lie ahead.' William also spoke of how important the visit was to the Queen. He said, 'The affection that my grandmother the Queen has for this nation is infectious. Her Majesty spoke recently of how, since her first visit here sixty years ago, she has been privileged to witness Australia's growing economy and flowering self-confidence.' He added, 'For Catherine, Harry and me, born in the early eighties, we've never known anything else – Australia and Australians have always been for us a beacon of confidence, creativity in the arts and sporting ability.'

It was clear that this was a different type of tour. The crowds were packed with youngsters, enthusiastically greeting this new royal family. A new younger generation of Australians clearly wanted to keep the monarchy. Figures showed that more than 60 per cent of younger Australians – the eighteen to twenty-four-year-olds, who were just children when Diana had died in Paris in 1997, wanted William and Catherine as a future King and Queen. The Diana/Catherine comparisons obviously and understandably irritated the principals and royal aides. The palace courtiers on the trip even made a point of mentioning it to the accompanying press corps. They explained that the 'Cambridge' tours, William, supported by Catherine, would be done in his way, and this was a curious hybrid of formality and more populist, photo-led events. William wanted to carve out his unique style, one which combined his passions with the traditions of the royal system. The Antipodean tour showed William's passion for the conservation of endangered species and indeed the planet itself. His support for the military at home and in Commonwealth realms was key, too, as was the couples' support for their own charitable patronages, such as Catherine's for children's hospices.

It was all part of William's development as he tried to work out the role. It was a hybrid of the old and the new, a back-to-the-future monarchy. It was less Charles and Diana, more the Queen and Prince Philip on their great Commonwealth tour of 1953 and 1954. William did not give any TV interviews on this trip, relying solely on speeches to express his thanks and views. The formal, 'tiara moments' glamorous events with Catherine decked out in diamonds while meeting the great and the good of a country were also subtly avoided. A trip to Royal Randwick racecourse, where the Queen's horse Carlton House was running in the second biggest race in the Australian calendar, was sidestepped, too. Instead, on a night off, the royal couple took their team for downtime at an evening rugby match.

Geoff Gallop, a respectful and erudite man, acknowledged that the republican movement would have to restate its argument. He said that it, too, had to get mainstream political support, something that was not currently on the agenda. Australian Prime Minister Tony Abbott, a Liberal and staunch monarchist, was one step behind the royal couple on many of the engagements. He introduced the couple to his favoured Manly Beach in Sydney's northern coastal suburbs, where he surfed regularly, and also joined them for an Anglican Easter Sunday service, despite being a Roman Catholic. Gallop was right when he said opinion polls are fickle, and the results depend on which questions are asked.

The new royal family inspired the leading Australian television networks to broadcast live coverage for two hours in the afternoon and it was wall-to-wall coverage on the popular morning shows such as *Sunrise*. If the monarchy is to remain relevant in a modern, vibrant, cosmopolitan country like Australia, the royals need to be a regular presence, not just a glamorous roadshow every seven or so years.

They need to spend more time than they do in the Commonwealth countries. Supporting the Commonwealth, as the Queen has done tirelessly since its inception, is clearly the big policy. Whether that will be enough for Prince George to be King in Australia and New Zealand one day is doubtful. But, for the moment, those wonderful images of him playing with the endangered bilby at Taronga Zoo with a proud and relaxed mum and dad looking on did the monarchist cause no harm at all and established William, Catherine and George as the most famous family unit in the world.

William was still developing his role. He is, after all, even now, still the understudy's understudy. But the press wanted more. The young royals helped sell newspapers and editors didn't want to put the golden couple back in the box. In 2014, the press had accused William of sending mixed messages after he went wild-boar hunting in Spain, the weekend before he joined his father at a London symposium to speak out against the illegal wildlife trade. He did not appear worried by the criticism, just as he wasn't concerned when it emerged that he hadn't paid the full fee for a crash course on agriculture at the University of Cambridge.

Then, just weeks after Catherine had returned from a break in Mustique with her parents, with George but without her husband, she and William headed for a holiday in the Maldives, staying at the Cheval Blanc Randheli on Noonu Atoll for seven nights. George remained at home with their Spanish nanny. Social media lit up, one message reading: 'Seriously? ... it seems it's just one long holiday for the D and D of Cambridge.'

CHAPTER THIRTEEN

FAMILY GUY

'It's one of the most amazing moments of life but it's also one of the scariest'
Prince William, on becoming a father[69]

On William's instruction, Kensington Palace officials issued a statement that Catherine was expecting their second child in the spring. His wife had been due to accompany him on an engagement in Oxford on 8 September 2014 but had decided to stay at home at Kensington Palace on doctors' advice. Once again, it emerged, she had been struck down with debilitating hyperemesis gravidarum, better known as acute morning sickness – the same condition that she had suffered with so badly during the early stages of her pregnancy with Prince George.

'It's been a tricky few days. But obviously we are basically thrilled. It's great news but early days. We're hoping things settle down and she feels a bit better,' William said to a crowd gathered outside a centre devoted to the study of China that he had just opened at the University of Oxford. 'I've got to get back and look after her now,' he added, before getting into his car and being driven away.

Catherine had not been seen in public for more than a week when she was photographed arriving at King's Cross station with her husband and their family dog, Lupo, after returning from a short break in Norfolk. She was already in the early stages of pregnancy. Only those closest to the Cambridges, including the Queen and her parents, had been told and only because once again her sickness had come on so quickly. It was soon apparent that Catherine was not able to continue her schedule of public engagements. They included her first solo foreign trip, to Malta. Her condition meant they had to go public, even though she was not yet twelve weeks pregnant.

The announcement, fourteen months after George's birth, did not surprise many; after all, the royal couple had made no secret of the fact that they had always wanted more children. Family members and political leaders issued congratulatory statements. Buckingham Palace said the Queen and members of both William's and Catherine's families were 'delighted'. Prince Harry, who was set to be bumped further down the line of succession, said it was 'exciting' and joked that he could not wait for his brother to 'suffer more' with another child. UK Prime Minister David Cameron released a statement moments after the announcement, saying: 'I'm delighted by the happy news that they're expecting another baby.' Labour leader Ed Miliband tweeted, 'Fantastic to hear that Prince George will soon be a big brother! Congratulations to the Duke and Duchess of Cambridge on their happy news.' The then Scottish National Party leader Alex Salmond also tweeted his congratulations, referring to the royal couple by their Scottish titles. He said: 'Congratulations & best wishes to the Earl & Countess of Strathearn. Wonderful to hear they're expecting their second baby – very happy news!'

It capped a fabulous year for the Cambridges following the overwhelming success of the royal tour to New Zealand and Australia. They were seen as the darlings of the global media without having to over-exert themselves. The Queen had also gifted them a country home, Anmer Hall, a Georgian mansion on her Sandringham estate in Norfolk, that used to be leased by Prince Charles's lifelong friend Hugh van Cutsem in the nineties. William had often played there as a child with the Van Cutsem boys.

The two-hundred-year-old, ten-bedroom mansion underwent a £1.5-million refurbishment paid from private funds; the refurbishment brought the décor into line with the royal couple's taste. It involved an extensive tree-planting to give the Duke and Duchess and their young family greater privacy. It included a new kitchen, a new roof, a conservatory and a tennis court, which Charles paid for. The renovation also included additional living quarters for the children's nanny, Maria, and will undergo a garage conversion to create sleeping space for their security and protection officers.

Catherine devoted her spare time on her maternity leave to adding her personal touches to make the couple's new house a home. An entirely new kitchen and a garden room with a glass roof were fitted for entertaining friends comfortably. It meant the Middletons could now join William and Catherine for Christmas when the Queen and the rest of the royal family were at Sandringham.

William had also left his job as an RAF search-and-rescue pilot in Wales in September 2013. During his seven years flying Sea King helicopters, he carried out more than 150 missions and completed more than 1,300 flying hours. Leaving the services was a real wrench, but he soon qualified to work for the East Anglian Air Ambulance, flying missions mainly from Cambridge airport but occasionally from Norwich. The couple began to split their time between their official home in Kensington Palace and the privacy they craved that Norfolk afforded them. The job had given him freedom, a sense of normality and another purpose in life, other than his predestined duty to reign one day. He became the first future king of the United Kingdom to receive a PAYE (Pay As You Earn) – that is, taxed – salary (outside of military service pay). His pay was £40,000 before tax, which he gave to charity.

William loved flying, as he described in 2021, during his *Time to Walk* Apple podcast: 'I could talk for hours about flying. As a young boy, I went and did a couple of trips, which I was very lucky to have with my father in a Wessex, a very, very old helicopter, [that] no longer flies. And I got to sit in the front. And I didn't realise at the time how much of an impression it would make on me, but I absolutely adored it.'

'And they gave me a photograph from the trip. And I had it on my wall, and I kept looking at it, and it kept calling to me like it was saying, "Come on, what's the next step?" And the RAF came along, and I went and did search and rescue with them.'

He went on, 'The moment I started the helicopter training, I realised that it was better than anything. It was one of those things that I just instantly took to and thought, "This is really cool." I really enjoy it. In 2015, I started with the Air Ambulance out of Cambridge, the East Anglian Air Ambulance it's called. And we were flying night-time operations, which is what kind of attracted me to, to doing it there. The other interesting thing about HEMS or air ambulance work was the medical side. So, as a HEMS pilot, you are fully involved in every job in terms of helping the team with the bags and getting the aircraft ready to transport a patient, or, in some cases, you're there providing

CPR and actually helping the guys with the casualty. Because you can be very remote, very rural. And so, there is only four of you at the scene. In HEMS, you've got to really solve some quite difficult situations together.'

After he helped to save the life of a gravely injured boy only a few years older than his son, George, while working for the service, William experienced a mental health crisis. In a remarkable display of frankness, he graphically described how his torment had left him depressed and feeling as if 'the whole world was dying'. He was deeply affected by what he experienced that day. Overwhelmed, he said it was as if 'something had changed' inside him.

Weeks later, his despair intensified. As he described it, it was 'like someone had put a key in a lock and opened it, without me giving permission to do that'. 'You just feel everyone's pain, everyone's suffering. And that's not me. I've never felt that before.' His blunt honesty in the podcast shows the calibre of the man. He is not afraid to wear his heart on his sleeve. He revealed how talking to colleagues and meeting the boy's family enabled him to overcome the trauma and conquer his demons, over time.

William was referring to a car accident in March 2017 which left five-year-old Bobby Hughes brain-damaged when he was knocked down by a learner driver while playing with friends outside his house in Saffron Walden, Essex. The driver had accidentally pressed the accelerator instead of the brake when she saw Bobby on the road. William kept in touch with Bobby, now ten, and his family, telling his parents, 'Anything I can ever do for you, don't hesitate to ask me, for Bobby's rehabilitation.' Speaking to the *Mail on Sunday* in December 2021, the boy's mother Carly, forty, said, 'William told us how it affected him as a father and how he felt our pain. He's amazing, a credit to our country … I've looked into his eyes and, genuinely, he has got a kind heart.'

William revealed how the shock of Bobby's case remained with him and, weeks later, sent him into a state of deep distress. 'I went to this one job. And it wasn't very far,' he says. 'The maximum we flew was fifteen minutes. And that was the great thing – you get the aircraft out as quick as you can. It was a short distance. I still remember the crew who were on, great mates of mine. We had a paramedic and a doctor on and another pilot flying with me. And the call we get is very brief, not very detailed. So, we were expecting a minor injury case.

'Immediately it became clear that this young person was in serious difficulty, sadly been hit by a car. And, of course, there are some things in life you don't really want to see. And all we cared about at the time was fixing this boy. And the parents are very hysterical, as you can imagine, screaming, wailing, not knowing what to do, you know, and in real agony themselves. And that lives with you.

'But our team got to work, and they stabilised the boy, and then it was a case of getting him out of there and into hospital. It all happened very fast. And we had the patient there in under an hour. It gives the patient the best chance of survival.

'I went home that night pretty upset but not noticeably. I wasn't in tears, but inside I felt something had changed. I felt a sort of, a real tension inside of me. And then, the next day, going back in again to work, you know, different crew. On to the next job. And that's the thing, you're not always all together. So then you can't spend a day processing it.

'And so, you sort of have a reluctance to talk about it because you don't want to hold each other up. You, you don't want to, you know, burden other people. You also don't want to think, "Oh, is it just me? Am I the only one who's really affected by that?"'

The emotional impact of Bobby's ordeal sent William into a state of mental anguish. 'And that's not me. I've never felt that before. My personal life and everything was absolutely fine. I was happy at home and happy at work, but I kept looking at myself, going, "Why am I feeling like this? Why do I feel so sad?" And I started to realise that, actually, you're taking home people's trauma, people's sadness, and it's affecting you. But I can't explain why I had that realisation what was going on because a lot of people don't have that realisation. And that is where you can slip unnoticed into the next problem.

'I think, until you've been through it, it's hard to understand. I was lucky enough that I had someone to talk to at work in the Air Ambulance because mental health where I was working was very important. Talking about those jobs definitely helped, sharing them with the team, and ultimately, in one case, meeting the family and the patient involved who made a recovery, albeit not a full recovery, but made a recovery. That definitely helped.'

William said he is marked by memories of the day. 'It even makes me quite emotional now. When they come in and say thank you, and, "Here he is. He's OK." It's ... you know, it still even affects me now. But I think, as a human being, when you see someone in such dire circumstances, basically at death's door, you can't help but be affected by that.'

His very personal experience puts his recent work – to raise awareness of the mental health of emergency service workers – into context. During an event at Kensington Palace in November 2021 he said that he had found cases involving children much harder to cope with since becoming a father.

His working role and family commitments meant he could not devote as much time to royal duties as some in the media felt he should, particularly with the Queen and Duke of Edinburgh's advancing years. The tabloids were having none of it. In a February 2016 spread, a *Sun* headline labelled William 'throne idle', a play on 'bone idle', and went on to unfairly accuse him of a reluctance to carry out public engagements while enjoying the life of a huntin', shootin' and fishin' 'gentleman country farmer'. There was, said the article, 'little doubt about William's desperation to shun the role he was born to do'. He is 'the very essence of a reluctant royal'. It seemed to completely ignore the mentally draining nature of the work he was doing.

On the eve of the Queen's ninetieth birthday, two months later, in April 2016, William agreed to speak to the BBC about his grandmother and his interpretation of royal duty as well as address the criticism he faced that he is a somewhat 'reluctant royal'. It fell to the corporation's veteran royal correspondent, Nicholas Witchell, to question William on camera about his role and his own ambitions for the monarchy he would one day lead.

William was calm and measured in his responses, in no way defensive. Without flinching at the somewhat impertinent line of questioning, he insisted he was still developing into his 'duty role' and that he 'didn't lie awake waiting to be king'. His position was clear; when the time was right, he would be ready to shoulder more royal responsibilities. But he also acknowledged that the royal family needed to modernise and said he was already thinking about how to keep the monarchy 'relevant in the next twenty years'. For now, however, he was clear that his focus was on being a father, husband and an air-ambulance pilot.

His grandmother and father, in the meantime, he said, had given him the 'time and space' to explore another means of doing a worthwhile job. Addressing the 'work-shy' jibes William just shrugged it off. 'It's something that I don't completely ignore, but it's not something I take completely to heart.' Respecting his grandmother was at his core, he revealed: 'Having lost my mother at a young age, it's been particularly important to me that I've had somebody like the Queen to look up to and who's been there and who has understood some of the more complex issues when you lose a loved one.'

William said his grandmother, the Queen, was not afraid to scold him if she felt he deserved it, relating the story of a childhood incident when he and his cousins, Peter and Zara Phillips, had got into trouble at Balmoral, the Queen's Scottish estate. 'We were chasing Zara around, who was on a go-kart, and Peter and I managed to herd Zara into a lamp-post. And the lamp-post came down and nearly squashed her, and I remember my grandmother being the first person out at Balmoral running across the lawn in her kilt; [she] came charging over and gave us the almightiest bollocking, and that sort of stuck in my mind from that moment on.'

Inevitably, his public role, or lack of it, raised questions with the public. Were the family effectively moving out of their London home, Kensington Palace? It had after all cost an astonishing £12 million and required more than one hundred workers, to carry out renovations for them to 'move in safely' to their home, the palatial four-storey, twenty-room Apartment 1A. Indeed, architects and builders working on the project spent eighteen months renovating the apartment, installing new heating, electrics and re-plastering the property. At the time William's PR team had assured the media, critical of the cost, that it was to be their base, both to live and work, when William became heir to the throne. The cost to the taxpayer was later revealed to be £4.5 million, sixteen times the cost of the average UK home. It raised eyebrows, but the couple's popularity and the fact that Charles paid the shortfall tempered the controversy. Significant structural work to restore the Grade II-listed property to a single home over a period of six months was covered by the sovereign grant, which funds the Queen and her family's official activities. The couple paid for fixtures and fittings privately.

William's PR team went into overdrive. They insisted that the Cambridges had not abandoned Kensington Palace, but would simply spend most weekends at Anmer Hall, the Norfolk residence on the Sandringham estate that the Queen had offered them. Kensington Palace would remain their primary residence both for now and when William became heir to the throne, they said. In time the assurances proved false as the Cambridges effectively took up practically full-time residence in Norfolk at the ten-bedroom mansion with swimming pool and tennis courts, until George was of pre-prep-school age, to focus on William's family and his flying career with the East Anglian Air Ambulance service.

William didn't show it publicly, or even discuss it privately with his wife, but his role in the air ambulance service was taking its toll. He found serving as an emergency responder tough on his mental health, as in the case of Bobby Hughes, referred to above. Years later, in November 2021, whilst addressing the Emergency Services Mental Health Symposium, he recalled his time working with both the Royal Air Force Search and Rescue Force and the East Anglian Air Ambulance. 'I remember the pressure of attending calls in the most stressful conditions, sometimes with tragic conclusions. I remember the sense of solidarity with my team, pulling together to do the best we could and sharing the weight of responsibility. I also remember returning home with the stresses and strains of the day weighing on my mind and wanting to avoid burdening my family with what I had seen,' he said. He eventually quit the emergency services in 2017 to focus on royal duties.

Their Norfolk residence also gave the Cambridge family the privacy they wanted. George had experienced issues with paparazzi, who had followed his nanny when they went for walks around the Kensington Palace Gardens grounds. William decided to act. Kensington Palace issued a statement about the privacy intrusions in August 2015 stating, 'a line had been crossed and any further escalation in tactics would represent a very real security risk'. How could royal security officials differentiate between paparazzi using evasive measures to elude detection and terrorists who might be posing a real threat to the third in line to the throne? The Cambridges realised their son had a future life in front of the cameras given his birthright, but were justifiably determined that he should enjoy as much of his childhood as possible before duty called. They requested a life for their son free from 'harassment and surveillance'.

After the arrival of their second child, a baby girl, Charlotte Elizabeth Diana of Cambridge, the couple announced they would take up residence in Norfolk. The royal baby was just the fillip the country needed after the humdrum general election that had been dominating the UK news. Pundits were predicting a hung parliament, but got it spectacularly wrong when the sitting prime minister, David Cameron, swept to power with a Conservative majority, abandoning the Tory/Liberal Democrat coalition.

Princess Charlotte's birth may not have created the same level of media frenzy as the arrival of her older brother, George, but it still dominated the front pages and led the television news bulletins around the world. This time, however, William was determined to avoid the media hype outside the hospital that accompanied the birth of his son and instructed his media team, led by new communications boss Jason Knauf, to keep a lid on it. The last time it had been a free-for-all, fuelled largely by foreign television networks and paparazzi putting their camera tripods and ladders down very early, to mark their positions opposite the Lindo Wing of the hospital. This time the Palace reminded everyone it was a working hospital, struck a deal with the UK media and arranged for accredited fixed positions on the pavement outside St Mary's Hospital. UK outlets would be told when the duchess had gone into hospital and were given priority and many of the foreign TV networks and agencies instead chose to set up their media tents outside Buckingham Palace at Canada Gate.

William knew it was a two-way street, but he felt he had conceded as much ground as he was prepared to. He did give the media a happy photo opportunity and took George to the hospital to see his new sister. The toddler gave a little wave to the photographers as his father whispered, 'Good boy,' to him. It was the first time he had 'officially' been seen by members of the public in Britain since the day after his birth. William drove his Range Rover to Kensington Palace to pick him up, returning minutes later and carrying him into the hospital as George obediently waved to the smitten crowd, earning a kiss from his father. After meeting Charlotte, which is a name that cost British bookmakers a small fortune, since it was one of the two favourites, George was taken back to Kensington Palace privately. Then the real show began: William, Catherine and the new little baby appearing on the steps of the Lindo Wing.

Immaculately turned out and composed, Catherine showed off the little sleeping beauty, Charlotte, to the excited crowd. The palace announced that the princess, at this stage unnamed, had been born at 8.34 a.m. on Saturday 2 May weighing 8 lbs 3 oz. Somehow the baby slept right through her big moment as her proud parents introduced her to the waiting world. She was covered in a shawl and with a bonnet over her head to protect her from the early evening chill.

'She's fast asleep,' said the duchess to her husband. William said he and his wife were 'very, very pleased', but after what had been an exhausting day, which had started with the duchess's admission to hospital at 6 a.m., they were clearly not in the mood for small talk and desperate to get home to the privacy of Kensington Palace. Catherine, now thirty-three, wearing a bespoke yellow-and-white silk shift dress with buttercup print by Jenny Packham, mouthed 'Hello' and waved to a cheering crowd, but looked incredible, having had a visit in the hospital from her hairdresser, Amanda Cook Tucker. William urged her to 'be careful' as she approached the steps. Once she had safely negotiated them, she looked up and said to him, 'This is nice. Lots of people out there. Look up there on the top.' Then, looking at her daughter, she said, 'Do you think she's cold?' William replied, 'No, she's fine, she's good.' The duchess, still looking a little concerned, said: 'Let's take her inside.'

William and Catherine had privately hoped for a little girl. The Prince of Wales, too, was thrilled at the news. Thousands of bets had been placed on the baby being a girl. The only people who did not want a girl were the UK bookmakers, who now faced collective payouts of £500,000 after the punters guessed right. As soon as the birth had been made public, there followed congratulatory messages for the couple. The Prince of Wales and the Duchess of Cornwall said they were 'absolutely delighted' by the arrival of the new princess.

The then UK prime minister and Conservative leader David Cameron, who was fighting for his political life at the time in the run-up to the general election, was among the first to congratulate the couple, writing on Twitter: 'Congratulations to the Duke and Duchess of Cambridge on the birth of their baby girl. I'm absolutely delighted for them.' Later America's President Obama, who had met George during his visit to London, would add his voice to the chorus of approval.

William opened the car door for his wife, then put his daughter in her cot seat before driving them back home. In private, he had already sent his brother, Harry, a photo of his baby girl. He and Harry had both shared the pain of losing their mother so young and William was proud that he could acknowledge her, as the name Diana was once more associated with a princess. William had run the full name past the Queen and of course Prince Charles, who was privately thrilled at the respectful nod to him, too, the name Charlotte being a female equivalent of Charles.

After two days at Kensington Palace, the Cambridges headed to Norfolk to escape the media glare. So serious were they about switching their life to Norfolk, it caught many off guard when instead of enrolling George in a London nursery, it was announced that George would be attending a Norfolk school a few days a week, starting in January 2016. This was the £33-a-day Westacre Montessori school, in East Walton near King's Lynn, a short distance from their home. It was another example of the couple putting family first and William being willing to forego convention for what he deemed best for his growing family. George would be attending classes with many ordinary students who received financial assistance and some children who had special needs. Westacre was thrilled and said George 'will get the same special experience as all of our children'.

It showed that William and Catherine wanted to give their son as normal an upbringing as possible. Instead of a posh nursery school in central London, requiring a child's name to be put on a waiting list at birth, the couple had chosen to let their son go to a school of a very different kind. While William and Harry had both marked their first day of school with a photo opportunity with scores of waiting photographers' cameras flashing, George's first day of school was private. His parents, like any other young family, dropped their son off away from the media glare. Catherine later released two photos of a smiling George in his blue hooded quilted jacket with brown suede patches and pale-blue backpack as he made his way into Westacre school.

Charlotte was christened at the Church of St Mary Magdalene, Sandringham, on Sunday 5 July 2015. She was baptised at the Lily Font by the Archbishop of Canterbury. The princess, wearing the royal christening robe, was taken to church in a Millson pram, previously used for Prince Andrew and Prince Edward. Members of the local community were invited to join in the occasion outside the church. The Cambridges, including George and Charlotte, were joined by the Queen, the Duke of Edinburgh, the Prince of Wales and the Duchess of Cornwall, Catherine's family and godparents and spouses at the service. The Duke and Duchess of Cambridge asked the following people to be godparents to Princess Charlotte, all of whom were friends or family members: Sophie Carter, James Meade, Adam Middleton, the Honourable Laura Fellowes and Thomas van Straubenzee.

★★★

With the birth of their third child, Prince Louis, at 11.01 a.m. on 23 April 2018, the Cambridge family was now complete. He was born weighing 8 lbs 7 oz at St Mary's Hospital in Paddington. William took George and Charlotte, Louis's older brother and sister, to visit him and Catherine at the hospital on the day Louis was born. It was later announced that they would name their child Louis Arthur Charles, a nod to Lord Louis Mountbatten who was Charles's mentor and great-uncle, and had been murdered by the IRA in 1979. Like his brother, Louis was baptised at the Chapel Royal at St James's Palace. An annoying republican self-publicist, shouting at the top of his voice on a megaphone, was loudly booed and drowned out by royal fans' cheers as Prince William and Catherine emerged on the steps of the maternity wing with their baby, wrapped in a G. H. Hurt & Son shawl. The shouter eventually moved on.

Louis was the first baby to be affected by the change to the ancient feudal law of male-preference primogeniture, which received royal assent on 25 April 2013 and commenced on 26 March 2015. Absolute primogeniture, for those in the line of succession born after 28 October 2011, means the eldest child, regardless of sex, precedes any siblings, so male heirs will no longer automatically leap-frog girls. Louis had replaced his uncle Harry as fifth in line to the throne, but, due to the new rules, he was still ranked lower than his sister, Charlotte. The following day Charles said the birth of his third grandchild was a 'great joy'. 'The only trouble,' he added affectionately, 'is I don't know how I am going to keep up with them.'[70]

Now a father of three, William said it had changed him forever. In an interview for the documentary, *When Ant and Dec Met the Prince: 40 Years of the Prince's Trust*, he said, 'I'm a lot more emotional than I used to be.'

'I never used to get too wound up or worried about things. But now the smallest little things, you well up a little more, you get affected by the sort of things that happen around the world or whatever a lot more, I think, as a father. Just because you realise how precious life is and it puts it all in perspective.' He clearly adores his children, and they adore him. They have a special name for him too, that they all use – 'Pops'.

The family were by now spending less time in Norfolk and were based during the week at their spacious apartment, 1A in Kensington Palace. The previous year, the Palace had announced that George would enrol as a pupil at co-educational private Thomas's Battersea Prep School, in south London, in September 2017, where the most important rule is, 'Be Kind'.

In a letter to parents, the £6,000-a-term preparatory school's headmasters, Ben Thomas and Tobyn Thomas, wrote, 'This is clearly a significant moment for their family and most certainly for Thomas's. Like so many parents, the Duke and Duchess have put a great deal of thought into the choice of their eldest child's first 'big school'. We are honoured that the aims and values of Thomas's reflect those that Their Royal Highnesses would like for Prince George's education. We are deeply conscious of the trust that they, like all Thomas's parents, are placing in us and we hope very much to live up to their expectations. The Duke and Duchess have made it clear that they do not wish Prince George's attendance at Thomas's to change its aims, values or ethos in any way. They would like, as far as is possible, for him to enjoy the same education that all of our pupils receive and for them to join the school community as all of our new parents do.'

On his first day, 7 September 2017, wearing his smart uniform of navy shorts and blazer, long, red socks and black shoes, George, then four, posed with his dad outside their house before William dropped him off at school. At the time, Catherine, who was expecting baby Louis, was suffering from severe morning sickness, and was still too unwell to join them. William carried George's bag and held his hand as the pair walked up to the entrance where they were greeted by

Helen Haslem, head of lower school. George shook her hand before being accompanied to his first class. William told Ms Haslem that George had been eagerly watching and he had noticed the other boys going into the school in their uniforms. Afterwards the proud father said, 'It went well. There was one other parent who had more of an issue with their children – so I was quite pleased I wasn't the one.' Two years later, Charlotte joined her big brother at the same school.

William has made no secret of the fact that his children are his motivation and inspiration behind everything he does, including the cause that drives him: trying to stop mankind destroying the planet. 'I've always loved nature,' he said. 'But fatherhood has given me a new sense of purpose. Now I have got George, Charlotte and now Louis in my life – your outlook does change. You want to hand over to the next generation, the wildlife in a much better condition.'

CHAPTER FOURTEEN

LASTING LEGACY

'I too have felt – and still feel – the emptiness on such a day as Mother's Day'
Prince William[71]

As far as William was concerned, it would be a one-off. He admitted that he didn't know if co-operating so publicly on such a personal film about his late mother had been wise, but he hoped that he and his brother, Harry, would not live to regret it. 'Not only is this the first time we've spoken so openly and at length about our mother, it is also the last time,' he said. His younger brother, Harry, however, clearly had other plans.

William appeared uptight as he walked into a room in July 2017 to address a select group of journalists to introduce a documentary, *Diana, Our Mother: Her Life and Legacy*. He admitted that the prospect of speaking candidly about her so publicly had been a daunting experience. 'At least, at first,' he added. In time, though, he said the ordeal had developed into a sort of healing process, too. It was a watershed moment. Watching William and Harry speak so candidly about their late mother, raw and painful as it clearly was, was compelling television. On occasion they looked close to tears.

The film hinted at a more 'in touch' style of monarchy, with a sovereign, when William's time comes, determined to do things his way, not necessarily a 'Diana-style' monarchy, but certainly one influenced by her and her compassion for humanity, and those who were suffering. Throughout, William seemed happy to abandon the stiff-upper-lip style, effectively telling the older generation of the Queen and Charles: 'That was then, this is now.'

The Prince of Wales, who had to raise his sons alone after Diana's death, did not get involved in the film. His aides said he had been kept informed, but he was not asked to be in it, or needed for the documentary, as it was clearly about the princes' mother. It was surprising, however, that they didn't think their father warranted a mention, even in passing, and the lack of acknowledgement from them privately irked Charles. He had, after all, done his best for them and loved them unconditionally.

It chronicled Diana's personal journey, her campaigns supporting the homeless, people living with AIDS and her courageous efforts to ban landmines. Despite the princes' calls for openness about mental health in the months that preceded it, it did not, however, tackle her mental frailties or touch on her clandestine affairs. It was a lovely documentary, as seen through a rose-tinted lens, a candy-coated portrayal of somebody who was, in person, far more complex, and frankly far more interesting, than her sons had shown. Perhaps this is unsurprising as they were, after all, children at the time of her death and found they could remember very few specifics about her when they began the filmmaking process. Indeed, Harry has had to carry out considerable research into Diana's life for his forthcoming book due to be published by Random House in late 2022. William and Harry even felt the need to caution their collaborators, filmmakers Ashley Getting and Nick Kent, not to expect too much from them. 'They prefaced their interviews saying, "We don't actually have that many memories of our mum,"' Getting and Kent recalled.[72]

The reality was that their grief and bereavement had suppressed, or in some cases wiped out, many memories. When filming started, somehow some memories, stored deep inside them, returned to the surface relatively quickly. William revealed how he keeps his mother's memory alive for his young children; and opened up about his final conversation with Diana, and the trauma of having a loved one ripped from their lives so suddenly. William says he thinks of his mother every day and even felt her presence at his wedding.

Among their revelations, the brothers describe how they are haunted by the final phone call Diana made to them from Paris, hours before her death. The boys cut the conversation short because they were busy playing with their cousins – something that has caused them heartache to this day. 'I have to deal with that for the rest of my life,' Harry now says of the fateful decision. He adds that: 'This is the first time the two of us have ever spoken about her as a mother. [It was] arguably probably a little bit too raw until this point. It's still raw.'

Prince Harry has revealed how William encouraged him to seek counselling after two years of 'total chaos' as he struggled to come to terms with his mother's death. The then thirty-two-year-old said Prince William implored his younger sibling to get help after 'shutting down all his emotions' for nearly twenty years following Diana's death in 1997. Harry, who was twelve years old when his mother died, admits that he ignored his grief during his teenage years, only addressing it when he was 'on the verge of punching someone' in later life.

Before that point, he endured two years of 'total chaos' when he became 'a problem' to himself – a period which included the infamous Nazi fancy dress and intimate photographs from a party in Las Vegas – but 'did not know what was wrong'. But the royal, who even turned to boxing to help ease his aggression, says he was saved by opening up about his feelings, leaving him 'in a good place' and wanting to do all he can to help remove the stigma around mental health.

Sadly, the hackneyed narrative of Diana, the saintly, wronged young wife and, by default, Charles the sinful older husband who should have treated her better, returned ahead of what would be a pretty tough month in public-relations terms for Charles. Unwittingly, perhaps, his sons and their film had added to his woes. William explained, 'Part of the reason why Harry and I want to do this is because we feel we owe it to her. I think an element of it is feeling like we let her down when we were younger. We couldn't protect her.' He went on, 'We feel we at least owe her twenty years on, to stand up for her name and remind everybody of the character and person that she was. Do our duty as sons in protecting her.'

William and Harry knew that going ahead with their documentary was a risk. It was touching and made compulsive viewing and the way they spoke of her, with a modern openness, was a natural resistance to pain. It was a film about the love of a mother for her two sons and, in crass terms, the scoop on their last conversations with her previously unshared reflections and private photos.

The Guardian newspaper praised it: 'What this programme was mainly about: two brothers, remembering the mum they lost too early, thinking about her every day, regretting not saying more that last time on the phone, still feeling those massive hugs, twenty years on. It doesn't matter who they are: that is normal, human, and moving.'

Diana's memory had clearly always been a driving force in William's life, although he doesn't wear his heart on his sleeve quite like his younger brother, Harry. 'Time makes it easier,' he said. 'I still miss my mother every day.' He went on, 'I never realised quite how much of an impact she had. I applaud her for all her dedication and drive, and I think the infectious enthusiasm and all the energy she had really rubbed off on me for causes such as [AIDS research in Africa].' He has learned to cope with his grief and to channel his energy into charitable causes, such as homelessness, which were important to the princess.

'What I understand now is that grief is the most painful experience that any child or parent can endure,' he said. 'Initially, there is a sense of profound shock and disbelief that this could ever happen to you. Real grief often does not hit home until much later. For many, it is a grief never entirely lost. Life is altered as you know it, and not a day goes past without you thinking about the one you have lost. I know that over time it is possible to learn to live with what has happened and, with the passing of years, to retain or rediscover cherished memories.' He added, 'Losing a close family member is one of the hardest experiences that anyone can ever endure. Never being able to say the word "Mummy" again in your life sounds like a small thing. I too have felt – and still feel – the emptiness on such a day as Mother's Day,' he said.

As they prepared for the next period in their lives, both princes had an eye on the past, hoping that what they have achieved as men would have made their mother proud. As Harry said, 'It's a huge shame she's not here, but I hope she'd be incredibly proud of what we managed to achieve.' For Harry, making her proud seems to be a personal mission, admitting: 'We will do everything we can to make sure she's never forgotten.'

What really emerged was that Diana's most significant legacy was the two young princes themselves, who – even in the act of recalling their mother with unqualified love and joy – were beginning to transform the face of the royal family by being its most openly approachable and compassionate members yet. The entire period was excruciating for Charles. He decamped to Birkhall, Scotland, perhaps to escape the furore and let it blow over. Diana, after all, had been a mistress of manipulation in life; twenty years after her death many still bought into the narrative that she had created. When Harry eventually praised Charles for looking after and trying to protect him and William in the aftermath of the tragedy in another film, it felt like 'too little, too late' to some close to the prince, an afterthought amid all the Diana nostalgia.

Seeing his older brother William's family grow made singleton Prince Harry think seriously about his future and he yearned to join his brother in parenthood. At the age of thirty, Harry gave a significant interview in which he made it clear he was waiting for the right moment, and of course the right woman, to come along. 'There come times when you think now is the time to settle down, or now is not, whatever way it is, but I don't think you can force these things; it will happen when it's going to happen,' he said in an interview with Sky News royal reporter Rhiannon Mills in May 2015, whilst on tour in New Zealand. 'Of course, I would love to have kids right now,' he said, 'but there's a process that one has to go through.' It was his choice of wife, however, which would lead to one of the most seismic crises in the monarchy since the abdication in 1936.

CHAPTER FIFTEEN

'THE PEACEMAKER'

'You have not been forgotten'
Prince William, during a visit to Jalazone refugee camp
in the Palestinian territories in 2018

When the Foreign and Commonwealth Office requested that he take on his most challenging diplomatic task to date, he jumped at the opportunity. The prince was well prepared before boarding the RAF Voyager that was usually used by his father as heir to the throne and the prime minister. Sir David Manning, a former British ambassador to Israel and the US, and foreign affairs adviser on the Kensington Palace team, was the perfect mentor for the prince. William spent a number of months in 2018 getting ready for his forthcoming summer visit to Israel and the occupied Palestinian territories. He was aware that he would have to carefully balance competing concerns of Jerusalem and the Palestinians.

Irritated at what has been regarded as a long-running snub, Israeli politicians had liaised with the Foreign and Commonwealth Office about a possible royal visit. The Queen and Prince Charles both felt William was ready. Until this visit, British policy had been not to sanction an official royal visit to Israel and the occupied territories until the Israeli-Palestinian conflict had been resolved. Peace talks between Israel and the Palestinians collapsed again in 2014 and once again the chasm between the two sides had widened in the ensuing years, with violence flaring up. The conflict revolves around the Palestinians wanting East Jerusalem, captured by Israel along with the West Bank and the Gaza Strip in the 1967 Middle East war, as the capital of an independent state they seek to establish in the two separate territories.

William's four-day tour marked the first time a member of the British royal family has paid an official visit to Israel. It was painstakingly designed to be non-political. He was welcomed as a 'prince and a pilgrim' by the Israeli president, Reuven Rivlin. He split his time between sites in Jerusalem which are of religious importance to Judaism, Islam and Christianity. He also honoured Holocaust victims at the Yad Vashem memorial. He paid a visit to a school and a medical facility in a Palestinian refugee camp, met the people of Tel Aviv on the seafront, and talked with tech entrepreneurs.

William took it in his stride when President Rivlin asked him to pass on a message of peace to Palestinian President Mahmoud Abbas. He shared his own desire for peace in the Middle East. As he left Ben Gurion airport in Tel Aviv for home, the British embassy tweeted, in Hebrew, that they felt the prince's trip had been a success. What may have been seen as some as 'mission impossible', appeared to have gone well. Welcoming the future king to his official residence in Jerusalem, Israel's President Reuven Rivlin said, 'I know you are going to meet President Abbas. I would like you to send him a message of peace and tell him it is about time that we have to find together the way to build confidence. Build confidence as a first step to understanding that we have to bring to an end the tragedy between us that goes along for more than 120 years.' He told President Rivlin: 'I very much hope that peace in the area can be achieved.' The move came during an extended period of tension in the area.

Before he visited the West Bank, William had walked along a street in Tel Aviv beside Israeli Eurovision winner Netta Barzilai. Despite there being no 'chicken dance', those watching were charmed. Prince William praised Tel Aviv's distinctive character and its diversity. He drew a comparison between Israel's innovation and talent, and that of the United Kingdom, and pointed to strong ties between the two nations. At the home of the UK Ambassador to Israel, William commented on Israel's vibrancy. He had noted this during a football event involving both Jewish and Arab children, and during his walk along one of Tel Aviv's beaches. He appeared completely relaxed at being in Israel, which will have had an impact on how the country is seen. In his speech at the UK ambassador's residence, he appealed for peace: 'This region has a complicated and tragic history; in the past century the people of the Middle East have suffered great sadness and loss. Never has hope and reconciliation been more needed,' he said, adding that he shared a desire with everyone present, and their neighbours, for a 'just and lasting peace'.

William was later given the full red-carpet treatment at the hilltop offices of President Abbas in the occupied West Bank. He inspected an honour guard at the Muqata, Abbas's headquarters, where the president asked him what he hoped to achieve. 'My sentiments are the same as yours in hoping that there is a lasting peace in the region,' William replied without a pause to think out his answer. He had his script, and he was not going to deviate from it.

After meeting President Abbas, William visited a UN health centre and school in Jalazone refugee camp. The camp is home to over 9,000 Palestinian refugees. It comprises closely packed concrete buildings, bordering an Israeli settlement. Armed Palestinian security men guarded the road and watched from the rooftops. On the door of the clinic there was a sign picturing an AK-47 with a red line through it.

Prince William looked on as babies had check-ups and were vaccinated. He asked camp resident Suhair Moussa, 'Is this your first child?' Her daughter Naifa was one month old. Told that it was Moussa's fifth child, he said, 'So you are well used to this now.' Outside the clinic, a Palestinian protested at Britain's colonial-era involvement in Palestine. He referred to the 1917 Balfour Declaration, which expressed British support for 'a national home for the Jewish people' in Palestine. Prince William's visit took place on the seventieth anniversary of the foundation of the state of Israel, but Palestinians remember this as the Nakba (the Catastrophe) with hundreds of thousands of Palestinians driven from their homes or fleeing the violence that ended in war between Israel and its Arab neighbours. Forty-four-year-old Nasser Migdad, who was born in Jalazone, said that he would tell William that he was responsible for the Nakba, that through the Balfour Declaration, Britain had brought the Jews to Palestine. Migdad did not get the opportunity to speak to William.

The prince's next meeting, with pupils at the girls' school in the camp, was more positive. The girls, sitting in a circle around William, asked questions through a translator. Layan Wissam, fourteen, was happy that William was visiting because 'he used his time to sit with [them] and listen to [them]. [The girls] sat with an important figure.' Another girl, fifteen-year-old Rahaf Ziyad, told the prince about the educational challenges they faced. He asked what could be done to help. She suggested expanding the school as there are many students and the classrooms are small. She said they would create a garden and name it after Princess Diana. William liked the idea. Later, UN director of operations in the West Bank Scott Anderson described Jalazone was 'emblematic', next door to a settlement and with much higher unemployment than the settlement. He was grateful for the opportunity to show the prince some of the challenges faced by the camp resident, also some of the opportunities it gave them.

In the centre of Ramallah, the prince watched Palestinian dancers and listened to a young man sing '*Ya Watani*', 'Oh, My Homeland', popularised by the Lebanese singer Fairouz. He also enjoyed traditional dishes, such as falafel, shawarma and kanafeh, and had a game of football with local children. He was given football shirts with the names of his children.

Speaking alongside President Abbas, Prince William said, 'The Palestinian side is committed to the peace process with the Israelis, so both states could live peacefully together within the borders of 1967.' The West Bank has been mostly peaceful recently, compared with outbursts of fighting along Israeli border with Gaza, which is ruled by Abbas's main Palestinian rival, Hamas. 'My message tonight is that you have not been forgotten' the prince said. 'The United Kingdom stands with you.'[73]

As he travelled back to Jerusalem, where earlier he had been photographed wearing a kippot and touching the Western Wall, William had good reason to believe his visit had been a success. He reserved a wry smile at one overblown headline emblazoned across the front page of the *Daily Express*. It read: 'WILLIAM THE PEACEMAKER'. As one senior diplomatic aide said, putting it into perspective, 'Yes he did well, but he's no Henry Kissinger.'

To clarify what he meant, it needs explaining that Henry Kissinger, born in 1923, is a German-born American academic and politician who played a dominant role in US foreign policy in the late sixties and seventies and won the Nobel Peace Prize for his part in negotiating an end to US involvement in Vietnam. His guiding philosophy was that foreign policy should serve the national interest – a pragmatic outlook dubbed 'realpolitik'. Kissinger arranged Nixon's two famous summit visits, to China and the Soviet Union, in 1972. These visits introduced the policy of détente, by which the US sought to defuse tensions with the communist powers.

CHAPTER SIXTEEN

FAB FOUR

'Catherine has been absolutely ...' said Prince Harry. 'Wonderful,' said Meghan.

Prince Harry and Meghan, praising the Duchess of Cambridge

William had always looked out for his younger brother. Perhaps, then, it was no surprise that he was a little anxious that Harry's whirlwind relationship with divorced American actress Meghan Markle had resulted in his brother's marriage proposal so soon after they had first met. He felt, close sources confirmed, that Harry had been too impetuous, given what is expected of any woman who marries into their family. Did he really know her well enough? Did she know what being a member of the royal family would entail? William, having always been close to Harry, was probably the only person qualified to raise this delicate issue directly, and so he felt duty-bound to do so.

No matter how well-intentioned William's questions were, they sent Harry into a spin. He had become almost unhealthily protective of Meghan, and William's 'big brother' chat riled him. Indeed, he took his brother's remarks as a criticism of his judgement. In his view, it was evidence that William didn't support the marriage or his choice of bride. Without doubt, it was an overreaction; Harry was being far too sensitive. But relations between the two men never recovered. It was the start of the so-called royal feud between the brothers.

To be fair to William, Harry and Meghan's relationship had moved on apace since they first met on a blind date in early July 2016. That night they spent three hours together at Soho House's Dean Street townhouse, where Meghan had been staying during her trip to London. The stunning, biracial divorcee and Harry hit it off straight away, in fact the couple seemed obsessed with each other from the start, both of them admitting they 'felt a real chemistry'.

Meghan Markle was co-star of the Netflix drama series *Suits*, in which she played paralegal Rachel Zane. In 2015 she explicitly stated that she identifies as biracial, and she told *Elle* magazine in December 2016, 'Being biracial paints a blurred line that is equal parts staggering and illuminating.'

Despite Harry's international fame, Meghan, who had posed for snaps outside the palace on an earlier visit twenty-one years earlier, claimed she didn't have preconceived notions about Harry being a prince before the date. 'Because I'm from the States, you don't grow up with the same understanding of the royal family,' she explained during the BBC interview carried out after their engagement. 'I didn't know much about him, so the only thing that I had asked [our mutual friend] when she said that she wanted to set us up, was, "Well, is he nice?" because if he wasn't kind, it just didn't seem like it would make sense.'

When news of Meghan Markle's engagement to Prince Harry broke, in 2017, her childhood best friend Ninaki Priddy said, 'I'm not shocked at all. It's like she has been planning this all her life. She gets exactly what she wants, and Harry has fallen for her play. She was always fascinated by the royal family. She wants to be Princess Diana 2.0. She will play her role ably, but my advice to him is to tread cautiously.'[74]

Describing their first meeting, Meghan said, 'We met for a drink and then I think very quickly into that we said, "Well, what are we doing tomorrow? We should meet again."' From there, romantic holidays followed and as far as Harry was concerned all the stars aligned. She was the one. At the photocall at Kensington Palace which followed their engagement announcement, Harry was asked when he knew Meghan was the woman for him. He quickly replied, 'The very first time we met.'

After their second date, Harry invited Meghan to accompany him on a trip to Africa just three or four weeks later. She obliged and they camped out with each other under the stars. Their romance was natural, he said, continuing to say: 'We were really by ourselves, which was crucial to me to make sure that we had a chance to get to know each other.' After four months of dating in secret, news of their romance was revealed by journalist Camilla Tominey in her brilliant scoop on 31 October 2016. A source told the *Sunday Express* that Harry was 'happier than he's been for many years' and was 'besotted' with Miss Markle. On the same day, she posted a sweet photo on her Instagram of two bananas spooning, possibly hinting at the new love in her life.

A few days later Harry confirmed his relationship in a formal statement on 8 November 2016, in which he pleaded with the press and trolls on social media to stop the 'wave of abuse and harassment' that had been directed at his girlfriend. He claimed he had been involved with 'nightly legal battles' to stop the media from publishing defamatory stories about Meghan and their relationship. Many thought the actress would be prepared for the attention, although she said she had 'never been part of tabloid culture'.

William had been against issuing the formal statement. His father, who was on an important visit to the Gulf states and had just arrived in Bahrain, was also opposed to the statement. Prince Charles was given just twenty minutes' notice that the statement was going to be released. The prince had given an interview to the *Evening Standard* on climate change, having just collected a prestigious award, but his aides knew that the statement, much of it hurriedly drafted by Harry himself, in which he criticised the press and the racist undertones of some commentaries, would dominate the news cycle. Far from being 'crushed', as some later claimed, Charles was disappointed by his son's lack of deference. 'He would never have done such a thing if the Queen was on tour. There is a grid system, but Prince Harry seemed to think when it came to Meghan Markle, she would always take precedence,' one former aide said.[75]

William, too, privately thought his brother had overreacted. 'It was all a bit dramatic, a bit OTT,' one of his ex-aides later recalled. On 27 November 2016, William released a statement to clear up speculation that he had been unhappy with Harry's decision to open up about his relationship, saying, 'I absolutely understand the situation concerning privacy and support the need for Prince Harry to support those closest to him,' he stated, backing up his brother. After spending New Year's Eve in London, the couple embarked on a romantic trip to Norway to catch the Northern Lights. Harry put a lot of thought into its planning and wanted to make the holiday as romantic and special as possible. In early 2017, Harry introduced his girlfriend to his sister-in-law Catherine and Princess Charlotte at apartment 1A at Kensington Palace. They reportedly 'got on fabulously'.

Meghan spoke openly about her relationship for the first time in the October 2017 issue of *Vanity Fair*. 'We're a couple. We're in love. I'm sure there will be a time when we will have to come forward and present ourselves and have stories to tell, but I hope what people will understand is that this is our time,' she said in the cover story. 'This is for us. It's part of what makes it so special, that's just ours. But we're happy. Personally, I love a great love story.' That month, for the first time she accompanied Harry to an official royal appearance at the Invictus Games opening ceremony. They also spent time with Meghan's mother, Doria Ragland. The couple even shared a sweet smooch at the closing ceremony of the Games. Their engagement was finally announced on 27 November 2017 and was marked with a photoshoot and a formal interview.

Meghan, at the outset, had been seen as a breath of fresh air. She vowed to rise to the challenge and throw herself into her new role even before they married. Their whistle-stop tour of the UK, including visits to Edinburgh, Cardiff, Belfast, Lisburn and London, was greeted by enthusiastic crowds wherever they went. They, as 'the new kids on the block', were hogging the newspaper headlines. William, who in adulthood expected to be treated with deference as he would one day be king, was put out when his brother and soon to be sister-in-law slotted in an engagement to Cardiff on 18 January 2018 that clashed with one of his. William, who is competitive by nature even when it comes to media coverage, chose to debut his new and dramatic buzz cut as he cheered up patients at a London hospital that same afternoon, knowing the papers would feature him on their news pages too.

When Meghan first arrived on the scene and met her future father-in-law Charles, she was bowled over by his gentlemanly charm. Her warmth for Harry's father led to a softening of relations between the prince and his second son, too. Harry now had somebody other than his older brother with whom to discuss family matters, and Meghan's opinion really mattered to him. In turn, Charles, charmed by the beautiful actress, was completely taken with her, but not 'taken in'. 'She is so intelligent and so nice,' Charles remarked. 'She makes Harry happy. We could not like her more.'

The Queen, too, had been taking a keen interest in Meghan, thanks not least to their shared love of dogs. The day before the wedding, the Queen, who weeks earlier had lost her last corgi, appeared to share a car with Meghan's beagle, a rescue dog called Guy. During Harry's engagement interview, he claimed that when Meghan took tea with the Queen the corgis took to her immediately, even going so far as to lie on her feet. It raised a few insiders' eyebrows, especially as any newcomers who try to get into her good books by patting the dogs are sharply told, 'Don't do that, they don't like it.' The insider said, 'What she really means is she doesn't like it.'

What happened next shocked the world and rocked the British monarchy to its foundations.

On the surface, everything seemed fine. On 26 April, the Palace confirmed that William would be Harry's best man at his wedding. 'The Duke of Cambridge is honoured to have been asked and is very much looking forward to supporting his brother at St George's Chapel, Windsor, on 19 May,' the statement said. But in the preceding months William and the rest of the family had noticed a difference in Harry. He seemed to be permanently on edge.

Charles is a stickler for showing deference to the Queen and her office. His two sons weren't the same, however, at acquiescing to him and his office. But in the build-up to the royal wedding and beyond, Harry had begun to show his father, who was, after all, bankrolling the entire event, much more respect. Charles did everything he could to ensure his youngest son had the wedding he wanted. To this day, however, Charles admits he often finds it difficult to gauge either of his sons' occasionally unpredictable moods. 'In that aspect of their nature, both princes are very much like their mother,' one close source confirmed. 'They both have quite extreme mood swings, just as Diana did,' said a former courtier. 'She could be your best friend one minute and the next your worst enemy.'

The stress seemed to be getting to the couple, who by now were being treated by acupuncturist to the stars, Ross Barr in the lead-up to the wedding. Barr's treatments dealt with anything from infertility to hair loss and relationship problems but seemed to have failed to have a lasting impact on Harry. Staff and family said he was 'petulant and short-tempered' with members of staff. On occasion, he raised his voice and even swore, 'What Meghan wants, she gets,' he said to the

Queen's royal dresser and confidante Angela Kelly. When his tiresome behaviour reached the Queen's ears, she was disappointed in the way he spoke to a valued member of staff and addressed the issue with him personally.

'Angela is very special to the Queen,' said a senior figure. 'She is an essential part of the Her Majesty's inner circle, and the two women have developed a friendship over the years. When she heard what happened she was a little disappointed, especially as the Duke of Sussex would have known Angela was just trying to do her best for him and his bride-to-be and wouldn't really be able to answer back,' the source added. The insider pointed out that some people had thought it was Meghan who had been behaving like a demanding Hollywood star, but it wasn't that at all, it was her groom-to-be, perhaps, just trying a little too hard to please her.

The Queen also questioned why Meghan, as a divorcee, even needed a veil for the ceremony, given that this was her second marriage. In the end, the Duchess wore Queen Mary's diamond bandeau tiara, made in 1932.

William waded into the furore, too, when he asked the Queen to ban Meghan from wearing jewellery from the royal collection. He also sought assurances that his brother's bride-to-be would not wear any jewellery in the collection once worn by Diana, Princess of Wales, even though his wife Catherine had been allowed to wear some, due to her seniority and position as the next Princess of Wales and future Queen Consort.

The whole affair had, it seemed, been another cause for a period of bad blood between the two princes, that had been triggered when they discussed the speed of Harry's relationship with Meghan. William could see his brother was smitten, and it became obvious, almost immediately, that his younger brother wanted to marry her. It was clear that the close bond between the brothers had been damaged. During the pre-wedding walkabout, which echoed what had happened before his brother William's wedding, Prince Harry was greeted with shouts of 'good luck' and thanked one woman who had travelled from Canada for coming so far.

Tens of millions of people from around the world tuned in to see the couple wed at Windsor Castle on 19 May 2018. Celebrities Oprah Winfrey and ex-footballer David Beckham and his ex-Spice

Girl/fashion designer wife, Victoria, were among the stars who joined the royal family. But all eyes were on the bride, who wore a Givenchy gown for the ceremony and a chic Stella McCartney halter dress for the reception at Frogmore House. On 15 October, Kensington Palace announced that the Duke and Duchess of Sussex were expecting their first child. The announcement came as the couple landed in Australia for their first joint royal tour and on 6 May 2019, baby Archie Harrison Mountbatten-Windsor arrived. The baby boy was seventh in line for the throne and the Queen and Prince Philip's eighth great-grandchild. Everyone was delighted with the royal baby's arrival. But, beneath the surface, all was not well between the brothers.

It emerged that not only had the brothers fallen out, but Catherine and Meghan's relationship had soured when they had clashed over a misunderstanding involving a bridesmaid dress. In November, the *Daily Telegraph* reported that Meghan made Catherine cry at a dress fitting for Princess Charlotte.[76] Meghan confirmed there was a disagreement between the women in the days before her 2018 royal wedding to Prince Harry. However, during the now infamous Oprah interview, she denied making her sister-in-law cry, saying, 'The reverse happened.' At the time, everyone kept silent, but the simmering resentment between the couples was about to blow up into a full-scale feud.

CHAPTER SEVENTEEN

DIFFERENT PATHS

'We are certainly on different paths at the moment, but I will always be there for him,
and as I know he will always be there for me'

Prince Harry, Duke of Sussex, discussing his relationship
with his brother Prince William, 21 October 2019

A humorous exchange at the Royal Foundation Forum on 28 February 2018, whilst being light-hearted banter, had the ring of truth about it. The hand-picked interviewer, Tina Daheley, asked the royal group if they ever have family disagreements – which prompted awkward giggling.

"Oh, yes,' Prince William said in response.

'[They are] healthy disagreements,' Harry added quickly.

When Daheley asked for more detail about the disagreements, Harry, in his clever self-effacing and funny manner side-stepped revealing anything concrete, saying, 'I can't remember, they come so thick and fast.'

And when Daheley pushed a little further and asked if any of their most recent disagreements had been resolved, William said, 'Is it resolved? We don't know,' before elaborating a little.

His words were telling. 'We've got four different personalities and we've got the same passions to make a difference, but different opinions,' he said. 'I think those opinions work really, really well. Working as a family does have its challenges and the fact that everyone is laughing shows they know exactly what it's like. We're stuck together for the rest of our lives.'

He seemed to say it all. The expression 'stuck together' suggested it was a bond neither the Cambridges or the Sussexes were comfortable with. Indeed, he had a point. For decades, William and Harry had always been 'the boys' — Diana's tragic sons robbed of their mother by a car crash — almost joined at the hip. When William married Catherine, Harry had become the happy gooseberry, always seen larking around with his sister-in-law at events. When he did go it alone, with the formation of his Lesotho-based HIV/AIDS charity Sentebale, in memory of Diana, and then the Invictus Games, his brother and sister were always there to support him. When they united for Heads Together, the successful initiative to end the stigma surrounding mental health, again they all seemed to dovetail perfectly, partnering with inspiring charities with a common goal of changing the national conversation on mental wellbeing. Front-line veteran Harry focused on the military, working with Contact; Catherine concentrated more on helping youngsters and schoolchildren with Young Minds and Place2Be; and William advocated causes concerning men's mental health, later using his connections in the football world to reach out to those who were suffering in silence. In PR terms, it seemed to work; there appeared to be a fun, positive chemistry between them all.

When single mother Karen Anvil, aged forty, snapped the four young royals walking arm-in-arm on Christmas Day 2017 as they walked to St Mary Magdalene Church, on the Sandringham estate in Norfolk, she had no idea what she had done. But when the snap was distributed via a clever photographer's syndication agency to publications around the world, earning Karen more than £50,000, a new, but short-lived, phenomenon was born.

Behind the scenes and smiles, however, all was not well. Harry, a war-worn veteran now, was not comfortable being lectured by his older brother. He had found a woman he loved and married her. Yes, it had been a whirlwind romance; yes, she was biracial; yes, she was a divorced actress; but emphatically yes, he was besotted with her and was going to marry her no matter what. When William advised caution and urged his impetuous younger brother, out of love and concern, to take his time getting to know Meghan, Harry took umbrage. William had failed to see that Harry was changing, becoming his own man. It was a resentment that, sadly, would fester.

The *Mail on Sunday* columnist, Rachel Johnson, the feisty and sharp-witted sister of UK Prime Minister Boris Johnson, was among the first to see the cracks in the enforced joint 'foundation' straight away. As the Fab Four sat in their safe smart casuals in front of a bright-blue backdrop burbling about 'making a difference together', headliner William said his few words. He was used to being the star turn, except, this time, he wasn't — newcomer Meghan was.

She didn't hold back. Women don't need to 'find' a voice, Meghan replied, women already HAD a voice. The problem was they didn't feel 'empowered' to use it and people, i.e., men, had to be 'encouraged' to listen. 'There is no better time to shine a light on women feeling empowered, and people really helping to support them,' she said, namechecking the #MeToo and Time's Up movements. It was enough to make William shift in his seat, which he indeed appeared to do.

'This was risky on a couple of fronts. Over here, we secretly don't like women who speak out too loudly and often (I should know), let alone women who order other women to speak out and men to listen,' Ms Johnson wrote. 'And as a nation, we certainly prefer royal women who don't really speak, like the Queen, or the Duchess of Cambridge, as demonstrated by that number-one hit about a perfect girlfriend with the lyric "you say it best when you say nothing at all".'

She went on to point out the problem for this cosy new arrangement for the 'Fab Four' and the new band member. 'If you look at the Royal Foundation, it divvies things up, so Harry is armed forces, Kate is young people and mental health, and William is across conservation. Meghan — mark my words — will be banging the drum for "wimmin". We will have our first feminist-activist princess. Which is great and could be fine (though I feel women are not victims in need of charity but continued advocacy), but equally it could end up with tensions in the band — and royalty is a far harder show to keep on the road than rock 'n' roll.'

Then she hit the nail on the head: 'Meghan would do well to remember she is becoming a member of a constitutional hierarchy, which depends on everyone knowing their exact place in the pecking order and toeing endless invisible lines.'

Meghan, as her track record showed, was not one for conformity, or worrying about chains of command. Even as a little girl if she saw what she deemed injustice she did something about it, including destroying a sexist television commercial at the age of eleven. As a schoolgirl, Meghan had been asked to evaluate messages in commercials and she was struck by an ad for Ivory Soap, a Procter & Gamble product, which showed a sink full of dirty dishes, with a voiceover saying, 'Women are fighting greasy pots and pans with Ivory Soap'. 'I don't think it's right for kids to grow up thinking that Mom does everything,' she said in her first-ever TV appearance, in 1993. She wrote to Procter & Gamble, asking them to change the commercial to say, 'People all over America are fighting greasy pots and pans,' not just women. P&G complied.

Even before the wedding, Meghan talked of 'hitting the ground running'. It was a great in a soundbite, but perhaps it would have been better to pace herself, to learn the royal ropes slowly but surely, not to upset members of the family by treading on their toes. After all, everything in the Royal Foundation had been running smoothly for years, there wasn't any need for a radical shake-up.

In truth, despite the enforced smiles at that event, it was doomed from the outset, and it had nothing to do with differing personalities or egos. The concept was simply impractical and didn't leave much room for independence for either the Cambridges or Sussexes. There wasn't any room for them to grow or to express themselves individually. Far from enabling them to achieve their goals it somehow shackled them, forcing them to perform under one banner. Rather like the original 'Fab Four' [The Beatles], who split after bitter infighting, the same fate would befall the royal quartet, only it took months, not years.

Within twelve dramatic months, it had all come crashing down. The following February, it was announced that William and Harry's households were to split to create separate courts. The spin doctors tried to dress it up as just part of the plan, but why then had there been the fanfare for the foundation the previous year?

The work to create the two separate households, Kensington Palace aides claimed, had been underway since the wedding of Harry and Meghan the previous May. Add to this the imminent arrival of the Sussexes' first child and it was decided that the carve-up would start sooner.

A possible move next door to William and Catherine's palatial Apartment 1A was turned down by the Sussexes, it emerged later, due to timing and not to the fact that the two brothers didn't want to be neighbours. When they had gone round to have drinks at William's apartment whilst living at the compact Nottingham Cottage opposite, Meghan had been surprised by the disparity between the brothers.[77] The reason given was that the extensive renovations on the residence, including the removal of asbestos, would have to be done before they could move in, and by now they were tired of being cooped up in their modest accommodation inside the Kensington Palace 'compound'.

It was announced that the Sussexes would move to Frogmore Cottage, on the Windsor Estate, in the shadow of the Queen's castle. Significantly, the main division involved is said to be of their communications team, which, it was said, would allow the couples the freedom to shape their own media approaches. Under the surface, there were growing tensions and stories started to emerge that the Sussex household was not a happy place to work. There were claims of bullying and complaints about what some staff deemed unacceptable behaviour by Meghan.

Simultaneously, the shake-up of the press team left William with all the key players. Christian Jones, who was thirty, had joined Kensington Palace as Deputy Communications Secretary from the Department for Exiting the European Union. He had been photographed in Notting Hill with the Duchess of Sussex, when the joint Kensington Palace press office had been headed up by Jason Knauf. Jason, who had joined the Palace in 2015, would soon move to a new role as Chief Executive of the William and Catherine Royal Foundation. Instead of looking after Meghan and Harry, sharp operator Jones took the job running the Cambridges' media affairs. Civil Service highflyer Simon Case CVO, briefly director of strategy at GCHQ, had also been appointed as William's private secretary, so the future king had got all his ducks in a row with regard to assembling a top team. Simon Case was soon poached back by Prime Minister Boris Johnson, in September 2020, after two years as William's right-hand man, to run Whitehall as head of the Civil Service. At forty-two, he became the youngest ever cabinet secretary, replacing Sir Mark Sedwill.

Meghan enlisted Amy Pickerill, who had worked for the joint Kensington Palace team in communications, as her first private secretary and American Sara Latham as the couples' communications secretary. Pickerill, a Nottingham University graduate, didn't last long. She quit in May 2019 becoming the fourth member of Meghan's team to leave in quick succession, following the planned departures of the Queen's former assistant private secretary, Sam Cohen, and the resignations of Meghan's personal secretary Melissa Touabti. Her female personal protection officer also left after the visit to Australia, Fiji and Tonga. Were the wheels falling off Meghan's wagon?

At the time, the Palace was at pains to dispel rumours that the Duchess was difficult to work with. Privately, however, Meghan believed that the Palace aides and the royal family were briefing against her and trying to discredit her, as bullying accusations emerged. She was worried that claims that she had reduced staff members to tears by her behaviour were gaining credence. One courtier said that the duchess 'governed by fear'. The swirl of negativity around her helped make up her mind, that leaving 'the Firm' was the right thing for her and Harry to do. It was clear 'Diana's boys' – as mentioned previously, always seen as almost joined at the hip as youngsters – had become different adults, with very different outlooks on life.

William was alarmed at some of the stories that had come to his ears about his sister-in-law's treatment of staff. Although William had been known to be short-tempered, he had always tried to adhere to his father and grandmother's directive to be polite and cordial to staff because they were not able to answer back. On occasion, he had exploded, but if he did, he would be the first to personally reach out and apologise. Despite denials, both from her lawyer Jenny Afia, and from Meghan herself, claims of her 'bullying' circulated.

Schillings lawyer Jenny Afia denied that the Duchess of Sussex ever bullied staff or inflicted 'emotional cruelty' on underlings and 'drove them out' in a BBC documentary, *The Princes and the Press*, presented by BBC Media Editor Amol Rajan in November 2021. Ms Afia insisted that Meghan didn't 'repeatedly and deliberately hurt anyone'. But she added that she 'wouldn't want to negate anyone's personal experiences'. She also claimed there were 'massive inaccuracies' in Valentine Low's report in *The Times*. The veteran reporter responded via Twitter, saying, 'How odd. Perhaps she would care to let me know what they were.'

It was later discovered that Jason Knauf had made the allegations of bullying the Palace's human resources department in October 2018. He had also emailed Simon Case, Prince William's private secretary, having already raised bullying concerns with head of HR Samantha Carruthers. Knauf had been appointed communications secretary to the Duke and Duchess of Cambridge in 2015. He later took on the same role for the Duke and Duchess of Sussex after their marriage in 2018. Mr Knauf resigned one month after reporting the allegation, but then returned to head up the new Royal Foundation of the Cambridges. Knauf, who stood down from his role as CEO of the Royal Foundation in December 2021, also gave advice to Meghan on her letter to her father, which was at the centre of her privacy action against Associated Newspapers, publisher of the *Mail on Sunday*. William was concerned that the situation was out of control, but his relationship with his brother had deteriorated so badly that he couldn't go to him and ask him to try to calm the situation down by speaking to his wife.

Not only was the brothers' relationship strained, but their wives weren't on the best of terms either. This dated back to a story first revealed by Camilla Tominey, an executive and respected royal writer at the broadsheet *Daily Telegraph*, that Meghan had made Catherine cry over a spat involving a 'flower girl' bridesmaid's dress for Princess Charlotte to wear on Meghan and Harry's wedding day. In the Oprah Winfrey interview, Meghan claimed it was the other way round, and that it was Catherine who had made her cry. So, relations between the Cambridges and the Sussexes were at rock bottom.

Charles feared the worst if his two sons clashed, especially when the women they loved were involved. He knew that they were both strong-willed, stubborn even; conflict would be very difficult to manage and could have a detrimental impact on the monarchy itself. Occasionally the level of belligerence between the princes and, indeed, towards him, had shocked the prince. On occasion, both his sons have challenged him. William has even been known to speak firmly in his father's face, reminiscent of his mother's hot temper, which Charles had to deal with on a frequent basis during their marriage.

Whilst wanting to knock his sons' heads together, Charles stayed out of the quarrels, hoping that they would all stop being so sensitive, see the bigger picture and come to their senses. 'He hates confrontation,' said one source close to the prince. 'He tends to think along the lines of least said, soonest mended.' In this instance, with hindsight, it appears to have been the wrong call. Meghan and Harry were now set on a course that would have damaging repercussions for William, Charles and the monarchy as an institution.

The Duke of Sussex has responded to speculation about a rift between him and his brother. Prince Harry said, in an ITV documentary, that the two were 'on different paths at the moment', but that he loved William 'dearly'. During an interview for ITV News's exclusive documentary, *Harry & Meghan: An African Journey*, Meghan, Duchess of Sussex, opened up about the difficulties of living under the intense media scrutiny she's experienced ever since she married into the royal family.

Of the British tabloids' treatment of her, she told ITV's Tom Bradby, 'I never thought that this would be easy, but I thought it would be fair and that's the part that's really hard to reconcile.'

She began by saying, 'I've said for a long time to 'H' – that's what I call him – it's not enough to just survive something, right? That's not the point of life. You've got to thrive; you've got to feel happy. I really tried to adopt this British sensibility of a stiff upper lip. I tried, I really tried. But I think that what that does internally is probably really damaging.'

After Bradby noted that the wealth and status associated with her and the royal family inevitably goes hand in hand with media attention, Meghan responded, 'I think the grass is always greener. You have no idea. It is really hard to understand what it's like. The good thing is that I have got my baby and I have got my husband and they are the best.'

In the same interview, Meghan said that her British friends had warned her against marrying Prince Harry. 'When I first met Harry, my friends were so excited. My US friends were happy because I was happy,' the duchess said. 'But my British friends, they were sure he was lovely, but they said I shouldn't do it because, "The British tabloids will destroy your life".'

The Sussexes' tour of southern Africa, which ran from the end of September to early October 2019, had been going smoothly. The couple went to South Africa at the request of the UK's Foreign and Commonwealth Office and Meghan stayed in South Africa with baby Archie. The first section of the tour appeared to have gone well.

They had posed beautifully for a photo opportunity with Archie and revered anti-apartheid campaigner Archbishop Desmond Tutu in Cape Town, and danced and spoke eloquently in Nyanga township on the outskirts of the city. Harry then went on to visit Angola, Malawi and Botswana for his charity work, accompanied mainly by television crews, as it was too expensive for most print media to follow.

Harry was clearly unsettled as he snapped at Sky correspondent Rhiannon Mills. This unjustified reaction happened when she tried to squeeze in an unscheduled line of questioning during a visit to Mauwa Health Centre in Malawi. Perhaps he was on edge because he knew what was about to break imminently. Hours later, the Sussexes issued an unprecedented statement in which he accused sections of the British tabloid press of pursuing a 'ruthless campaign' against his wife. Harry's public statement was released on the couple's website on 1 October, coinciding with the announcement that Meghan was suing the *Mail on Sunday* newspaper after it had published a private letter she wrote to her father, Thomas Markle. The paper denied wrongdoing and confirmed it would defend the case. Harry claimed some newspapers had 'vilified (his wife) almost daily for the past nine months' and published 'lie after lie' at Meghan's expense because she was out of public view on maternity leave. It was an unprecedented move that took place on what was, after all, a Foreign and Commonwealth Office-backed official royal visit.

On the same tour, away from the accompanying accredited journalists, the couple were filming a documentary with ITV and their 'friendly' journalist Tom Bradby, in which both Meghan and Harry would speak out. Meghan told ITV about her serious difficulties coping with being a member of the royal family, and Harry, for the first time, publicly confirmed his relationship with his brother William was not good, appearing to support all the speculation of a rift between them.

Tom Bradby spoke to Meghan about her experience of a year which had seen her face ever more public attention before and after giving birth to Archie in May. She looked pained as she described her private struggle to cope through the pregnancy and the early stages of motherhood amid the pressures of the media interest in her public life as a member of the royal family. She said the intense spotlight and incessant negative press coverage from some sections of the media had made it harder at a time when she was already feeling 'really vulnerable'. Asked by Bradby how she was coping, Meghan said, 'Thank you for asking because not many people have asked if I'm OK. But it's a very real thing to be going through behind the scenes.' Bradby then added, 'And the answer is, would it be fair to say, not really OK? That it's really been a struggle?' Looking close to tears, the professional actress replied, 'Yes.'

Harry then spoke for the first time about his strained relationship with his brother. It came after reports of tensions between William and Harry had been stoked by a decision for them to have separate offices and to split their charitable foundation. He said that because they were both under pressure it was inevitable that 'stuff happens'. He added, unconvincingly, 'But we are brothers. We will always be brothers. We are certainly on different paths at the moment. But I will always be there for him, as I know he will always be there for me.'

The cat was now well and truly out of the bag, and there was no way of putting it back. The break-up of the so-called 'Fab Four' was now complete; over and above that, William was deeply disappointed that his brother had broken the bond of trust between them.

CHAPTER EIGHTEEN

ROYAL RIFT

'We're very much NOT a racist family'
Prince William

Finding a workable balance between private life and public duty has always weighed on William's mind. Ironically, this was central to his brother Harry's decision to walk away from fulfilling a meaningful role in the royal family, too. There had long been talk that Harry and his wife Meghan were unsettled with their role before it emerged that they had decided to shun a traditional royal Christmas with the Queen and the rest of the senior royals at Sandringham and instead head off on holiday to Canada. In private, however, all hell had been let loose, with Prince Charles and his youngest son exchanging correspondence and calls after Harry had bluntly told his father he wanted to find a new semi-attached role within the system for him and his wife: half in, half out.

On 8 January, the excellent journalist Dan Wootton, then assistant editor of *The Sun*, revealed this 'civil war' at the heart of the royal family as Meg and Harry 'quit the Royals', writing that the Queen and Charles were furious. The headline writers coined the term 'Megxit' for the banner headline – a word that the Collins Dictionary would later announce had received an official entry as it became firmly ingrained in our lexicon in 2020. It even became their official word of the year. Within hours, the Duke and Duchess of Sussex issued a statement that they were looking to 'carve out a progressive new role' for themselves within the monarchy. As part of this they said they would divide their time between North America and the UK, confirming Wootton's scoop and creating a rift within the royal family who were said to be 'disappointed' by the move.

Presumptuously, the Sussexes seemed to think that the Queen would back them, even when she had not indicated that she would, and when any adjustments would have to be sanctioned by Harry's father. It did not stop them telling the world that they would no longer take part in the royal rota reporting system, which grants media access to official royal engagements, and would instead engage with 'grassroots media organisations' and 'young, up-and-coming journalists', while inviting 'specialist media' to select events.

In reality, the writing had been on the wall for some time. The newspapers reported that an 'emergency summit' had been called with the Queen, Charles and William coming together at Sandringham to formulate a plan and a joint reaction. Harry was there, of course, but reports that his wife, Meghan, would join them on speakerphone from Canada did not prove to be true. William arrived at the Queen's Norfolk estate at 1.45 p.m., just fifteen minutes before the talks began on 14 January. The following day, William, who was said still to be seething about the way his brother had tried to back the Queen and his father into a corner, went back to work and smiled through his anger at an investiture. Among those receiving honours that day were Theresa May's chief Brexit negotiator Olly Robbins and former England cricket captain Andrew Strauss, who were both being knighted.

Harry was in for a surprise at the 'summit'. Much was discussed, including funding and security for the couple and that the departure of the Sussexes would be subject to a twelve-month review. He walked away with very little from his wish list. A personal statement released by the Queen read:

'Today my family had very constructive discussions on the future of my grandson and his family. My family and I are entirely supportive of Harry and Meghan's desire to create a new life as a young family. Although we would have preferred them to remain full-time working members of the royal family, we respect and understand their wish to live a more independent life as a family while remaining a valued part of my family. Harry and Meghan have made clear that they do not want to be reliant on public funds in their new lives. It has therefore been agreed that there will be a period of transition in which the

Sussexes will spend time in Canada and the UK. These are complex matters for my family to resolve, and there is some more work to be done, but I have asked for final decisions to be reached in the coming days.'

On 31 March, the Sussexes completed their final official engagements before leaving for a new life in North America. They flew to Canada before making the inevitable move to California, Meghan's home state. Talk of a private, quiet existence started to unravel almost immediately. In April, details of the couple's new foundation, called Archewell, after their son, emerged, which was to replace their 'Sussex' royal brand. In May, it emerged that a book about the Sussexes, written by journalists Omid Scobie and Carolyn Durand, who were sympathetic to their cause, called *Finding Freedom* was to be published, apparently with the Sussexes' blessing (although the couple denied it at the time), giving what the authors claimed was an 'accurate version' of the couple's relationship and departure from Britain. Then, in September, the couple signed a major deal with Netflix thought to be worth multi-millions to provide 'content that informs but also gives hope'. Meanwhile, they paid back the £2.4 million of taxpayers' money used to renovate Frogmore Cottage where the couple had lived before they left the UK.

Meghan was rightly widely praised for her brutal honesty in an article in *The New York Times*, where she revealed she had had a miscarriage in July and experienced an 'almost unbearable grief'. It must have been extraordinarily hard. The Duchess said that she and Harry had been left holding the 'shattered pieces' of her heart. But the big commercial deals for the Sussexes kept on coming and, with them, increasing cynicism in the UK from the public and media alike, who believed that the couple has simply sold out for megabucks. With each announcement, the royal family and their aides and the media prickled at what looked like blatant profiteering on the royal brand. In December, Harry and Meghan signed a deal with audio-streaming service Spotify, thought to be worth millions. Fleet Street hit back, slamming the couple as hypocrites who hadn't escaped to North America for privacy, but to cash in and make fistfuls of dollars. The worm turned among the largely pro-Harry and Meghan US newspapers, with *New York Post* columnist Maureen Callahan spelling out the disquiet in her op-ed on 3 October 2020. Under the headline, 'Hypocrites Meghan and Harry beg for privacy – but are hungry for attention', she wrote: 'It's only been ten months since Prince Harry and Meghan Markle announced they were leaving the British royal family in search of "privacy" – yet they have never been so much in our faces, sanctimoniously and hypocritically telling us how to live and who to vote for, all while signing a reported $100-million deal with Netflix. Also, Markle is reportedly eyeing a run for president of the United States in 2024. Yes, this formerly unknown C-list actress who couldn't hack the cosseted existence of a senior royal, whose entire adult life has been spent in search of a spotlight she now claims to disdain, thinks she has the grit, intellect and real-world experience necessary for the top job.'

It was a powerful point, well put, and it showed that the public mood towards the couple on both sides of the pond was growing less sympathetic. Harry and Meghan knew they needed to do something dramatic to own this new narrative. They already had a plan, and it was devastating. On 11 February 2021, it was announced that Meghan had won her high-court privacy case after a two-year legal battle with the *Mail on Sunday*, with the judge granting a summary judgment in Meghan's favour over the newspaper's publication of a 'personal and private' handwritten letter from the duchess to her estranged father, Thomas Markle. In her statement, Meghan spoke of 'illegal and dehumanising practices'. She went on, 'These tactics – and those of their sister publications *Mail Online* and the *Daily Mail* – are not new … For these outlets, it's a game. For me and so many others, it's real life, real relationships and very real sadness. The damage they have done and continue to do runs deep.'

Three days later, on Valentine's Day, the couple announced that they were expecting another baby – the Queen, Charles and William all said they were delighted. But hours later, it was confirmed that the couple would be interviewed by Oprah Winfrey on her television show, just as the Duke of Edinburgh was being admitted to hospital in central London. The Palace played the duke's illness down, but he would be dead within weeks. On 19 February, Harry and Meghan's departure deal was confirmed, done and dusted. It left Harry fuming as they had been stripped of their patronages and he had lost several honorary titles, including Captain-General of the Royal Marines, which cut the Afghanistan veteran to his core. In a statement, the couple said they have 'offered their continued support to the organisations they have represented regardless of official role', adding, with a swipe at the royal triumvirate of the Queen, Charles and William, who had moved decisively, by saying 'service is universal'.

Bitter, the fiery prince came out punching. He didn't seem bothered that the Queen would be caught in the cross-fire; indeed, she may even have been his ultimate intended target. Whatever the case, he was taking no prisoners. On 26 February he described the 'toxic' atmosphere created for the couple by the British press, which had forced the family to quit Britain. In a bizarre interview with James Corden, host of the US talk show *The Late Late Show*, he discussed his son's first word, and how he kept in touch with the Queen and Prince Philip via Zoom and, predictably, considering his megabucks deal with Netflix, how he doesn't mind *The Crown* as it is 'fictional'. He also insisted that he will 'never walk away' from the royal family and he did 'what any husband or father would do' by emigrating to America. He claimed he had 'stepped back, not stepped away' because his mental health was being 'destroyed' and insisted that his 'life is public service'. Compared to what was to come next, it was tame.

Next to enter the crowded stage was the queen of the talk show, Oprah Winfrey, who was poised to destroy the image of the institution of monarchy that the real Queen had led with vision and fairness for close to seventy years. Worse still, the attack came from within. Harry and Meghan's interview was packed with jaw-dropping, but largely inaccurate, soundbites. To add to being betrayed by their own, the royal family's pain was heightened by the way the explosive claims were teased with a series of tempting preview clips to promote it in the US. First, Harry said his biggest fear was that 'history would repeat itself' in a reference to the death of Diana. Then, in another, Oprah asks Meghan how she feels knowing the royal family will be hearing her speaking out about them. 'I don't know how they could expect that after all of this time we would still just be silent when there is an active role that "the Firm" is playing in perpetuating falsehoods about us,' she says. 'And if that comes with risk of losing things … there's a lot that's been lost already.' The final clip talks about it being 'liberating' to be able to have the 'right and privilege' and say 'yes' to Oprah. It was gripping stuff, but agonising for the Queen, Prince Charles and Prince William. But there was worse to come.

The teasers had done the job they were designed to do and when the full interview aired, on 7 March 2021, it would secure a huge global television audience of nearly fifty million viewers. Anyone in Harry and Meghan's sights, and that included Charles, William and even Catherine, not to mention the so-called 'men in grey suits', the palace courtiers, was in for a tough time. Meghan came out firing in all directions, not seeming to care who she took down, or what the wider implications for her husband's estranged family might be.

The most startling allegations came from the duchess, who claimed that becoming a member of the British royal family had left her feeling suicidal. Then came another: that the royals are racist and Archie, their son, was not given a princely title due to the colour of his skin. 'In those months when I was pregnant,' she said, 'we have in tandem the conversation of "you won't be given security", "not going to be given a title", and concerns and conversations about how dark his skin might be when he's born.' Oddly for an interviewer of Oprah's calibre, she chose not to question the veracity of the duchess's claims.

When he eventually joined the interview, Harry appeared uncomfortable about the racist theme and went on to contradict his wife about the timing of the so-called racist comment and her version of what had happened. 'That conversation, I'm never going to share. But at the time, it was awkward. I was a bit shocked. That was right at the beginning when she wasn't going to get security, when members of my family were suggesting that she carries on acting because there's not enough money to pay for her, and all this sort of stuff,' he said. When accusations against specific people followed, he contradicted himself by ruling out from the line-up of possible culprits his grandmother, the Queen and Prince Philip, who was seriously ill at the time.

It was one almighty mess.

The Palace came under increasing pressure to respond to the allegations of racism within the highest echelons of the royal family as the furore threatened have a devastating effect on the reputation of the monarchy. Meghan and Harry's accusations of racism seemed to be supported when *The Guardian* reported, in March 2021, that the Queen's courtiers banned 'coloured immigrants or foreigners' from serving in clerical roles in the royal household until at least the late sixties, according to documents that newspaper reporters uncovered at the National Archives. They revealed how, in 1968, the Queen's chief financial manager informed civil servants that 'it was not, in fact, the practice to appoint coloured immigrants or foreigners' to clerical roles in the royal household, although they were permitted to work as domestic servants. It is unclear when the practice ended.

There had, of course, been the embarrassing incident in December 2017 when the wife of the Queen's first cousin, Princess Michael of Kent, had to apologise for having worn a 'blackamoor' brooch which critics called racist at a Christmas banquet at Buckingham Palace. Meghan, then Harry's fiancée, was also a guest at the lunch. A spokesman said the princess was, 'very sorry and distressed that it has caused offence'. [Blackamoor figures and sculptures are exotic figures which usually depict African men and were widespread in the seventeenth and eighteenth centuries.] Camilla, the Duchess of Cornwall, known for her risqué sense of humour, stopped using an inappropriate golliwog novelty key ring that she had been given to avoid it being misinterpreted.

The finger pointers online wrongly accused Charles of being the one who had made the crass remark about the possible colour of his future grandchild's skin. Some based this on the fact that a former black employee of his, Elizabeth Burgess, had taken him to a tribunal in 2001, claiming constructive dismissal, alleging she had been racially abused and forced out of her job as a Palace secretary. She said she was subjected to racist jokes and name-calling while working at Charles's Highgrove Estate in Gloucestershire. Burgess claimed constructive dismissal and breach of contract, also that she had been sexually discriminated against because she was being prevented from working her normal hours on her return from maternity leave. But she lost her claim, with the employment tribunal panel ruling that Mrs Burgess, who worked for Charles's household, had failed to prove any of her allegations. Charles employed a black press secretary, the indomitable Colleen Harris MVO DL, and later made Eva Omaghomi deputy head of communications and subsequently promoted her to be his director of community engagement, a role aimed at improving diversity. One senior member of the royal household dismissed talk of him having made a racist comment. 'It goes against everything the Prince of Wales believes in. He believes diversity is the strength of our society. It is a bit rich coming from Harry given the prince had to defend him when he was forced to apologise for dressing up in a Nazi unform and filming himself making a racist remark to a fellow Sandhurst officer cadet back in 2009.'

During the interview, throughout the discussion of racism and his family, Harry shifted in his chair, awkwardly not making eye-contact with Oprah most of the time. He then repeated his earlier remarks made to ITV's Tom Bradby: that he and his brother William were on 'different paths'. Worse, with echoes of his late mother Diana's BBC *Panorama* interview in which she suggested her husband wasn't suited to the top job as king, he claimed that both Prince William and Prince Charles were 'trapped' by their roles', explaining that:. 'I was trapped but I didn't know I was trapped. Like the rest of my family are, my father and my brother, they are trapped. They don't get to leave, and I have huge compassion for that. For the family, they very much have this mentality of, "This is just how it is. This is how it's meant to be. You can't change it. We've all been through it." What was different for me was the race element, because now it wasn't just about her. It was about what she represented.' He also went on to reveal the full extent of his fractured relationship with his father. It was devastating stuff. The payoff line, 'My brother can't leave that system, but I have,' stopped William in his tracks.

Prince William was infuriated. He let it be known to friends that, far from feeling trapped, he now fully embraced and understood the path laid out before him and appreciated both its advantages and its pitfalls. Prince William's circle explained that he, rather like the Queen, 'totally accepts' his role and all that it entails. He acknowledges that it has difficulties but 'service and duty are at the core if his being'. One senior aide said, 'He knows, accepts and embraces what is expected of him. He is all about service and duty.' William was staggered at his brother's discourtesy and presumptuousness in thinking he was able to publicly speak on his behalf about his beliefs, especially as he had got it so badly wrong. One senior figure put it more strongly, saying, 'He was furious. He thought it was not only bad manners, but frankly bloody rude to make those claims on his behalf, with no authority and made worse because it was total nonsense.' William felt totally let down by somebody he had once trusted implicitly. Their shared experience, grieving the loss of their mother, had bonded them. But the Oprah interview has destroyed his trust in his younger brother. Friends said William thought Harry had 'totally lost the plot'. William was particularly enraged by the way Meghan had brought his wife, Catherine, an innocent party, into the frame, when she was falsely accused of deliberately making Meghan cry. Mostly, he was enraged that his brother had had the impertinence to slander his own family by labelling them racist. As the Queen and Charles suffered in dignified silence, William couldn't leave such an outrageous accusation hanging for the public to chew over without addressing it.

Just four days after the Harry and Meghan show, William showed his mettle. Palace aides had laid down the law before a visit by William and Catherine to 'School 21' in Stratford, east London, saying that the couple would not be answering questions, so the press should not shout them out. Sky News's fearless correspondent Inzamam Rashid had different instructions from his newsdesk and wasn't going to be dictated to by overzealous Palace PR staff. His pointed questions got a response from William, who was wearing a mask due to the Covid-19 restrictions at the time: 'We are very much not a racist family,' William said without turning round to look at the reporters. When asked if he had spoken to his brother after the Oprah interview, he added, 'No, I haven't spoken to him yet, but I will do.'

According to the postscript written for the paperback edition of Omid Scobie and Carolyn Durand's bestselling book, *Finding Freedom*, written with Meghan's co-operation, the couple had seriously considered naming the identity of the member of the royal family who had made the alleged racist comment about Archie's skin colour. They weighed up shaming the person but chose not to because they felt that if it was known who it was it would be very damaging to the royal family. But the guessing game which followed led to Harry confirming during the interview that it was not the Queen or Prince Philip. Of all of the claims made during the two-hour long interview, these were without doubt the most damaging to the family. This author has been told by whom and when a comment was made, and that it was said during a light-hearted exchange. The source said, 'It was not meant to be taken seriously and the entire situation has been taken out of context. What followed and the way in which it has been twisted is frankly unfair and appalling.'

William was again left aghast, just days later, when his private chat with his brother made headlines around the world after US television presenter Gayle King, from the CBS network, another media friend of Meghan Markle, announced on air that the brotherly conversation had not gone well: 'I did actually call them to see how they were feeling. Harry has talked to his brother, and he had talked to his father, too. The word I was given was that those conversations were not productive.' Again, William was astonished by his brother and sister-in-law's total lack of discretion. How could William possibly trust his brother again if their private conversations were being passed down the line and blurted out to a US television anchor, who, in turn, divulged all the details on her show for public consumption? It was then, friends said, that for William, the shutters came down.

In the immediate aftermath of the Oprah Winfrey interview, William felt he had to take the lead and that the royal family needed a clear strategy and action plan in dealing with the renegade royals. He was, therefore, a key figure in the ongoing conversations between the Queen and Charles on how to counter Harry and Meghan's 'groundless' verbal attacks. Of course, the Queen would have the final say, but she needed Charles and William, her key liegemen, to guide her. William believed it was critical to address the racism issue and said that it was imperative that it was noted in Her Majesty's planned statement as one of the key issues that would be addressed.

Prince William has always been a decisive person. He has always been right on top of his brief, approaching his work with a clear-mind strategy, always trying to look at the bigger picture. All the charitable causes he has championed, from homelessness, which he took on in memory of his mother's work in this area, to trying to end the stigma associated with mental-health problems, and from racism in football, as president of the Football Association, to the conservation of endangered species in the wild, preserving the natural environment and saving the planet as a whole, really matter to him. He is a traditionalist, too, and understands the real need to represent the country and the Commonwealth and its peoples. He believes wholeheartedly in a co-operative approach to finding solutions, working with partners across the world to create positive change for good.

Breaking down old barriers can increase the prince's reach and make a real difference for good in the world. We've seen this approach in 2015 when on the eve of President Xi's state visit to the UK he urged China to stop buying illegally traded wildlife products such as ivory and horn, to save elephants and rhinos. In front of a small audience at King's College, London, which included the broadcasters Sir David Attenborough and Bear Grylls, and was later shown to millions on Chinese television station CCTV1, he said, 'We have to accept the truth: that consumers are driving the demand for animal body parts, for art, for trinkets, or for medicine. Only we, as consumers, can put the wildlife traffickers out of business.'

Two years later, he accepted an invitation to visit China, but, before going, he stuck to his demands, and got what he wanted. Just one week before the prince arrived in China, the government promised to shut down its ivory trade by the end of the year. For William, who has campaigned against the ivory trade for years, there is no such thing as that extra mile; he believes in pursing an issue until it has been resolved. William, who is president of umbrella conservation group United for Wildlife, welcomed the news: 'China's decision to ban its domestic ivory trade by the end of the year (2017) could be a turning point in the race to save elephants from extinction. I congratulate the Chinese government for following through on this important commitment. This battle can be won.'

He believes it is a strategy that works. He is hugely popular with the public, and although the royal family don't live their lives vicariously through opinion polls, post-Oprah, he ranks just below the Queen at the top of a YouGov poll on the popularity of the royal family. All the claims of him being 'work-shy' or somebody who was 'reluctant' to commit to duty had just evaporated into the ether.

There is no doubt that the adage 'Behind every great man there is a great woman' has never been truer than in the case of William and Catherine. William's marriage to Catherine has grounded him. They are equals and they are friends, as well as lovers and parents. She has helped him appreciate a modern media and use it to further his good causes and improve his public image. A privileged and unelected institution like the monarchy has to ensure that the public, who it relies on for its existence, feel they're getting proper access to the principal players.

Charlie Mayhew, chief executive of the conservation charity Tusk, has known William since he was twenty. In 2005, Tusk and Centrepoint, the homelessness charity championed by Princess Diana, were the first patronages William took on. 'In those early years,' Mayhew said, in an interview with *The Sunday Times*, 'I kept having to pinch myself to remember how young he was,. He was much more mature than his age and very aware of his destiny coming down the track. He had a sincerity, but never without wicked humour. His teasing is merciless.'

It was of course, William's mother, Diana, who was determined to take him to see real life outside the gilded cage of the palace to give him a greater understanding of real life and the pressures and difficulties people face. He recalled she took him to a homeless shelter to meet people who were down on their luck and who had a very difficult time in life. 'She wanted to make sure that I understood that life happens very much outside of palace walls, and this is what's going on. This is the real world here. And we sat there, and we listened. It really brings it to life when you hear somebody sit in front of you and talk very movingly and very openly about the challenges they've been up against,' he said. Helping the homeless through Centrepoint has been another core cause that drives him. He is always looking for new solutions to the growing problem of homelessness. In December 2021, it emerged that he was interested in using property on the Duchy of Cornwall estate, which he will inherit from his father when his father becomes king, as housing for the homeless. With the impact of Covid causing a greater strain for many people, William started investigating how royal property could be used for those on the streets, to provide a roof over their heads. It is the sort of forward thinking that makes him stand out.

William knows some people see his passion for conservation as a posh man's part-time hobby, but Mayhew says the Duke's 'genuine and huge knowledge' undermines that view. 'He'll call and WhatsApp to flag up something that I haven't even seen in the conservation space,' Mayhew says. 'He can be impatient to get things done.' His father and grandfather, Prince Philip, were of course guiding lights on his journey to be a champion for conservation, but the father of his former girlfriend, Jecca Craig, also greatly influenced his approach to the issue. He met Ian Craig when he and Prince Harry visited the family's 55,000-acre Lewa Downs conservation ranch in the foothills of Mount Kenya in 1995. The prince fell for Ms Craig when he returned to Kenya during a gap year after Eton, but they drifted apart before he went to St Andrew's University. 'I had such an amazing experience, where I got to see [Ian] darting an elephant for research purposes, and I must have been sixteen, seventeen, something like that,' he recalled on the *Time to Walk* Apple podcast. In the podcast he went on to say:

'Touching an elephant, seeing it lying there in front of you, breathing very slowly, its enormous ribs going up and down, and picking the trunk up and listening to the breathing coming out of [it] in your ear – it's a really special, very privileged experience. And that, for any young guy, is like: "Wow, this is cool".

'Back then, conservation was very much a case of: put wildlife over here, put people over there. Don't let them meet. And Ian came along with a pretty radical idea, which was: "You can't keep these two entities separate. They need to be together." This is where I started to realise what the job is. A large part of it was community engagement, getting to meet people and really understand what their challenges were.'

'Ian's ability to convene was something that was really impressive and stuck with me quite a lot. He could go to some of the hardest-to-reach communities in the most rural areas. And he'd sit down with the elders in the village, and rather than telling them what to do and disregarding their opinion, he actively brought them in at every opportunity, sought their advice, sought their consent, sought their experience because most of the time, these local communities know better than everyone else.

'That was what was so impressive, was his ability to listen. He went many, many times to these meetings. And once he'd given his pitch why he was there, he would sit for hours and hours in the baking sun, listening to the elders talk, and the young people, about what it meant for them. How would it work for them? Could they go along with it? And I really loved that idea and that sort of model as how to really get the best out of everyone.

'Ian's model very much reaffirmed what I'd learned from my younger days. We live in these little echo chambers where you're only subjected to what you want to be subjected to. But Ian showed me a very different way which is, go looking for those people who challenge you. Go looking for the viewpoints you didn't think you wanted to hear because, if you listen, you're empowering the other person and allowing them to feel like they matter. And that is really, really important because if we don't let each other feel valued, then you can become very disenfranchised, lost, lonely, isolated. I think listening is one of our greatest tools, one of our greatest assets to understand each other,' William said in the podcast.

Like William, Ms Craig, now a mother of two who has remained his friend, is a conservationist and helped to found Panthera, which campaigns to save wild cats, and Stop Ivory, which seeks to protect elephants.

Last year, William launched the Earthshot prize, a £50-million Nobel-style environmental award to galvanise solutions to global problems over the next decade. 'He believes "conservation and the environment ... shouldn't be a luxury, it's a necessity," Mayhew says. 'That's the drum he wants to beat. He's got a megaphone and wants to use it in the most constructive way. He speaks for that next generation, and I think they can relate to it.'

★★★

It was clear from their body language at the Windsor funeral of the Duke of Edinburgh on 17 April that tensions were running high between the two brothers. Their cousin Peter Phillips walked between them as they followed their grandfather's coffin, reunited in grief but not in spirit. The mood was helped by the royal family's "peacemaker", the Duchess of Cambridge. The brothers had clearly decided to press pause on a family rift an opted to put the grandfather's memory first.

As it turned out the Queen's birthday parade was again disrupted by COVID-19 restrictions and a scaled-down version was held at Windsor Castle, with only the Queen's first cousin, the Duke of Kent in attendance.

In July, they unveiled a statue of their mother at Kensington Palace, marking what would have been Diana's sixtieth birthday, an emotionally charged occasion with the world watching. The brothers posted a joint statement. "Today, on what would have been our Mother's sixtieth birthday, we remember her love, strength and character – qualities that made her a force for good around the world, changing countless lives for the better. Every day, we wish she were still with us, and our hope is that this statue will be seen forever as a symbol of her life and her legacy. Thank you to Ian Rank-Broadley, Pip Morrison and their teams for their outstanding work, to the friends and donors who helped make this happen, and to all those around the world who keep out mother's memory alive." At the event itself Harry appeared to offer his brother a chance to engage, but without Catherine, his wife, there to mediate he didn't seem inclined to try.

'In many ways he was able to take the emotion out of the situation. The decision over the Duke of York was very difficult for the Queen and the Prince of Wales. They were obviously closer to Andrew than his nephew. He could evaluate just how damaging his uncle was to the long-term future of the monarchy,' said the former aide.

For William, the enduring reputation of the institution is paramount. He has never been particularly close to his uncle. They share a love of helicopters, but really, Andrew and William are diametrically opposed to each other. As the sex scandal and Andrew's relationship with dead convicted paedophile Jeffrey Epstein and jailed sex trafficker and disgraced socialite Ghislaine Maxwell, daughter of the media tycoon Robert Maxwell, engulfed the royal family, William became increasingly angry. The Duke of Cambridge has very little sympathy towards his uncle. His only concern is the serious damage the allegation has had on the institution he was born to lead. Unlike his father, the Prince of Wales, who had heart-to-hearts with his brother, or the Queen, who believes her son and funds his hugely expensive legal team, Prince William has cut all contact with his uncle. William was incensed when he heard that a senior female member of the royal household was told to 'f★★★ off' when she offered what she thought was constructive advice on how to deal with the growing crisis. She was left close to tears by Prince Andrew's foul-mouthed admonishment. A senior source said, 'There will be no public role or comeback for York, if the Duke of Cambridge has any input on the matter and let me assure you, he does. He should be banished, as far as Prince William is concerned.

He is clear that his uncle should not be allowed back into public life representing the sovereign.'

In January 2022, when Manhattan federal court judge Lewis Kaplan ruled that the civil case brought by Andrew's accuser Virginia Giuffre had to proceed to trial, again William showed his ruthless qualities. His father, who was in Scotland, had erred on the side of caution, believing it is wrong to pre-judge situations and that everyone is innocent until proven guilty. William, who had been with his grandmother at an investiture at Windsor Castle the day before the decision, spoke to the monarch, calmly but clearly. He told her he believed Andrew's role in the royal family had become untenable and that she had to strip him of his military titles, patronages and use of 'His Royal Highness'. On the telephone, Charles backed his son's assessment, counselling the Queen that drastic action was needed. They said that if Andrew intended to fight the civil trial over sex-abuse allegations to clear his already tarnished name, he had to do it as a private citizen.

William and Charles made it clear to the Queen that as far as they were concerned the royal family could not permit its association with Andrew to damage the institution that they are obliged to serve and protect. One senior person in the royal household said, 'The Prince of Wales and the Duke of Cambridge had to do their duty, no matter how painful personally, for the good of the institution of monarchy that they both serve and will one day lead.' Buckingham Palace was then told to issue what was seen as brutal statement confirming Andrew's removal from official royal life. It read: 'With the Queen's approval and agreement, the Duke of York's military affiliations and royal patronages have been returned to the Queen. The Duke of York will continue not to undertake any public duties and is defending this case as a private citizen." For guidance, they advised that, just like Harry, he could keep his birthright 'His Royal Highness' title, but he could no longer use it. He was out. The former Falklands War helicopter pilot and Royal Navy officer's military titles and royal roles will go to other members of the family, although he will retain his service rank of vice-admiral.

A senior member of the royal household said: 'This means they won't be coming back to Prince Andrew whatever the outcome of any legal proceedings. There really is no way back for him, full stop." The Duke of York, crestfallen and humiliated, issued his own thoughts, not officially, but via a source close to him: 'Given the robustness with which Judge Kaplan greeted our arguments, we are unsurprised by the ruling. However, it was not a judgment on the merits of Ms Giuffre's allegations. This is a marathon, not a sprint, and the Duke will continue to defend himself against these claims.' But it was a marathon he will have to run on his own.

Charles and William are understood to have advised the monarch that the royal family had to clearly distance itself against fall-out from the allegations against Andrew, who is accused by Ms Giuffre of having sex with her three times when she was under eighteen, after being trafficked for sex by his friend, Jeffrey Epstein.

CHAPTER NINETEEN

EARTHSHOT

*'We are alive in the most consequential time in human history ... The actions
we choose or choose not to take in the next ten years will determine
the fate of the planet for the next thousand'*
Prince William, Duke of Cambridge, 2021

Sir David Attenborough joined William's star-studded prize council
and inspired the whole Earthshot enterprise. William's son and heir,
Prince George, was so upset by what he saw in one of the brilliant
veteran BBC broadcaster's shows that his father decided to act. Then
the environment champion of champions, Sir David, ninety-five years
young, with his mop of grey hair, enters the fray as the headliner,
doing what he does best, describing the wonders of the world, whilst
issuing some warnings. His rich, honest voice – the voice that narrated
231 episodes of *Wildlife on One* from 1977 to 2005 – resonated with
viewers of all generations. This, we all know, is a wise man who speaks
the truth. When he speaks about nature, we all listen. This, however,
was not another doomsday 'edge of the cliff' assessment of our planet's
future, but one that offered real hope and was driven by the idea of
finding solutions.

Sir David Attenborough has made an unsurpassed contribution in
opening people's eyes to the incredibly diversity, beauty and fascination
of the natural world during a career which has lasted over six decades.
Both he and William engaged well with their audience, showing how
everyone, if they put their minds to it, can make a real difference
to saving the planet, so that future generations can enjoy it as we
have done. It highlights how individual projects are helping offset
the effects of climate change, taking us across the globe, travelling

from the Maasai people of Kenya to Yellowstone Park in the United States and to the Knepp Estate in Britain. Fans of Attenborough's programmes were not disappointed. There is a wealth of skilfully composed and edited footage of remarkable wildlife, God's creatures that face being wiped out unless we, humanity, the most selfish of all species on earth, change our ways. The five-part television series, *The Earthshot Prize: Repairing Our Planet* was watched by people all over the world. Part of its appeal is that it is both informative and inspiring, but without lecturing its audience. Brazilian football star Dani Alves is a member of the Earthshot Prize Council. His home country is the world's largest exporter of beef, but in explaining that we need to change how we farm cattle, Alves acknowledges that the still eats meat and we don't all have to become vegetarians. While in Borneo, conservation manager Cat Barton is attempting to devise a way to produce palm oil sustainably, without endangering orangutans. The series aims to instil hope rather than create feelings of despair; we may have very little time left, but we do still have time to address the challenges we face, if we act now.

As mentioned before, Prince William first went to Africa in Easter 1995, with Harry and his father, and it changed his life. He explains: 'I met Ian Craig, who's a conservationist out there in charge of running Lewa Downs, which is a conservation ranch just outside of Nairobi in Kenya.'

William longed to go back, so, before he went up to university, he called up Ian, and said, 'Remember me? Can I come back?' Craig said, 'Yeah, no problem at all. I've got plenty of things you can do. You can muck in and help out, learn the ropes.' So, William spent several months with Craig and his team learning about African conservation, African wildlife, rural communities and generally getting Kenya under his skin. At that time, when he was in his late teens, he was just thrown in at the deep end with people he'd not met before, speaking a different language.

In Davos, in January 2019, Sir David Attenborough was handed a Crystal Award for his leadership in the fight against climate change and issued a stark warning that the 'Garden of Eden is no more'. He also took part in several panel discussions on the future of our planet, including a one-on-one interview with his long-term admirer Prince William. The prince asked Sir David about his career, the precarious state in which the natural world finds itself, and also to tell young people and leaders how to care for the planet.

Sir David responded that when he started as a broadcaster in the 1950s, 'The natural world then seemed like an unexplored world ... I went to West Africa for the first time, and it was a wonderland. You'd just step off from the beaten track ... and it seemed to me as a newcomer, unexplored and exciting and everywhere you turned you saw something new. The human population was only a third of the size of what it is today ... you really did get the feeling of what it might have been like to be in the Garden of Eden.'

With regard to climate change, he explained, 'I don't think there was anybody in the 1950s who thought that there was a danger that we might annihilate part of the natural world ... the notion that human beings might exterminate a whole species was not something people thought about, and if it did occur ... it seemed the exception. Now, of course, we are only too aware that the whole of the natural world is at our disposal, that we can do things accidentally that exterminate a whole area of the natural world, and all the species that live within it.'

He added that it's difficult to overstate the level of urgency with regard to tackling climate change: 'We are now so numerous, so powerful, so all-pervasive, the mechanisms that we have for destruction are so wholesale and so frightening, that we can exterminate whole ecosystems without even noticing it. We have now to be really aware of the dangers of what we are doing. And we already know the plastic problems in the seas are wreaking appalling damage upon marine life. The extent of which we don't yet fully know.' Both men were singing from the same hymn sheet and William was determined to harness Sir David's wisdom and respect for the Earthshot idea that he had been developing privately.

That September, Sir David was at Kensington Palace for a private screening of his new documentary, *A Life on Our Planet*, hosted by the Duke of Cambridge. Sir David gave Prince George a fossilised tooth from an extinct shark, *Carcharocles megalodon*. George was thrilled by the prehistoric sea predator's tooth, found by Sir David during a family holiday to Malta in the late sixties. It was embedded in the island nation's soft yellow limestone and is about twenty-three million years old.

Sir David chatted to the duke and duchess and their three children, George, Charlotte and Louis, after the screening. William and Catherine shared photos of the meeting on their official Instagram page, saying that Attenborough had visited the palace. In the photo of the family with Sir David, Charlotte has her hands on her face in excitement because she was meeting the world-famous conservationist.

Ahead of the Earthshot Prize celebrations at Alexandra Palace in London on 17 October 2021, William gave a series of interviews, firstly on BBC Radio 4's *Today* programme, in which he praised his father for his passion for the topic. 'He's talked about this for a long time and long before people sort of cottoned on to climate change. So, I've always listened to and learnt and believed in what he was saying. But I know it's a very hard sell, you know, forty years ago to kind of predict and see some of the sort of slow-moving catastrophes that we were headed towards.' William also said that he 'feels there must be some hope and optimism' when discussing the impact of climate change on the planet, explaining, 'I do feel you have to have the urgency and the importance of what's going to happen and the seriousness of what's coming along. There are plenty of people talking about that. But I personally feel we must have some hope and some optimism. It's all very apocalyptic about things.'

But, in a thirty-five-minute interview with Adam Fleming on BBC *Newscast*, in which he watched back and reflected on some of the moments in his TV series, William warned, 'If we're not careful we're robbing from our children's future through what we do now … I want the things that I've enjoyed – the outdoor life, nature, the environment – I want that to be there for my children, and not just my children but everyone else's children. If we're not careful we're robbing from our children's future through what we do now.'

Looking ahead to COP26, the United Nations Climate Change Conference held in the UK in 2021, William warned against 'clever speak, clever words, but not enough action' and said it was critical for the climate conference to 'communicate very clearly and very honestly about what the problems are and what the solutions are going to be, and that's why the Earthshot Prize is so important, because we're trying to create action.' He also got headlines for speaking about the space race and space tourism saying, 'We need some of the world's greatest brains and minds fixed on trying to repair this planet, not trying to find the next place to go and live.

'You know, for me, it would be an absolute disaster if George is sat here talking to you or your successor, Adam, you know in like thirty years' time, whatever, still saying the same thing, because by then we will be too late. And I think for me, it sort of formulated and sort of cemented itself a bit in my mind in Namibia about three years ago. I love community conservation and [in] Namibia have been some of the sort of world leaders in community conservation and for people who don't know what that is, it's effectively the locals wherever you are in the world taking an interest in management of the wildlife, nature, the environmental assets around them. So, they very much manage them, they protect them, they nurture them for their own prosperity … I came away having met loads of good people there and I felt really inspired, really energised by what I'd seen. But then coming back to the UK and seeing the headlines around the world, and you know the media also like to concentrate sometimes on the negativity. And I felt you know you're losing people every single time you have those headlines. We all get that there's a really big, urgent message and I'm not saying we shouldn't talk about the urgency or the big issues but ultimately if we want to tackle this, if we want to get on the front foot, we've got to bring people with us. And people have got to feel like there's hope, there's a chance we can fix this.'

The inaugural awards ceremony proved an unmitigated success. The royal couple arrived in an Audi electric car. Catherine looked radiant on the green, rather than red, carpet in the cinch-waisted, powder-purple Alexander McQueen dress that she had first worn in 2011 on tour in Los Angeles at a BAFTA black-tie event at the Belasco Theater. This was one of the first events of this kind that she experienced after tying the knot with William in April 2011. William looked dapper as he moved away from classic black evening dress, instead opting for a black polo neck and green velvet jacket.

Inside, William issued a rallying cry to the next generation to keep on demanding change and not to give up hope as he announced that the US would be hosting the next awards ceremony. At the end of the event, televised by the BBC, William, who was joined by Catherine, took to the stage and said, 'I want to say something to the young watching tonight. For too long, we haven't done enough to protect the planet for your future. The Earthshot is for you. In the next ten years, we are going to act. We are going to find the solutions to repair our planet. Please keep learning, keep demanding change, and don't give up hope. We will rise to these challenges.'

No stars flew to London for the event and guests were asked by organisers to consider the environment when choosing their outfit for the awards. Winners included projects to restore coral reefs, schemes to redistribute surplus food and an organisation attempting to tackle issues contributing to air pollution in India. Catherine presented the winner in the Protect and Restore Nature category to the Costa Rican government, which has initiated a project to pay citizens to help restore ecosystems. She said, 'Nature is vital to us all. A thriving natural world regulates our planet, nurtures our physical and mental health and helps feed our families. But for too long, we've neglected our wild spaces and now we're facing several tipping points. If we don't act now, we will permanently destabilise our planet and we will rob our children of the future they deserve.'

Liverpool's star striker Mo Salah presented the first prize in the Revive Our Oceans category. The winner was the Coral Vita project which grows coral on land to replant in oceans, thereby injecting new life into stressed and dying ecosystems.

Actor and activist Emma Watson awarded the Fix Our Climate prize to AEMElectrolyser technology, which turns renewable electricity into emission-free hydrogen gas. She said, 'I've spent much of my working life acting in fictional, make-believe worlds where the impossible can be made possible. Now, we need to do the same thing with climate change here in the real world. There have been many other times in history when it's been said something couldn't be done, and then people believed in a better world and made it so. This time is no different, I know that we can.'

Appearing via video link, the winner's delight at receiving a million pounds each to develop there various initiatives was readily apparent. When Dame Emma Thompson was struggling with her microphone while presenting the award for Build a Waste-free World to the city of Milan for its pioneeering food-waste project, she joked, 'I broke my mike by dropping it down the lav.' Coldplay's pre-recorded performance was powered by sixty people pedalling bicycles; Ed Sheeran followed. William spoke to the winners via video, saying, 'I am so proud of you. Everyone here is amazed by the solutions. Real positivity and the fact it is solutions-based keeps people smiling and feeling hopeful.'

Just before the event, William's father publicly praised his son for his bold initiative, saying, 'I am very proud of my son, William, for his growing commitment to the environment and the bold ambition of the Earthshot Prize. As a world, we need to come together to inspire, reimagine and build the sustainable future we so desperately need. Over the coming decade, with future generations in mind, the Earthshot Prize, and its inspirational nominees, will help us find the innovative solutions. In parallel, through my Terra Carta and Sustainable Markets Initiative, we will work to mobilise the trillions of dollars required to transition the global economy onto a more sustainable trajectory. Together, with all those who join us, we have a real opportunity to deliver a brighter future for humanity while restoring harmony between nature, people and planet.'

Even whilst heaping praise on his son's ambitious project, the Prince of Wales was keen to remind people that he had been there first and that his new charter, putting sustainability at the heart of the private sector, marked fifty years of campaigning for the environment. Charles's Terra Carta, he says, offers the basis of a recovery plan to 2030 putting 'Nature, People and Planet' at the heart of global value creation, 'One that will harness the precious, irreplaceable power of nature combined with the transformative innovation and resources of the private sector,' says Charles.

The two Windsor men, who have not always seen eye to eye, had at last found common ground that has brought them much closer than they have ever been. One aide, however, said, 'The Duke of Cambridge has done a brilliant job, injecting hope into the debate over climate change, instead of always saying we are at the cliff edge. His initiative is about finding ways to stop and slow the damage. The Prince of Wales, whilst passionate, offers a doomsday scenario.'

That's as may be, but Charles certainly deserves credit for his pioneering in the field of sustainability and highlighting the dangers of global warming and climate change. 'It wasn't that long ago that Prince William was driving around in his petrol Audi, now it's all electric cars!' said a member of the household. Indeed, until the

'Megxit' calamity and its painful fall-out, Charles had been much closer to his younger son than his heir. Harry used to talk with his 'Pa' (as before the troubles he used to affectionately call his father) for hours. In a clip unearthed from Charles's stint as a guest editor of Radio 4's *Today* show before the pair fell out, he spoke to him about fighting climate change. Harry can be overheard saying, 'I know that the two of us can end up talking on about this for hours and hours, which we always do, but not with a microphone in front of us.'

The Prince of Wales's relationship with his elder son has, at times, been strained. Occasionally, it has needed Catherine's deft diplomatic touch to smooth things over between the two men. William is particularly touchy and overprotective about his children, to the point of checking what photos of his children are in shot if his father is posing for a PR shot or doing an interview. The Duchess of Cornwall, however, is not as accommodating as Charles towards his son, nor as conciliatory as Catherine when it comes to resolving disagreements between them. One senior former member of the royal household who has witnessed the father/son relationship at close quarters says William, as a direct heir, sometimes appears to forget – whether purposely or not is unclear – that there is a hierarchy in which he ranks below his father. 'Deference doesn't appear to be in his vocabulary when it comes to his father,' one well-placed source said. 'It must seem odd to the Prince of Wales, who has always honoured his mother and late father.' Another senior ex-member of the royal household said, 'Of course, he is very respectful to Her Majesty the Queen. But when it comes to his father it is as if he thinks they are, as direct heirs to the throne, on a level,' the ex-courtier said.

Camilla's clever handling of this, and subtle reminders to William and other members of the family that the Prince of Wales is not only the next monarch but also patriarch of the family, was highlighted when she felt William didn't show Charles enough deference and respect. A courtier recalled, 'I remember one occasion when they were leaving Windsor Castle after a joint event, the Duke of Cambridge learned that his father had police outriders from the Special Escort Group for a journey as his royal status warranted. He asked his father if he and Catherine could tag along behind in convoy, making it easy to get through the traffic. The Prince of Wales agreed. But when the Prince and Duchess of Cornwall were kept waiting several minutes by Prince William and his wife, the Duchess of Cornwall insisted they go without his eldest son in tow. As William and Catherine emerged all they could see were the blue flashing lights of the motorbikes disappearing in the distance.'

It is an example of how Camilla, rightly more confident in her role as future Queen Consort, is happy to put William in his place if she feels he is abusing the Prince of Wales's generosity and kind character. 'The truth is the prince will do anything for his sons, and the falling out with Harry has hurt him, but the Duchess feels it is her duty to protect the Prince of Wales from himself sometimes. He is going to be king, and she doesn't mind reminding others in the family of that now and again, and that includes his son and heir.'

CHAPTER TWENTY

REACHING OUT

'I think listening is one of our greatest tools, one of our greatest assets to understand each other'

Prince William

William was incandescent. His tone was calm, but nobody doubted the severity of his feelings for the broadcaster that had historically always bent over backwards to please the royal family. As well as being furious with the BBC for the way in which it had handled the Martin Bashir *Panorama* issue, William also expressed his 'indescribable sadness' at the failings surrounding the airing of the programme in 1995. He said that these had exacerbated his mother's 'fear, paranoia and isolation'. He had no doubt, he said, that Bashir's lies had 'substantially influenced' what his mother had said in the interview and had significantly contributed to the worsening of his parents' relationship. His deeply personal recorded statement followed the devastating findings of an independent report by former Master of the Rolls, Lord Dyson in May 2021. Lord Dyson had carried out a six-month investigation into the scandal and ruled that 'Mr Bashir deceived and induced him [Earl Spencer] to arrange a meeting with Princess Diana'. Bashir was exposed as having faked documents to convince Diana to give her sensational 1995 interview.

The prince went further than anyone expected, saying *Panorama* 'holds no legitimacy and should never be aired again'. 'It effectively established a false narrative which, for over a quarter of a century, has been commercialised by the BBC and others,' the prince said. The BBC was adjudged to have 'covered up' what it knew of Mr Bashir's catalogue of deception as well as having been 'woefully ineffective' in investigating claims against Bashir after allegations surfaced that he had used fake bank statements to falsely claim Diana's inner circle were selling information on her to the press.

Prince William went on to say: 'It is my view that the deceitful way the interview was obtained substantially influenced what my mother said. The interview was a major contribution to making my parents' relationship worse and has since hurt countless others. It brings indescribable sadness to know that the BBC's failures contributed significantly to her fear, paranoia, and isolation that I remember from those final years with her.

'But what saddens me most is that if the BBC had properly investigated the complaints and concerns first raised in 1995, my mother would have known that she had been deceived. She was failed not just by a rogue reporter, but by leaders at the BBC who looked the other way rather than asking the tough questions.' The then culture secretary Oliver Dowden said that in the wake of the 'damning' inquiry findings, the government would consider whether the broadcaster's governance should be reformed.

Meanwhile, BBC Director-General Tim Davie said that while Dyson's report states that Princess Diana 'was keen on the idea of an interview' with the broadcaster, the 'process for securing the interview fell far short of what audiences have a right to expect'.

Peter Hunt, the former long-term diplomatic and royal correspondent of the BBC, was in no doubt about the seriousness of William's criticism and the long-term impact it would have. He wrote in *The Spectator*, 'This was the most damning criticism a senior royal has ever unleashed on the national broadcaster. Once lauded for its Diana scoop, the BBC will now forever be haunted by the accusation that its failures contributed significantly to the 'fear, paranoia and isolation' that Diana experienced in the final years of her life. William's statement was both damning and audacious. At its heart was a bold attempt to recast recent royal history.' He was right. Then came the judgement of the corporation's 'rising star', media editor Amol Rajan, aged thirty-eight, who said on BBC's *News at Ten* that the BBC had been 'severely injured and probably scarred.' It was to prove an ironic intervention, as Rajan would be at the centre of the BBC's next clash with the royal family, which would also create a media storm.

Within months, the Palace and the BBC were at loggerheads over a 'disgustingly one-sided documentary fronted by Mr Rajan, the host of Radio 4's flagship *Today* programme and former editor of *The Independent*, which dared to delve into William and Harry's troubled relationship with the media. It was a high risk move by the corporation and one that backfired spectacularly, raising the stakes in William's row with the BBC, putting future TV projects with the broadcaster at risk.

William was so incensed by the BBC2 documentary airing what he claimed were 'unfounded' claims about his office leaking information about his brother that the television rights to the Christmas concert at Westminster Abbey, featuring him and his wife and other royals, were offered to ITV instead. Many predicted that this royal snub to the BBC was merely the tip of the iceberg. Clearly, the BBC bigwigs had underestimated both William's temper and his tendency to hold a grudge. William was not only angered by what they saw as fanciful claims made in the documentary, called *The Princes and the Press*, but also by the broadcaster's approach to the project.

It was not only one-sided, even allowing Meghan's lawyer Jenny Afia to appear on it, but the duke also felt elements of it were not true and the Palace were not given the courtesy of previewing it. Mr Rajan, a republican, was soon on the back foot again. Amid a growing media storm, he later apologised for what he called 'rude and immature' comments he had made about the royal family a decade earlier when it emerged that he had described the late Duke of Edinburgh as a 'racist buffoon', the Prince of Wales as 'scientifically illiterate' and said events to celebrate the Queen's Diamond Jubilee were 'little more than the industrialisation of mediocrity'. The comments were made in a 2012 article for *The Independent*, in which he was also critical of Princes William and Harry. In a series of tweets, after liaising with the BBC Press Office, Mr Rajan, in what seemed to be an enforced apology, said he now 'deeply regretted' the comments he had made in a 'former life'. He added, 'I look back on them now with real embarrassment, and ask myself what I was thinking, frankly.' It seemed like the BBC Press Office was shutting the gate long after the horse had bolted, given that Mr Rajan's opinions had been in the public domain for years. It wasn't as if his contempt for the British monarchic system was not already well known, after all.

Only time will tell how far the future king will take his grudge against the BBC. In time, he will probably be guided to let it go, for the sake of the monarchy. But there is no doubt that he, perhaps more than any other senior royal, has embraced new ways to reach his future subjects, whether it is appearing in documentaries, online, in podcasts, on YouTube or via social media, he seems to be in touch with the modern world, whilst still maintaining the traditions of the past.

The Duke of Cambridge likes to talk directly to people, not just when he meets them one to one, but using whatever new communication platforms are available to him that have a far greater reach. He has mastered his presenting skills, banishing his nerves to reveal a man comfortable talking openly about deeply personal and difficult issues. In December 2021, he broadcast a thirty-eight-minute audio ramble and conversation called *Time to Walk*, an Apple initiative, available internationally on the digital radio station Apple Music 1 and on demand via Apple's Fitness+ subscription.

William was not just talking to Britain, but to the world – the broadcast is available in 165 countries. The series, in its second season, invites celebrities to lead listeners on a walk around somewhere they know, discussing the health benefits of walking among reflections from their own lives, as well as picking a few of their favourite songs. Previous walk leaders have included singer-songwriter Dolly Parton and boxer Anthony Joshua.

William shared with listeners a walk he had used to take as a child at Christmas with his grandfather, Prince Philip, through the Sandringham estate towards Anmer Hall, now his Norfolk home. Sounds of feet on wet grass, unoiled gates and flying geese provided a peaceful backdrop. As he walked, he spoke about some of the causes he is most passionate about. But in addition to talking about environmental conservation, he talked about keeping 'mentally fit', about looking after one's mental health. One song he opted to share was 'The Best' by Tina Turner. He remembered how his mother had used to play it in the car on the drive to take William and his younger brother Harry back to boarding school. Singing along with personal protection officer Ken Wharfe, an accomplished baritone, had helped to overcome their nerves. The next song he chose was Shakira's 'Waka Waka', much loved by his own children. He was happy to talk about when Taylor Swift had asked him to join her in singing 'Livin' on a Prayer' on stage with Jon Bon Jovi at a fundraising event. 'Sod it,' he remembers thinking, 'I can't be the doofus who's going to ruin it for everyone.'

It was wonderfully calm, warm and open. His revelations about his experiences working for the East Anglian Air Ambulance service, when he was audibly close to tears, showed the real man he is. When he said, 'I felt like the whole world was dying ... You just feel everyone's in pain, everyone's suffering,' you couldn't help but be moved by his courage to reveal his inner fears and feelings. He is clearly a man of honesty and inner power.

The lighter moments shone through, too, as well as his sense of growth as a person. 'The sound of the wildlife is so crucial for a walk. And I love the peace, but I'd much rather hear the songbirds than peace. You've got to look out for the little guys,' he said, with a sense of real affinity with nature. William says that he and his brother Prince Harry, like most other children, did their best to resist their father's efforts to encourage them out of doors, but that he now shares Prince Charles's appreciation of the countryside.

'When I grew up, my father used to love his walking, and still to this day loves his walking and used to try to force Harry and me out of the house,' he says. 'And we weren't really having any of it. Now, as you get older, you appreciate it a lot more,' he said, acknowledging his father's influence on his life, which is seldom given the recognition it deserves.

His normalcy shines, too. He chuckles as he reveals he hasn't yet abandoned all his youthful habits of loving a lie-in. 'I'm not an early riser, if I can help it,' he admits. 'I quite like watching nature put itself to bed in the evening and the sounds and smells that come with it. It's quite therapeutic. It stimulates all your senses, and so you really feel like you're in a calmer space, that you can process stuff and think, and I come home feeling better and feeling more relaxed.' Listeners can hear his footsteps as he walks along describing the animals in fields around his home.

In that short podcast he shatters so many illusions about him. He discloses that unlike his grandmother the Queen, who is awoken by a Scottish piper, he starts his day rocking to AC/DC, the Australian rock band formed by Scottish-born brothers Angus and Malcolm Young, with one of his favourite tracks being 'Thunderstruck'. 'There's nothing better, when you're a bit bleary-eyed after the weekend and trying to get yourself back into the grind of the week, than listening to 'Thunderstruck', he says of the track that reached number thirteen in the UK charts in 1990. 'It absolutely wakes you up, puts your week in the best mood possible, and you feel like you can take on anything and anyone ... It's a difficult song not to dance to or to nod along to.'

Throughout his walk, William's humour is evident. He describes how he 'had the giggles many times' during Christmas Day church service at Sandringham as he struggled to 'keep a straight face' with his cousins sitting opposite him. Beginning his walk at the sixteenth-century building, he says, 'So we're right outside St Mary Magdalene Church. The flag's up and I'm right beside the door we normally go in as a family. And what's very good about it is that we sit opposite each other as a family and, growing up, having my cousins sat opposite me [it] has always been quite difficult to keep a straight face at times.'

William spoke fondly of his grandfather, Prince Philip, who died in April 2021 aged ninety-nine. 'My family spend their Christmases in Norfolk at Sandringham, in the UK. You've got big pine trees that are quite synonymous with this part of Norfolk. And I love the smell of pine in the winter. It's very soothing. As we're walking along here, it's been a walk that my family have done for many, many years on Christmas Day. I have strong memories of walking down here, and my grandfather, he used to walk so fast that there'd be huge gaps and spaces between all of us, and there'd be us at the back with little legs trying to keep up.'

William gives a loving and moving account of his family's life: squabbling children with kitchen sounds in the background – a familiar soundscape to many, many of his future subjects. He recorded the *Time to Walk* podcast during a pandemic lockdown when he and his family were spending most of their time at their home in Norfolk.

He remembered that what he'd been most amazed by was how his children have inherited his family's love of music. 'Most mornings there's a massive fight between Charlotte and George as to what song is played. And I have to, now, basically prioritise that one day someone does this one, and another day it's someone else's turn. So, George gets his go, then Charlotte gets her go. Such is the clamour for the music. One of the songs that the children are loving at the moment is Shakira's 'Waka Waka'. There's a lot of hip movements ... There's a lot of dressing up. Charlotte, particularly, is running around the kitchen in her dresses and ballet stuff and everything. She goes completely crazy, with Louis following her around trying to do the same thing. It's a really happy moment where the children just enjoy dancing, messing around, and singing.'

Prince William's children and his wife are always in his mind. 'We've got hares running across the field over there, fat English partridges going over the hedge just here with a nice orange tractor up ahead,' he said. 'Louis is obsessed by tractors. It just feels very wild and very, very peaceful.' Tractors have, it seems, been a source of fascination to both William's sons. The walk concludes at Anmer Hall. 'We're finally here ... We spend as much time as we can here. It's very special, it's very peaceful. And we feel very, very lucky to be out in the countryside,' he said. 'We've got the sheep in the fields. We've got the pond here with the duck and the geese on. It's a fantastic place to be.'

In conclusion, William mentions his wife: 'It's been really nice to get out and have a walk,' he says. 'I feel like I've shared a lot of feelings ... Feels like I've been on a walk with a best mate, or my wife. I'll be heading back inside now, going to see what the children have been up to before I, hopefully, put them to bed exhausted.'

His tone and demeanour leave us all with a sense that this is a man who has grown into his role. He is a listener and believes listening is one of humanity's greatest tools, 'one of our greatest assets to understand each other'. One is left in no doubt that when the moment in history comes, William will meet the challenge and rise to it. Our thousand-year-old monarchy is safe in his hands, a future, modern monarch with an appreciation of tradition and the past, but an eye on the future, not just of this country, the realms, or the wider Commonwealth, but the whole planet, which we must preserve and share.

FIT FOR A QUEEN

'All the time William and I are so struck by the Queen's sense of duty and commitment. And I think to do that by yourself would be a very lonely place to be. But I think to have the support of your husband there by your side on those occasions – and behind closed doors as well – I think is really special. William and I have got quite a long way to go. But, no, it really, really is fantastic.'

Catherine, revealing that she and William were inspired by the Queen's closeness to her husband the Duke of Edinburgh in an interview for ITV's *Our Queen at Ninety* documentary

Princess Diana's life may have been lovelorn. She knew, however, that her eldest son, as a future king, would have to find the right partner to be Queen Consort. Despite his tender age, she wasn't afraid to tell him either. The head that wears the crown may be uneasy, but it is far worse without the right partner at his or her side to share the burden. To find peace in his future role, his wife, she advised, would not only have to love him unreservedly, but to serve him and the institution his birthright burdens him to lead. In many ways, Diana knew she had failed in that role for Charles, because he ostensibly broke the contract by loving another. Moreover, they were incompatible as a couple – emotionally, intellectually and sexually. The media created a global superstar almost overnight, who put her husband forever in her shadow. Diana knew William could not be a happy king without the strength of a devoted queen.

William was only fifteen when Diana died in Paris, but before the tragedy, he had witnessed her own personal unhappiness up close, and she had shared many confidences with him. Her emotional frailty pained him. As a ten-year-old, he tried to help his tearful mother feel better by slipping her a loving note under the door after he heard her crying in the locked bathroom following an altercation with Charles. It read simply, 'I hate to see you sad.' [This was described by Penny Junor in her book *Born to Be King: An Intimate Portrait*.] Diana later revealed they discussed his future, too. 'I put it to William, particularly, that if you find someone you love in life, you must hang on to that love and look after it. You must protect it.' Clearly, as he matured into a man, he never forgot her wise words.

William adores his wife. When Prince William met a British florist, Paula Pryke, the loved-up future king confessed to her that he loves to buy Kate bunches of flowers. Paula revealed, 'He told me that he liked buying flowers for Kate and how much she loved flowers.'[78] On their wedding day, in 2011, he vowed to 'love and cherish' her in his wedding vows; Catherine, in turn, agreed to 'honour' him. But she also knew that she would have to respect his future role as king and carry through her duties with the institution he was born to lead. She couldn't usurp his authority; she couldn't upstage him. Like Prince Philip, the late Duke of Edinburgh, Catherine recognised early on the limitations and the constraints of her future role. The difficulty would be to instinctively know, as throughout his long life as consort Prince Philip always seemed to, when it was time to step back and let the monarch take the lead. Catherine's role is, after all, to allow William's star to shine.

As the late King George VI prophetically said when he told a guest at Elizabeth and Philip's wedding, 'I wonder if Philip knows what he is taking on. One day Lilibet will be Queen and he will be consort. That's much harder than being a king, but I think he's the man for the job.' Perhaps that is why the Queen encouraged her grandson and heir to have a long courtship, as he did, so that the woman he loved understood exactly what her role would entail, with all its downs as well as ups. And Philip's wise words would not have been lost on the well-read Catherine, when, speaking at his golden wedding anniversary in 1997, he said, 'I think the main lesson that we have learnt is that tolerance is the one essential ingredient of any happy marriage. You can take it from me that the Queen has the quality of tolerance in abundance.'

There is no doubt since the death of Prince Philip, the sudden departure of Prince Harry and Meghan and the ongoing Jeffrey Epstein sex crisis that has engulfed the Duke of York, that William and Catherine have become the most influential royal couple when it comes to the long-term future of the monarchy. William, the Queen and Charles have ensured that he has been consulted on all the big decisions that have had a bearing on the institution in recent years.

As crisis followed crisis, smiling Catherine hasn't put a foot wrong. Throughout the Covid-19 pandemic the immaculate mother-of-three backed up her husband, taking on extra engagements, making scores of public appearances remotely, as the UK was forced into lockdown and, as soon as they could, publicly. The Cambridges, despite William being struck down by the virus, were ever present, it seemed, thanking NHS staff or Zoom-calling children of essential workers. With Catherine at his side, the prince seems more assured, their chemistry clear for all to see. Every step of the way, Catherine has put duty first.

Over time, her confidence has grown. She spoke candidly on podcasts about the guilt mothers feel when having to work and has not been afraid to talk about how she raises her family, conscious all the time of her financial advantages. Beneath that soft smile, there is a tigress, passionate about her husband and a modern woman who will fight tooth and nail for her family.

Her influence over William, whose presentation in the past used to be somewhat stiff and a little nervy, has helped him become more relatable, to be more himself. His sense of humour and warmth is now visible.

Catherine undoubtedly plays her cards very close to her chest. She never wants to let the side down. She pays close attention to detail. Not only is she William's most trusted adviser, she is someone who puts family and duty above all else. She can play bland with high-street fashions when it suits her. But when the moment is right, she knows exactly how to steal the show. After William asked Charles if he and Catherine could join his father and the Duchess of Cornwall at the world premiere of the new James Bond film, *No Time to Die*, on 28 September 2021 at the Royal Albert Hall, making it a joint engagement, it was Catherine, not 007 actor Daniel Craig in a dusty pink dinner jacket, who became the star attraction. She looked magnificent in a sparkling gold Jenny Packham gown, prompting actor Craig to comment when they met, 'You look jolly lovely.'

Sometimes William ruffles feathers amongst staff, because while he hasn't that big a household himself, which bolsters his image as a modern royal running a tight ship, he tends to sometimes rely on his grandmother's and father's staff, which causes disquiet in the ranks. Over Christmas 2021, the staff had to open Sandringham so that the annual shoot could go ahead. It meant that after dining at Windsor with the Queen, Charles and Camilla had to head to the royal Norfolk estate first for just two days so the shoot, attended by the Middletons, among others, could go ahead.

The Queen's influence on this remarkable woman, born into a middle-class family in Reading, has been clear. She and her siblings attended Marlborough College, thanks to her parents' thriving mail-order business. Then, in 2001, at university at St Andrew's, where she read history of art and met William, the path of her life changed forever. She suffered the humiliation of the 'doors to manual' jibe, a silly reference to her mother Carole's former role as a flight attendant, which said more about those using it than it did about Carole. It was pathetic, to bait Catherine about her mother's background: to refer to the fact that she had been born in a Southall council flat and was descended from Durham coal-mining stock. Catherine rose above it all with an in-built fortitude that seems to be at her core.

For somebody who once found making speeches nerve-racking, she now uses her voice to make a real difference to the lives of those less fortunate than herself. Her role, alongside her husband, in trying to end the stigma of mental health problems has been huge, particularly when it comes to schoolchildren. 'Together, with open conversations and greater understanding, we can ensure that attitudes to mental health change and children receive the support they deserve,'[79] she says. As somebody who suffered bullying at school, she means it wholeheartedly. Her message is clear: that children of all ages need to be listened to.

She has faced ridiculous criticism, such as in 2013, when novelist Hilary Mantel sparked outrage when she gave a lecture in which she described her as 'gloss-varnished'. The attack was totally unwarranted. 'Kate seems to have been selected for her role of princess because she was irreproachable; as painfully thin as anyone could wish, without quirks, oddities, without the risk of emergence of character.' It caused such a furore that even the then prime minister, David Cameron, was moved to comment, calling the remarks 'completely misguided and completely wrong' about what Mantel had called her 'perfect plastic smile'. Catherine kept her dignity and remained silent.

Her steely spine comes from her mother, Carole. Whenever she faces difficulties, she retreats to the Middletons' sprawling Berkshire mansion. William, too, remains very close to Carole and Michael Middleton. He loves them and it gives him a family life so different from his own. Unlike her much-loved late mother-in-law Diana, Catherine is careful not to be over-emotional in public. Quietly, and by just getting on with the job, she is, however, very widely respected. She has adopted a 'never complain, never explain' attitude to her official role, a throwback to the early days of the Queen's reign. Catherine's hard work, discretion and devotion have been rewarded, too.

In April 2018, the Queen recognised her dedication to duty on her eighth wedding anniversary, when she created Catherine a Dame Grand Cross of the Royal Victorian Order (GCVO), the highest rank in a form of chivalry personally granted by the sovereign to recognise one's service. Other royals with the rank at the time included Prince Philip, the Duchess of Cornwall, and Sophie, Countess of Wessex.

It's no secret that Meghan and Catherine never gelled. That is hardly the first case of royal sisters-in-law clashing. Diana and Princess Anne famously didn't see eye to eye. But Catherine enjoys good relations with William's cousins Zara, Beatrice and Eugenie and his uncle's wife Sophie. She has a warm relationship with Camilla, William's stepmother, too. When she hosted her Christmas Carol Service at Westminster Abbey in December 2021 all the young royals happily attended in deference to the future queen.

Throughout the protracted 'battle of the brothers' between William and Harry, despite her closeness to Harry in the pre-Meghan days, her loyalty has always been to her husband. She is loyal to her friends, too. She has remained close to her friends from Marlborough College, including Emilia Jardine Patterson and Trini Foyle, as well as blending with William's friends such as Lady Laura Meade and her husband, James Meade, and Thomas van Straubenzee and his wife, Lucy Lanigan O'Keeffe, who teaches at Thomas's Battersea, where Charlotte and George go to school.

Like other parents, Catherine has involved herself with the school and activities. She and William do the morning school run, she has attended coffee mornings, too, and doesn't seek special treatment ever. She is just one of the mums. But that's just it, she isn't. For Catherine has the innate ability to switch roles with ease, a skill not many possess.

When the time comes, King William V and his consort, Queen Catherine, will be a devoted royal couple, devoted to each other, the institution of the monarchy and their people; they are a dynamic duo, hell-bent on making as much of a difference as they can. Together, they have a perfect blend of warmth and steely determination which means the monarchy as a twenty-first-century institution will be safe in their hands. Reflecting on his wedding day, William admitted to ABC presenter Katie Couric that he wished his mother Diana had been able to be there: 'I think she would have loved the day and I think, hopefully, she'd be very proud of us both for the day. I'm just very sad that she's never going to get a chance to meet Kate.' Without doubt, she would have approved.

Britain's history has been littered with terrible, incompetent monarchs such as Edward II (r. 1307–27) and James II (r. 1685–88), or profligate ones like George IV (r. 1820–30) with a personal income 'exceeding the national revenue of a third-rate power, there appeared to be no limit to his desires, nor any restraint to his profusion', to the current Queen's uncle, the uncrowned Edward VIII (r. 1936), who had a series of scandalous affairs with married women, then fell in love with twice-divorced American Wallis Simpson, which resulted in his abdication. There have been tyrants, too, like King John, who, in the words of one contemporary chronicler, was 'brim-full of evil qualities' and Henry VIII (r. 1509–47), regarded as blood-soaked and murderous, who by the end of his reign had become incredibly capricious. Elizabeth II, our oldest and longest-reigning monarch, is the ultimate constitutional monarch. She is seen as our greatest ever queen, too, more popular than Queen Victoria, under whose reign Britain transformed into an industrialised nation, and Queen Elizabeth I, who oversaw a vibrant era of arts and many new discoveries. Queen Elizabeth II has helped guide her grandson through his formative years and has proved a great role model for the future king.

William is a very good listener. Those who have met him on royal engagements, usually complete strangers, say they really feel he embraces their problems and hears their stories. He gives them time. Indeed, like his mother, he believes listening is one of humanity's greatest tools, 'one of our greatest assets to understand each other'. It is an asset he will need to draw on when his moment in history comes as he takes the throne. His poise, kindness and natural nobility, along with his ability to communicate with his people will stand him in good stead for what lies ahead. William has the skills and strength of character to meet that challenge and to rise to it, with his wife and adviser Catherine at his side.

Behind all the royal paraphernalia, the rules and the regalia, William is a man of his time. He tries to be as normal as possible. He goes to watch his favourite football team, Aston Villa, when he can; he even used to play five-a-side at Battersea Park under lights with his mates. He has spoken in the past about how sometimes he just wants to chill out at home and play video games: 'It's very addictive. I'd like to get one [a PlayStation 4], but I'm not sure how my wife would feel about it!'[80] William doesn't profess to be perfect: 'I'm always open to people saying I'm wrong, because most of the time, I am,' he said in an interview in 2004. Ultimately, he is a twenty-first-century gentleman: he puts his wife's needs and those of others before his own and isn't afraid of looking foolish in public.

Behind William's smile is a steely determination. He has never been somebody who will let himself, his family, or his country down. Like his grandmother and father, he is a committed servant of the Crown. When he was asked about his role as future king, in a 2016 interview with BBC royal correspondent Nicholas Witchell, his answer was clear. 'I take duty very seriously. I take my responsibilities very seriously,' he said. He went on, 'But it's about finding your own way at the right time, and if you're not careful, duty can weigh you down at a very early age. I think you have got to develop into a duty role.' He said that 'considering what kind of king he wanted to be very much occupies my thinking space', but that it would not be a priority for twenty years or more. He added, 'The royal family has to modernise and develop as it goes along, and it has to stay relevant. And that is the challenge for me. How do I make the royal family relevant in the next twenty years?' Asked about becoming king, he said, 'I have no idea when that's going to be, and I certainly don't lie awake waiting or hoping for it, because it sadly means that my family have moved on, and I don't want that.' Sadly, or not, for William – with a grandmother who is ninety-six years old on 21 April 2022 and a father who is seventy-four on 14 November 2022 – his time is fast approaching.

ENDNOTES

1. From Robert Jobson's article penned for the *Radio Times*, 2020, about the film *Prince William: A Planet for Us All.*
2. Quoted from the Nick Kent film.
3. In a letter quoted in Jonathan Dimbleby's *Prince of Wales: A Biography* and elsewhere.
4. From *Diana: Her True Story – In Her Own Words*, Andrew Morton, 2019.
5. From *Diana: Her True Story – In Her Own Words*, Andrew Morton, 2019.
6. King Charles II was succeeded by his brother James II, a Catholic, who was overthrown by William III in the Glorious Revolution, following an appeal by some Protestant nobles to the Dutch Prince William of Orange, who was married to James's elder, Protestant daughter, Mary. William's army landed in Devon in November 1869. Deserted by his army and navy, James escaped abroad. Parliament declared, in February 1689, that James's flight amounted to an abdication, and William and Mary were crowned joint monarchs. The Hanoverians, from whom William's father is directly descended, came to power in circumstances which could have undermined the stability of British society. The first Hanoverian king, George I, was only fifty-second in line to the throne, but, according to the Act of Settlement, he was the nearest Protestant.
7. Reported to the author by a royal source.
8. Revealed in the *Mail on Sunday*, in October 2017, in an exchange of letters between McGlashan and Laurens van der Post.
9. From *Diana: Her True Story – In Her Own Words*, Andrew Morton, 2019.
10. Interview with the author.
11. Statement by Ms Barnes to the press.
12. From *The Diana Chronicles*, Tina Brown.
13. From a report in the Associated Press.
14. From a report in the Associated Press.
15. In an interview with Mervyn Wycherley and the author.
16. Interview with Wycherley and the author.
17. Interview with the author.
18. From *Diana: Her True Story – In Her Own Worlds*, Andrew Morton.
19. From *Diana: Her True Story – In Her Own Worlds*, Andrew Morton.
20. From *Diana: Her True Story – In Her Own Worlds*, Andrew Morton.
21. From *Charles at Seventy*, Robert Jobson, 2018.

22. From *Charles at Seventy*, Robert Jobson, 2018.
23. From *William & Harry*, Ingrid Seward, 2003.
24. From *William & Harry*, Ingrid Seward, 2003.
25. From *William & Harry*, Ingrid Seward, 2003.
26. From *The Diana Chronicles*, Tina Brown, 2007.
27. From *Harry: Conversations with the Prince*, Angela Levin, 2018.
28. From *Diana: Her True Story*, Andrew Morton, 1998.
29. From *Charles at Seventy*, Robert Jobson, 2018.
30. From *Diana: Closely Guarded Secret*, Ken Wharfe and Robert Jobson, 2016.
31. From *A Royal Duty*, Paul Burrell, 2003.
32. From *Diana: Closely Guarded Secret*, Ken Wharfe and Robert Jobson, 2016.
33. From *Harry's War*, Robert Jobson, 2008.
34. From *Harry's War*, Robert Jobson, 2008.
35. Prince William discussed his scare during an interview conducted by a ten-year-old cancer patient named Alice for CBBC's *Newsround*.
36. From an interview with Ken Wharfe by the author.
37. From the interview with Martin Bashir on the BBC's *Panorama*, 1995.
38. From *Diana: Her True Story – In Her Own Words*, Andrew Morton, 2003.
39. From *A Royal Duty*, Paul Burrell, 2004.
40. From *Charles: Victim or Villain*, Penny Junor, 1998.
41. From *Diana, Our Mother: Her Life and Legacy*, Nick Kent, 2017.
42. From *William and Kate: The Love Story*, Robert Jobson, 2010.
43. From an interview with Ken Wharfe and the author.
44. From an interview with an anonymous source by the author.
45. From an interview with an anonymous source by the author.
46. From an interview with a reporter from the Press Association.
47. From an interview with the Press Association.
48. Prince William in an interview with the Press Association.
49. From an interview with the Press Association.
50. From an interview with the Press Association.
51. From an interview with Broderick Munro-Wilson for Jeremy Paxman's Channel 5 documentary *Paxman on the Queen's Children*, 2019.
52. The engagement interview was conducted by Tom Bradby, 2010.
53. From an interview with the Press Association.
54. As reported in the *Daily Mail*, 2003.
55. From an interview with Duncan Larcombe by the author.
56. From an interview with a royal source by the author.
57. From an interview with Mark Stewart by the author.
58. From an interview with Niraj Tanna by the author.
59. From *Kate: The Future Queen*, Katie Nicholl, 2015.
60. From the ITV News engagement interview by Tom Bradby in 2010.
61. From Tom Bradby's ITV engagement interview.
62. From *William and Kate: The Love Story*, Robert Jobson, 2010.
63. From an interview with Arthur Edwards by the author.
64. From *Harry: Life, Loss and Love*, Katie Nicholl, 2018.
65. From the *Daily Mirror*, July 2011.
66. Reported in *News of the World* by the author, July 2011.

67. Statement by the Duke of Cambridge's spokesperson, 14 September 2012.

68. Reported by Katie Nicholl in *Vanity Fair* in September 2013.

69. From *Football, Prince William and Our Mental Health*, a documentary screened on the BBC in June 2020.

70. From a statement from the Prince of Wales, Clarence House office, April 2018.

71. From a speech on becoming the royal patron of Child Bereavement UK, March 2009.

72. Press Conference at Kensington Palace with filmmakers Ashley Getting and Nick Kent in 2017.

73. From a conversation between the author and a senior diplomat.

74. From an article in the *Daily Mail* by Rebecca English, 29 November 2017.

75. From an interview with a former aide by the author.

76. From 'Kate and Meghan: Is the royal sisterhood really at breaking point?' by Camilla Tominey, in the *Daily Telegraph*, 26 November 2018.

77. Confirmed for the author by a royal source.

78. William to florist Paula Pryke of his love of giving Kate flowers after he presented her with an OBE in 2014.

79. From a video of support for Place2Be in January 2019.

80. A comment made at the British Academy of Film and Television Arts, November 2013.

APPENDICES

The Royal Foundation

The Royal Foundation was originally established in 2009 by William and Harry with both Catherine and Meghan joining as patrons later. Since relinquishing their royal roles, however, the Duke and Duchess of Sussex have gone on to create their own charitable organization – the Archewell Foundation. The Duke of Cambridge, like his wife The Duchess of Cambridge, also directs his charitable activities through The Royal Foundation of the Duke and Duchess of Cambridge. The Foundation develops programmes and charitable projects based on the interests of Their Royal Highnesses by working with organisations which are already making a proven impact in their respective fields. The Royal Foundation provides additional investment, mentoring, support, and partnerships for these programmes, and lends its own profile and leverage to enhance the effect of their good work.

Heads Together

In 2017, the Duke spearheaded the Heads Together mental health campaign with the Duchess of Cambridge and Prince Harry, leading a coalition of eight mental health charity partners to change the national conversation on mental health. The campaign aimed to build on existing progress nationwide in tackling stigma, raising awareness and providing vital help for people with mental-health problems. The coalition of charities covered a wide range of mental-health issues and worked in areas that were in line with the Duke and Duchess and Prince Harry's interests. They were the Anna Freud National Centre for Children and Families; Best Beginnings; CALM – The Campaign Against Living Miserably; Contact (a military mental health coalition); Mind; Place2Be; The Mix; and Young Minds. Heads Together was privileged to be the 2017 Virgin Money London Marathon Charity of the Year, giving the campaign a positive platform to raise funds for the charity partners and to start millions of conversations about mental wellbeing.

Children and Charity

The Duke of Cambridge is committed to helping children and young people to build their skills, confidence and aspirations. Through his charitable work, His Royal Highness has strived to raise awareness of how serious issues can affect young people, for example, homelessness and bullying. In 2016, the Duke convened a new industry-led taskforce to develop a shared response to the online bullying of young people. The Duke also champions the benefits of equipping young people with essential skills and training to enhance both their personal and professional lives by highlighting youth-engaging programmes, such as those run by Coach Core and Skill Force, that work with the hard-to-reach and make a difference to young people and their surrounding communities.

The Armed Forces

After completing his forty-four-week training course, Prince William was commissioned as an army officer in December 2006 and joined the Household Cavalry (Blues and Royals) as a Second Lieutenant. A year later, he was promoted to the rank of Lieutenant. Having completed seven-and-a-half years of full-time military service, promoting the important role and the welfare of those who are serving or who have served their country in the Armed Forces is a key focus for the Duke's charitable activities. Through their programme of official engagements, both the Duke and Prince Harry have shone a light on the ongoing challenges facing service personnel making the transition to civilian life. As Patron of the Royal Air Force Battle of Britain Memorial Flight and Honorary Air Commandant of Royal Air Force Coningsby, His Royal Highness has also drawn attention to the crucial role played by UK air defence, alongside recognising and commemorating its important history.

The Environment

Protecting the natural environment for future generations is one of Prince William's key priorities. His Royal Highness has publicly supported initiatives to fund conservation, community development and environmental education programmes across Africa, and has led key programmes such as the United for Wildlife Financial and Transportation Taskforces to end illegal wildlife trafficking on a global scale.

Royal Titles

Prince William's current official title is His Royal Highness the Duke of Cambridge. He also holds the subsidiary titles of The Earl of Strathearn in Scotland and Baron Carrickfergus in Northern Ireland. The duke is also a Royal Knight Companion of the Most Noble Order of the Garter, a Knight of the Most Ancient and Most Noble Order of the Thistle, a member of the Privy Council of the United Kingdom, and a Personal Aide-de-Camp to the Queen. When his father, Prince Charles, becomes King, William will become the Duke of Cornwall, too, and inherit the lucrative Duchy of Cornwall estate, which at present generates an income of more than £20 million annually for the heir to the throne to fund his lifestyle in whatever way he sees fit. It is possible he will retain the Duke of Cambridge title and become the Duke of Cornwall and Cambridge. It is expected that as king, Charles will also bestow on William the coveted title of the Prince of Wales. The title, which is within the gift of the reigning sovereign, is granted to the heir apparent as a personal dignity and the title Earl of Chester has always been bestowed upon the recipient in conjunction with it. It is not automatically given, and the title is not heritable, either. It is seen as a great honour.

Prince William's Military ranks
As is customary for senior male members of the royal family, Prince William had a career in the Armed Forces before dedicating himself full time to the Crown. During his time in the forces, William earned ranks in the British Army, the Royal Navy and the Royal Air Force.

British Army
8 January, 2006: Officer Cadet
16 December, 2006: Cornet (Second Lieutenant), The Blues and Royals (short-service commission)
16 December, 2006: Lieutenant, The Blues and Royals
1 January, 2009: Captain, The Blues and Royals (and transferred to a full regular commission)
1 January, 2016: Major, British Army

Royal Navy
1 January, 2008: Sub-lieutenant
1 January, 2009: Lieutenant
1 January, 2016: Lieutenant Commander

Royal Air Force
1 January, 2008: Flying Officer
1 January, 2009: Flight Lieutenant
1 January, 2016: Squadron Leader

Bibliography
Dimbleby, Jonathan: *The Prince of Wales: A Biography* – Little, Brown, 1994
Hoey, Brian: *Prince William* – The History Press, 2003
Junor, Penny: *Prince William: Born to be King* – Hodder & Stoughton, 2012
Jobson, Robert: *The New Royal Family* – John Blake, 2014
Jobson, Robert: *Diana's Legacy: William and Harry* – MpressMedia, 2019
Jobson, Robert: *Charles: Our Future King* – John Blake, 2019
Lacey, Robert: *Battle of Brothers* – William Collins, 2020
Morton, Andrew: *Diana: Her True Story – In Her Own Words* – Michael O'Mara, 2017

Nicholl, Katie: *Kate: The Future Queen* – Hachette Books, 2015

Seward, Ingrid: *William & Harry: A Portrait of Two Princes* – Arcade, 2003

Seward, Ingrid: *William and Harry: The People's Princes* – Welbeck Publishing, 2008

Scobie, Omid/Durand, Carolyn: *Finding Freedom* – HQ, 2020

Wharfe, Ken: *Diana: Closely Guarded Secret* – John Blake, 2016

Wharfe, Ken: *Guarding Diana* – John Blake, 2017